Lecture Notes in Computer Science   13475

More information about this series at https://link.springer.com/bookseries/558

Irfan Awan · Muhammad Younas ·
Aneta Poniszewska-Marańda (Eds.)

Mobile Web and Intelligent Information Systems

18th International Conference, MobiWIS 2022
Rome, Italy, August 22–24, 2022
Proceedings

 Springer

Editors
Irfan Awan
University of Bradford
Bradford, UK

Muhammad Younas
Oxford Brookes University
Oxford, UK

Aneta Poniszewska-Marańda
Lodz University of Technology
Lodz, Poland

ISSN 0302-9743   ISSN 1611-3349 (electronic)
Lecture Notes in Computer Science
ISBN 978-3-031-14390-8   ISBN 978-3-031-14391-5 (eBook)
https://doi.org/10.1007/978-3-031-14391-5

This Springer imprint is published by the registered company Springer Nature Switzerland AG
The registered company address is: Gewerbestrasse 11, 6330 Cham, Switzerland

Preface

It is a great privilege to present the proceedings of the 18th International Conference on Mobile Web and Intelligent Information Systems (MobiWis 2022). The conference was held during August 22–24, 2022, in a hybrid mode. We were pleased that in addition to online presentations, the conference was held onsite in the historic city of Rome, Italy. According to UNESCO, Rome is a World Heritage site with magnificent monuments such as the Roman Forum, Colosseum, Trevi Fountain, St. Peter's Basilica, Spanish Steps, Piazza Navona, and many others. Rome is one of the most visited destinations in Europe, as well as the world, as millions of international visitors visit Rome each year.

MobiWis 2022 provided a good setting for discussing recent developments in various topics related to mobile web and intelligent information systems. The objective was to bring academic and industry researchers, engineers, and practitioners together to exchange ideas, experiences, and research results and discuss future challenges in mobile web and intelligent information systems. The use of mobile devices such as smart phones, tablets, and wearable gadgets has significantly increased in recent years. Though such devices provide various facilities to users, they also pose significant research challenges, which include, for instance, issues related to maintaining an appropriate level of security and privacy; managing and maintaining the underlying mobile networks as well as communication media and protocols; effective and user-friendly design of software for mobile devices by taking account of human–computer interaction and related principles; and deploying and applying mobile web systems and tools in prototype applications as well as in businesses and organizations.

The conference technical committee put together an exciting program which included papers on timely and emerging topics such as mobile technology acceptance, software-defined networks, user-interface design, intelligent services, and security and privacy with practical applications in healthcare, public transportation, etc. Papers accepted for the conference came from authors based in both academic research institutes and industry.

The COVID-19 pandemic had a negative effect on productivity in every sector, including education, research, business, industry, and the public sector. Researchers were unable to work at full capacity as they had limited resources and faced constraints in terms of access to required research facilities such as labs, equipment, and data. Despite these challenges, MobiWis 2022 received a good number of quality submissions from authors from different countries across the world. Members of the Program Committee rigorously reviewed all submitted papers. Based on the reviews, 18 papers were accepted for the conference, which is around 35% of the total submissions.

The success of this conference is truly attributed to the organizing and technical committee members who made serious efforts for the smooth running of the conference. We greatly appreciate all the committee members who contributed their time and efforts to organize the conference. We are sincerely grateful to the Program Committee members who provided timely, constructive, and balanced feedback to the authors. We are also thankful to the authors for their contributions to the conference.

We sincerely thank Markus Aleksy and Stephan Böhm (General Co-chairs), Filipe Portela (Workshop Coordinator), Nor Shahniza Kamal Bashah (Publicity Chair), and Natalia Kryvinska (Special Issue Coordinator) for their help and support.

We greatly appreciate the Springer LNCS team for their valuable support in the production of the conference proceedings.

August 2022

Irfan Awan
Muhammad Younas
Aneta Poniszewska-Marańda

Organization

General Co-chairs

Markus Aleksy   ABB, Germany
Stephan Böhm   RheinMain University of Applied Sciences, Germany

Program Co-chairs

Aneta Poniszewska-Marańda   Lodz University of Technology, Poland
Muhammad Younas   Oxford Brookes University, UK

Publication Chair

Irfan Awan   University of Bradford, UK

Journal Special Issue Coordinator

Natalia Kryvinska   University of Vienna, Austria

Workshop Coordinator

Filipe Portela   University of Minho, Portugal

Publicity Chair

Nor Shahniza Kamal Bashah   Universiti Teknologi Mara, Malaysia

Program Committee

Omar Abdel Wahab   University of Quebec at Outaouais, Canada
Fatma Abdennadher   National School of Engineering of Sfax, Tunisia
Pablo Adasme   University of Santiago de Chile, Chile
Novia Admodisastro   Universiti Putra Malaysia, Malaysia
Thomas Barton   University of Applied Sciences Worms, Germany
Christian Baun   Frankfurt University of Applied Sciences, Germany

Jozef Juhar   Technical University of Košice, Slovakia
Raquel Trillo   University of Zaragoza, Spain
Perin Unal   METU, Turkey

Contents

Mobile Applications and Technologies

Knowledge Behavior Gap Model:
An Application for Technology Acceptance

Agnis Stibe[1,2](✉) (iD), Nicolai Krüger[3], and Alina Behne[4]

[1] EM Normandie Business School, Metis Lab, Paris, France
agnis@agnisstibe.com
[2] INTERACT Research Unit, University of Oulu, Oulu, Finland
[3] IU International University of Applied Science, Düsseldorf, Germany
[4] Seedhouse Accelerator GmbH, Osnabrück, Niedersachsen, Germany

Abstract. Organizational change initiatives and societal health campaigns often fail or produce unsustainable outcomes. Intense trainings and knowledge sharing not necessarily lead to expected behavioral results. Is there a gap between what people know and what they do? This paper investigates ways for understanding and closing this gap. It reviews the literature related to innovation diffusion and technology acceptance. Based on that, it develops a Knowledge Behavior Gap model, containing four main constructs: knowledge, acceptance, intention, and behavior. To validate the model, a quantitative survey instrument was designed. Using it, eighty-three valid responses were collected. Partial least squares structural equation modeling method was used to analyze the data and test the model. The results demonstrate a strong and significant path from knowledge to behavior that leads through acceptance and intention. Interestingly, the paths from knowledge to acceptance and from intention to behavior both get even stronger with age. Meaning that for older people knowledge is a more powerful predictor of acceptance and intention is a more seriously influencing behavior. As the main contribution to science and practice, the model provides a more consistent way for measuring and predicting the success of envisioned organizational and societal changes. Thus, researchers are encouraged to advance Knowledge Behavior Gap model, while professionals are invited to apply it for enhancing desired transformations towards hyper-performance.

Keywords: Knowledge · Acceptance · Intention · Behavior · Model · Technology · Design · Persuasive systems · Hyper-performance

1 Introduction

Many novel ideas and initiatives often fail. New technologies emerge, but people are not rushing to start using them. With the continuous rise of novel digital innovations, users are more often than ever involved in permanent decision-making with regards to an acceptance and use of these technologies. While traditional user behavior studies distinguish between early adopters and late followers of innovations [28], an increasing everyday complexity is significantly affecting human decision-making capacity. This can

I. Awan et al. (Eds.): MobiWIS 2022, LNCS 13475, pp. 3–17, 2022.
https://doi.org/10.1007/978-3-031-14391-5_1

be seen with the fluctuating rates of adoption and use of wearables, conversational agents at home, autonomous driving, and artificial intelligence. Even after intense trainings and knowledge sharing there may be achieved dissatisfying levels of behavioral results. Is there an inherent underlying bias that people will always do the required right after they have acquired the relevant knowledge?

In the field of information systems, individual acceptance and use of technology has been a prominent research direction for decades [35]. There are available well-known models and theories, such as Theory of Reasoned Action [2], Theory of Planned Behavior [1], Technology Acceptance Model [8], and Unified Theory of Acceptance and Use of Technology [36]. The use of technology is related with the acceptance, but not often related with the knowledge about a technology.

Conversely, the Innovation Diffusion Theory by Rogers [27] states the knowledge is the first step of adopting or rejecting an innovation. Besides, in practice, there is often an expectation of a direct link between knowledge and usage behavior, i.e., that more information shall lead to the preferred behavior or an increase of the willingness of a person to do the behavior. However, knowledge is not always recognized as a relevant and powerful factor in the context of building user acceptance. This may be one of the key reasons behind lower technology adoption rates in many cases. Thus, we suggest that knowledge is an important instrument [24] that impacts acceptance and later technology related behaviors.

Based on that, we propose a hypothesis that knowledge about a technology is an entry point for the process of deciding about technology use. We argue that there is a direct link between knowledge and behavior, but more prominent relations are from knowledge to acceptance, then to intention using technology, and finally to actual use behaviors. We suggest that there can be a potential knowledge to behavior gap. Finally, we build and test a metamodel with the constructs of knowledge, acceptance, intention, and behavior. We aim at investigating our main research question:

What is the strongest path from knowledge leading to (technology use) behavior?

In this paper, we are addressing the research question in the following fashion. In Sect. 2, we review related literature and provide the relevant theoretical background. In Sect. 3, we describe the emerging hypotheses and build the research model. Section 4 outlines the methodological approach and data collection. In Sect. 5, we present our data analysis. Section 6 contains the study results. In Sect. 7, we propose a discussion of scientific and practical implications. Finally, Sect. 8 ends the paper with the conclusions of this study, limitations, and further research.

2   Theoretical Background of the Main Constructs

Existing scientific literature provides valuable insights from several well-elaborated theories and models in the field of technology acceptance and innovation diffusion. Ajzen and Fishbein [2] were working on one of the first behavioral theories, namely a Theory of Reasoned Action (TRA), that tried explaining the interconnectedness of attitude, behavioral intention, and behavior. A few years later, Ajzen [1] offered an extended view on TRA by adding perceived behavioral control, and thus suggesting a Theory of Planned Behavior (TPB). Nevertheless, TPB keeps the linkage of attitude to intention to behavior unchanged. Only clarifies, it is an attitude towards the behavior.

With the advent of rapid information technology progression, Davis et al. [8] expanded the list of independent variables that can impact the attitude towards using a technology and tailored their Technology Acceptance Model (TAM) specifically applicable to the cases of technology acceptance. Later, TAM was further advanced by Venkatesh et al. [36], suggesting more attitudinal variables determining behavioral intention, as well as introducing moderation effects into their Unified Theory of Acceptance and Use of Technology (UTAUT). Meanwhile, an Innovation Diffusion Theory (IDT) was developed by Rogers [27], suggesting that diffusion is the process by which an innovation is communicated over time among the participants in a social system. This perspective adds the important role that knowledge and its dissemination play into explaining the success of technology acceptance and consequent use behaviors. IDT states that knowledge is a key first stage in the adoptive process of an innovation [34], including novel technology.

According to the relevant literature (Table 1), the technology use behavior has been often studied is relation to a behavioral intention to use it and an attitude towards using it, but rarely in relation to the knowledge about the technology. That provides an opportunity to distill and synthesize theoretical background from the prior literature to develop more advanced research models that can better fit the needs of current times. For example, some of the technologies, which were discussed in earlier literature, are simply outdated (e.g., fax machines). A few decades ago, common knowledge about technologies might have been rare, as gathering technical knowledge was much more difficult than today. In contrast, the current world of digitally connected information society is filled with high-quality training videos, open education resources, and voice interfaces with an instant answer to almost every question referring to the internet [20].

Table 1. Main relevant constructs from behavioral and technology use theories.

Theory	Knowledge	Acceptance	Intention	Behavior
TRA [2]		Attitude	Behavioral intention	Behavior
TPB [1]		Attitude towards the behavior	Intention	Behavior
TAM [8]		Attitude towards using	Behavioral intention to use	Usage behavior
IDT [27]	Knowledge	Persuasion	Decision	Implementation
UTAUT [36]		Expectancy	Behavioral intention	Use behavior

Recent research provides evidence how researchers are carefully experimenting with the alterations and extensions of the listed models (Table 1) to increase their prediction accuracy. For example, Ko et al. [15] conducted a study about the Korean smart-work approach, which is a combinatory set of technological, geographical, and organizational freedom in the work style in South Korean. They found that the original TAM might not be fully suitable for the socio-technical, multidimensional complexity of smart-work environments. By testing six potential variables, they found significant influence of the technology appropriation on the tasked performed and the job satisfaction.

Another recent example is a study in the context of autonomous vehicles, conducted by Lindgren et al. [22]. It proposes a TAM extension for an innovation foresight and predicted acceptance of self-driving cars. An important contribution of this study for our research is the introduction of knowledge construct. They found that knowledge (especially, broader information technology knowledge, plus driver education of autonomous vehicles) plays an important role in the acceptance of self-driving cars.

Building upon this literature review, in the next section we are aiming at developing a research model that leverages the most relevant constructs from previous work on technology acceptance and innovation diffusion.

3   Knowledge Behavior Gap Model

More than a century ago, Tarde [31] was investigating the spread of ideas, concepts, and inventions in a society. He stated that any idea must be shared within a given social community to create a significant effect, which he calls a chain of ideas or chain of imitation, which basically describes the diffusional effect of an idea. Based on that, Rogers [27] constructed IDT and rendered more precisely that diffusion can be seen as a group phenomenon, which nowadays is often referred to as mass acceptance. Further, Rogers [28] explained adoption as the individual process of innovation decision or of accepting a new technology from knowledge to persuasion, decision, implementation, and confirmation.

The initial theoretical model by Rogers holds knowledge as the first variable to explain the personal adoption to an innovation. Other relevant literature provides additional examples of knowledge, especially system-related knowledge, as a variable dealing with pragmatic or instructional information enabling an individual to use a certain tool, e.g., [4, 19, 21]. As knowledge can be either broad or narrow and further conceptual or practical [13], for the purpose of this paper, we understand knowledge as the concrete (narrow) knowledge about a certain technology (practical).

Recent research by Moser and Deichmann [23] and Ochmann et al. [24] shows that knowledge is a highly individually perceived and powerful factor, which can vary between persons and cultures. This view follows the call for further studies by Awa et al. [5], where an integration of different acceptance models has been encouraged and knowledge can be used to reduce perceived risks in subsequent behaviors. Further, studies already revealed the influence of knowledge to the adaptation capability, e.g., [14, 30]. In our work, we treat *knowledge* as the understanding about a certain technology in terms of its functionalities and features, which differs from previous experience with the technology.

Measuring technology acceptance is a common denominator of the related theories and models (Table 1). We argue that acceptance is explained by the attitude of an individual based on the perceived usefulness and ease of use of a technology [36]. Moreover, Davis [9] underlines this with a statement that attitude means to accept or reject information technology. In this paper, we consolidate all the attitudinal aspects of previously listed theories under a unified *acceptance* construct. Further, for our research model we consider a construct of *intention* to use a technology according to Stibe [29], which is in alignment with in all the five previously reviewed theoretical models (Table 1). The same applies for the construct of *behavior*, which we treat as a synonym for use behavior [8, 36], implementation [27] and behavior [1, 2].

Based on the above, for the development of our research model (see Fig. 1), we argue that knowledge about a technology is the first aspect, which directly influences an attitude or acceptance of the technology. However, we also hypothesize that knowledge has a lower direct predictive power on the intention and actual use behavior, as such effects are mediated by an acceptance. Thus, we derive the following three hypotheses:

H1: More knowledge about a technology leads to higher technology acceptance.

H2: More knowledge about a technology leads to an intention to use the technology.

H3: More knowledge about a technology leads to an actual technology use behavior.

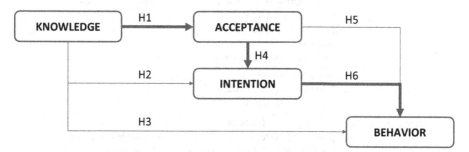

Fig. 1. Knowledge Behavior Gap model with hypotheses.

According to TRA [2], TPB [1], and TAM [8], there is already a scientifically proven correlation between an attitude towards a behavior and behavioral intention. For the research model of our study, we adopt that link as acceptance leads to intention (H4). TPB [8] also suggests that there is a direct impact of perceived behavioral control, another attitudinal construct, on actual behavior. A direct link that bypasses intention. Similarly, also UTAUT [36] suggests that there is another direct effect that bypasses intention. A link between facilitating conditions on actual use behavior. Thus, we also hypothesize that there can be a direct impact of acceptance on behavior (H5). Finally, we include a strongly validated link between intention and behavior (H6), in accordance with the similar model relationships in TRA [2], TPB [1], TAM [8], and UTAUT [36]. To finish developing our research model, we hypothesize that:

H4: Higher technology acceptance leads to higher intention to use the technology.

H5: Higher technology acceptance leads to an actual technology use behavior.

H6: Higher intention to use leads to an increased technology use behavior.

To reflect the main idea of how often there is a gap between people knowing something and whether they are actively applying that knowledge in practice or not, we decided to name it as a Knowledge Behavior Gap model. We hypothesize that in voluntary contexts the strongest path through the model leads from knowledge to acceptance, from acceptance to intention, and from intention to behavior.

4   Research Methodology and Data Collection

For testing and validating the hypotheses of the Knowledge Behavior Gap model, we created a quantitative questionnaire (Table 2) using persuasive systems [12] as a more specific subject for the study. For the questionnaire, we adapted the existing constructs from the reviewed literature.

Table 2. The key constructs and items of the Knowledge Behavior Gap model.

Construct	Items	Description
Knowledge [14, 23, 30]	I know what a persuasive system is I am familiar with what a persuasive system is I don't know what a persuasive system is I am unfamiliar with what a persuasive system is I don't understand what a persuasive system is	Knowledge about a certain technology, which differs from previous experience
Acceptance [35]	I think positively about persuasive systems I have nothing against persuasive systems I am afraid of persuasive systems I feel resistant to persuasive systems I am not accepting persuasive systems in my life	Acceptance can be explained by the attitude towards a technology
Intention [29]	I am sure I will use persuasive systems in the future I consider using persuasive systems in the future I think I will be using persuasive systems in the future I would rather avoid using persuasive systems I don't want to use persuasive systems	Behavioral intention of a person to use a technology

(continued)

Table 2. (*continued*)

Construct	Items	Description
Behavior [9]	I am using some persuasive systems currently I have used persuasive systems earlier I frequently use persuasive systems I don't use any persuasive systems at the moment I haven't really used any persuasive systems	Actual technology usage behavior

We collected 83 valid responses in six months. The participants were acquired with the help of social media networks, such as LinkedIn, ResearchGate, and Twitter, as well as direct email invitations and general student acquisition. We were able to generate a spread over four continents within our sample: Europe (Austria, Estonia, Finland, France, Germany, Greece, Ireland, Israel, Italy, Latvia, Lithuania, Netherlands, Norway, Portugal, and Sweden), North America (Canada and United States), South America (Brazil), and Asia (Turkey). More descriptive statistics in Table 3.

The main constructs of the Knowledge Behavior Gap model were tested for validity and reliability using SPSS 28 (Statistical Package for the Social Sciences), a statistical software suite developed by IBM for advanced analytics, multivariate analysis, and business intelligence. After that, we implemented a mathematical model in WarpPLS 8.0, a software with graphical user interface for variance-based and factor-based structural equation modeling (SEM) using the partial least squares (PLS). Practically, we analyzed our measurement model by applying PLS-SEM according to Hair et al. [11]. This approach has become popular and further a key approach in multiple research areas, including change management, to validate conceptual models [3].

Table 3. Descriptive statistics of the study sample.

Total number of respondents: 83		Number (#)	Percentage (%)
Gender	Male	50	60.24
	Female	33	39.76
Age	Range	20–74	
	Mean	35.00	
	S.D.	9.90	

WarpPLS software by ScriptWarp Systems as an effective analysis tool for predictive PLS-SEM cases based on existing theories [11]. When it comes to exploratory research, as in this paper, PLS-SEM is a well-accepted method for multivariate statistics [16]. WartPLS software is unique as it enables users to explicitly identify nonlinear functions connecting pairs of latent variables in SEM models and calculate multivariate coefficients of association accordingly [18]. That makes this tool very different from other available software offering only linear functions. It is the first to provide classic PLS algorithms together with factor-based PLS algorithms for SEM [17].

5 Data Analysis

General PLS-SEM analysis results include ten global model fit and quality indices: average path coefficient (APC), average R-squared (ARS), average adjusted R-squared (AARS), average block variance inflation factor (AVIF), average full collinearity VIF (AFVIF), Tenenhaus GoF (GoF), and Simpson's paradox ratio (SPR).

It is recommended that the P values (significance) for the APC, ARS and AARS all be equal to or lower than 0.05, which is the case for our main research model: APC = 0.384, P < 0.001; ARS = 0.426, P < 0.001; AARS = 0.413, P < 0.001. Ideally, both the AVIF and AFVIF should be equal to or lower than 3.3, particularly in models where most of the constructs are measured through two or more indicators. That is true for our model with the values of AVIF = 1.691 and AFVIF = 2.149.

GoF index is a measure of an explanatory power of the model, defined as the square root of the product between the average communality index and the ARS [32]. According to Wetzels et al. [37], there are thresholds for the GoF: small if equal to or greater than 0.1, medium if equal to or greater than 0.25, and large if equal to or greater than 0.36. Thus, our model has a large explanatory power as its GoF = 0.530.

SPR index tells if a model is free from Simpson's paradox instances, which may occur when a path coefficient and a correlation associated with a pair of linked variables have different signs. That may indicate a possible causality problem, suggesting that a hypothesized path is either implausible or reversed. Ideally the SPR should be equal 1, meaning that there are no instances of Simpson's paradox in a model, which is true for our model: SPR = 1.000. Thus, the direction of causality in the model is supported.

To ensure the validity and reliability of the reflective measurement model, we conducted various tests with the most frequent techniques according to Ringle et al. [26]. Thus, we tested the internal consistency reliability with Cronbach's Alpha (CA) and composite reliability (CR), the convergent validity with average extracted variance (AVE) as well as the discriminant validity with the Fornell-Larcker criterion [26]. Validity indicates the degree to which a measurement model can predict what it will be measured. Reliability, in contrast, checks the degree to which the same measured values lead to the same results, which represents the failure rate [6].

We also tested the internal consistency reliability, for which the average correlation of all individual items of the same construct are compared, showing how accurate a group of variables measures a latent variable. The internal consistency reliability is measured by CA and CR [26]. The higher the values of CA and CR the more congruent the items, so the higher the internal reliability. In our model, the CA of all constructs is considerably higher than the suggested threshold value of 0.7, ranging from 0.821 to 0.901 (Table 4). CR should have a value of at least 0.6, which is reflected in our model with values in Table 4 ranging from 0.874 to 0.927, thus our model is internally reliable.

Table 4. Reliability and validity measure (the square roots of AVEs in bold on diagonal).

	Knowledge	Acceptance	Intention	Behavior
CR	0.927	0.874	0.907	0.913
CA	0.901	0.821	0.872	0.882
AVE	0.717	0.584	0.662	0.679
Knowledge	**0.847**	0.381	0.464	0.415
Acceptance	0.381	**0.764**	0.757	0.318
Intention	0.464	0.757	**0.814**	0.554
Behavior	0.415	0.318	0.554	**0.824**

For testing convergent validity, we used AVE, which determines the average percentage of items that explain the dispersion of a latent construct. In the literature, a threshold of 0.5 is mentioned [10], which is the case for all constructs in our model (Table 4), ranging from 0.584 to 0.717. Last, we checked the discriminant validity with the Fornell-Larcker criterion [10]. Therefore, for each construct, the square root of each AVE in the diagonal needs to be compared with the correlation coefficients. Table 4 shows that in our model the AVE is higher in each case so that the discriminant validity is accepted. For more details, Table 5 provides structure loadings and cross-loadings.

6 Results

The structural model with key results is presented in Fig. 2. The β values that are noted next to each arrow demonstrate the strength of relationships between the constructs and the asterisks mark their statistical significance (P value), while the R^2 contributions are presented in brackets. All paths in the model are statistically significant.

The model results evidently demonstrate how the strongest (β = 0.400–0.689) and the most significant (P < 0.001) path emerges from knowledge to acceptance (H1), then to intention (H4), and then to behavior (H6). The other hypotheses are also supported. However, their strengths and significances are considerably lower comparing to the path described above. Knowledge to intention (H2) and to behavior (H3) paths are similar in their key parameters (β = 0.208, P = 0.024–0.023). And acceptance to behavior (H5) path is even comparatively weaker (β = 0.196, P = 0.031).

The total effects and effect sizes are also provided in Fig. 2. Effect sizes (f^2) determine whether the effects indicated by the path coefficients are small (.02), medium (.15), or large (.35). Our study reveals that knowledge has a medium size effect ($f^2 = 0.160$) on acceptance, while acceptance has a large effect size ($f^2 = 0.529$) on intention, and similarly large effect size ($f^2 = 0.337$) intention has on behavior. The coefficient of determination value (R^2) indicates the ability of a model to explain and predict the constructs [26]. The R^2 contributions are marked in the brackets (see Fig. 2). An overall explanatory power of our model is 49.1%, which shows a good predictive accuracy [11]. As the value is around 50%, it indicates that our measurements fit well to our model, and the independent variables well explain the variance of the dependent ones.

Table 5. Structure loadings and cross-loading.

	Knowledge	Acceptance	Intention	Behavior
Knowledge	**0.911**	0.352	0.471	0.357
	0.855	0.364	0.405	0.441
	0.850	0.294	0.412	0.387
	0.800	0.291	0.299	0.309
	0.813	0.304	0.350	0.227
Acceptance	0.219	**0.833**	0.688	0.213
	0.153	**0.742**	0.501	0.084
	0.401	**0.632**	0.388	0.124
	0.284	**0.754**	0.558	0.374
	0.386	**0.843**	0.692	0.338
Intention	0.437	0.521	**0.846**	0.622
	0.335	0.526	**0.815**	0.431
	0.442	0.543	**0.860**	0.631
	0.281	0.739	**0.765**	0.173
	0.370	0.765	**0.780**	0.345
Behavior	0.375	0.260	0.516	**0.875**
	0.379	0.290	0.469	**0.810**
	0.183	0.257	0.423	**0.802**
	0.284	0.219	0.424	**0.822**
	0.450	0.281	0.436	**0.808**

For exploratory research, WarpPLS software offers a unique opportunity to investigate the nonlinear functions of moderation effects on the connecting pairs of latent variables. In PLS-SEM analysis, moderating effects are providing deeper and richer insights into how various factors can possibly influence the strengths of model relationships. Typically, there are three ways. A moderator is increasing, decreasing, or having no significant effect on a relationship in the model.

In our model, we found that the age of an individual plays a positive (increasing with age) moderating role on the effects that knowledge has on acceptance ($\beta = 0.193$, $P = 0.033$) and intention has on behavior ($\beta = 0.261$, $P = 0.006$), depicted with green arrows in Fig. 2. To have a more detailed perspective on the moderating effects, Fig. 3 provides smooth 3D and focused 2D graphs with low-high values.

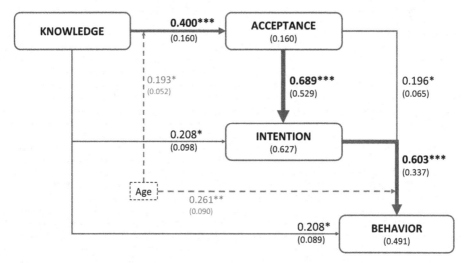

Fig. 2. Knowledge Behavior Gap model with PLS-SEM analysis results.

7 Discussion

The Knowledge Behavior Gap model clearly demonstrates that there is a strong and significant path from knowledge to behavior that leads first through an acceptance of the knowledge, and then through an intention to act upon or use the knowledge in practice, thus leading to an actual behavior.

The knowledge to acceptance relationship (H1) confirms an earlier perspective that has been suggested by Rogers [27, 28] in the Innovation Diffusion Theory, which postulates that the dissemination of knowledge predicts an acceptance of innovations. The further essential model relationships from acceptance to intention (H4) and from intention to behavior (H6) are well aligned with and reconfirming similar model connections from the earlier theories of technology acceptance, such as Theory of Reasoned Action [2], Theory of Planned Behavior [1], Technology Acceptance Model [8], and Unified Theory of Acceptance and Use of Technology [35, 36].

The other paths of Knowledge Behavior model are also significant, but less powerful and smaller effect sizes. It suggests there are people having shortcuts in their process from knowledge to behavior. For example, some people may bypass the acceptance step of the model, because they instantly trust that the new knowledge is relevant and meaningful for their future, so they go straight into planning their intentions (H2). Others can be even more advanced with a quick way for integrating the knowledge into their routines, so rushing directly to do the behavior (H3). Another shortcut in the model leads from acceptance to behavior (H5). Not very strong and significant, but still suggests that there are people that may need to accept the knowledge at first, and once that is achieved, they go straight into action to perform the required behavior.

The Knowledge Behavior Gap model has a potential to profoundly transform an earlier bias that has been commonly maintained in societies and organizations for a long time. An unspoken expectation that once people know how to do something, they

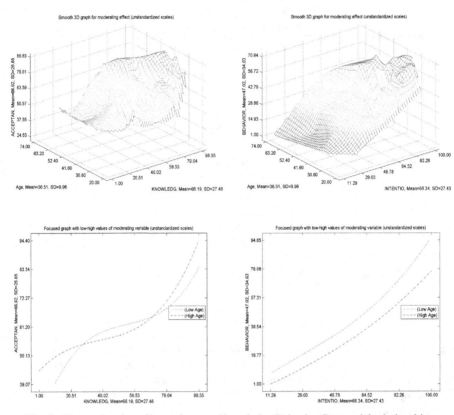

Fig. 3. The moderating effects of age on Knowledge Behavior Gap model relationships.

would go and start doing it, which is often not the case. For example, we can look at the contact tracing apps that have emerged with the recent pandemic. Generally, a large majority of people were aware of these apps. Many did have such an app installed on their smartphones. However, not many had it activated, or they did not use it regularly. If they had been asked about their awareness (knowledge) and importance of slowing down the spread of the virus (acceptance), most likely their responses would have been positive. However, their actions were incongruent with such a mindset.

Interestingly, our study also revealed that two of the main model relationships are shifting their strength and effect size depending on the age of individuals. It suggests that for older people knowledge becomes a stronger predictor for their acceptance, as well as intention becomes a stronger influencer of their actual behavior. Looking at that form the other side, younger people in comparison to older people need less knowledge about a technology to accept it, and lower levels of intention drive them to try using new technologies. This should not support the misperception that older people are less open or more averse for adopting technologies, e.g., [25].

This discovery of our research study demonstrates that older people may need more knowledge about technologies before accepting and using them. A reason might be that older adults consider technology usage more carefully and reflectively comparing to younger individuals [7], because they are not that skilled with technologies than digital natives, for example. These younger people are more likely to trust new technologies because their education and upbringing was generally different in the amounts and access to various technologies. Suggesting that older people need more knowledge about technologies, as well as more intention to use them, comparing to an intuitive trust that digital natives may possess. Thus, the technology adoption for older generations is usually slower than for younger people.

Overall, our findings are in line with and complimentary to the existing models and theories for behavioral and organizational change. Moreover, our work strives to these models with a deeper perspective of the essential steps towards personal technology acceptance. Additionally, we share deeper and richer insights on some of the most interesting moderating effects. That should be helpful for researchers and practitioners to interpret and apply the results with more accuracy and precision.

8 Conclusions

The major contribution of this research study is to propose a Knowledge Behavior Gap model as a response to the long-standing challenges with low efficacy of organizational transformation initiatives and societal wellbeing campaigns. Contrary to an intuitive, but maybe false, perspective that it is enough for people to know for their consecutive behaviors to emerge, our model suggests a more robust and reliable alternative. It describes that the strongest and most efficient path from knowledge to behavior leads through an acceptance first, and then through an intention to do the behavior.

As with many similar studies, our research has a few limitations. First, the amount of eighty-three respondents is not extremely large. Nevertheless, our study employs the PLS-SEM method, which has generated valid results already with even smaller sample sizes [33]. Second, the background of our surveyed sample has limited demographics, so cannot be easily generalized globally. Third, the chosen specific subject of persuasive systems in our questionnaire might have been interpreted differently by the participants. However, we did it on purpose to match the current global trend of more innovative technologies emerging that transform ho we live and work.

For future research, we invite interested scholars to test and validate the Knowledge Behavior model into diverse contexts and with larger sample sizes. Industry professionals and practitioners are welcome to apply and benefit from the model to enhance their desired and long-awaited corporate changes and business transformations. The model can be used to evaluate how people are going to accept and use such digital innovations as, for example, artificial intelligence, augmented reality, metaverse, and more. The Knowledge Behavior Gap model is a fundamental step towards empowering individual and organizational hyper-performance.

References

1. Ajzen, I.: From intentions to actions: a theory of planned behavior. In: Kuhl, J., Beckmann, J. (eds.) Action Control. SSSSP, pp. 11–39. Springer, Heidelberg (1985). https://doi.org/10.1007/978-3-642-69746-3_2
2. Ajzen, I., Fishbein, M.: Understanding Attitudes and Predicting Social Behavior. Prentice-Hall, Englewood Cliffs (1980)
3. Al-Emran, M., Mezhuyev, V., Kamaludin, A.: PLS-SEM in information systems research: a comprehensive methodological reference. In: Hassanien, A.E., Tolba, M.F., Shaalan, K., Azar, A.T. (eds.) AISI 2018. AISC, vol. 845, pp. 644–653. Springer, Cham (2019). https://doi.org/10.1007/978-3-319-99010-1_59
4. Assegaff, S., Dahlan, H.M.: Perceived benefit of knowledge sharing: adapting TAM model. In: International Conference on Research and Innovation in Information Systems, pp. 1–6. IEEE (2011)
5. Awa, H.O., Ojiabo, O.U., Emecheta, B.C.: Integrating TAM, TPB and TOE frameworks and expanding their characteristic constructs for E-commerce adoption by SMEs. J. Sci. Technol. Policy Manag. **6**, 76–94 (2015)
6. Burns, R.B., Burns, R.A.: Business Research Methods and Statistics Using SPSS. Sage Publications, Los Angeles (2008)
7. Czaja, S.J., et al.: Factors predicting the use of technology: findings from the center for research and education on aging and technology enhancement. Psych. Aging **21**(2), 333 (2006)
8. Davis, F.D., Bagozzi, R.P., Warshaw, P.R.: User acceptance of computer technology: a comparison of two theoretical models. Manage. Sci. **35**(8), 982–1003 (1989)
9. Davis, F.D.: User acceptance of information technology: system characteristics, user perceptions and behavioral impacts. Int. J. Man Mach. Stud. **38**, 475–487 (1993)
10. Fornell, C.R., Larcker, D.F.: Structural equation models with unobservable variables and measurement error. J. Mark. Res. **18**, 39–50 (1981)
11. Hair, J.F. Jr., Sarstedt, M., Hopkins, L., Kuppelwieser, V.G.: Partial least squares structural equation modeling (PLS-SEM). Eur. Bus. Rev. (2014)
12. Harjumaa, M.: On the Development of Persuasive Systems. VTT Science (2014)
13. He, J., Lee, J.N., Hsu, C.: The evolution of knowledge management: current and future application in China. In: PACIS 2003 Proceedings, vol. 88 (2003)
14. Hong, J., Sternthal, B.: The effects of consumer prior knowledge and processing strategies on judgments. J. Mark. Res. **47**, 301–311 (2010)
15. Ko, E.J., Kim, A.H., Kim, S.S.: Toward the understanding of the appropriation of ICT-based smart-work and its impact on performance in organizations. Technol. Forecast. Soc. Chang. **171**, 120994 (2021)
16. Kock, N., Hadaya, P.: Minimum sample size estimation in PLS-SEM: the inverse square root and Gamma-Exponential methods. Inform. Syst. J. **28**(1), 227–261 (2018)
17. Kock, N.: From composites to factors: bridging the gap between PLS and covariance-based structural equation modeling. Inf. Syst. J. **29**(3), 674–706 (2019)
18. Kock, N.: Using WarpPLS in E-collaboration studies: an overview of five main analysis Steps. Int. J. e-Collab. **6**(4), 1–11 (2010)
19. Lakhal, S., Khechine, H., Pascot, D.: Student behavioural intentions to use desktop video conferencing in a distance course: integration of autonomy to the UTAUT model. J. Comput. High. Educ. **25**(2), 93–121 (2013)
20. Lee, M., et al.: How to respond to the fourth industrial revolution, or the second information technology revolution? Dynamic new combinations between technology, market, and society through open innovation. J. Open Innov. Technol. Market Complex. **4**(3), 21 (2018)

21. Liebenberg, J., Benade, T., Ellis, S.: Acceptance of ICT: applicability of the Unified Theory of Acceptance and Use of Technology (UTAUT) to South African students. Afr. J. Inf. Syst. **10**(3), 1 (2018)
22. Lindgren, T., Pink, S., Fors, V.: Fore-sighting autonomous driving - an ethnographic approach. Technol. Forecast. Soc. Chang. **173**, 121105 (2021)
23. Moser, C., Deichmann, D.: Knowledge sharing in two cultures: the moderating effect of national culture on perceived knowledge quality in online communities. Eur. J. Inf. Syst. **30**, 1–19 (2020)
24. Ochmann, J., Laumer, S., Franke, J.: The power of knowledge: a literature review on socio-technical perspectives on organizational knowledge management. In: Twenty-Fifth Americas Conference on Information Systems (2019)
25. Olson, K.E., O'Brien, M.A., Rogers, W.A., Charness, N.: Diffusion of technology: frequency of use for younger and older adults. Ageing Int. **36**(1), 123–145 (2011)
26. Ringle, C.M., Sarstedt, M., Straub, D.W.: A critical look at the use of PLS-SEM. MIS Q. **36**(1), iii–xiv (2012)
27. Rogers, E.M.: Diffusion of innovations: modifications of a model for telecommunications. In: Stoetzer, M.W., Mahler, A. (eds.) Die Diffusion von Innovationen in der Telekommunikation. Schriftenreihe des Wissenschaftlichen Instituts für Kommunikationsdienste, vol. 17, pp. 25–38. Springer, Heidelberg (1995). https://doi.org/10.1007/978-3-642-79868-9_2
28. Rogers, E.M.: Diffusion of Innovations. Simon and Schuster, New York (2010)
29. Stibe, A.: Socially Influencing Systems: Persuading People to Engage with Publicly Displayed Twitter-based Systems. Acta Universitatis Ouluensis (2014)
30. Sussman, S.W., Siegal, W.S.: Informational influence in organizations: an integrated approach to knowledge adoption. Inf. Syst. Res. **14**, 47–65 (2003)
31. Tarde, G.: The Laws of Imitation. Henry Holt and Company, New York (1903)
32. Tenenhaus, M., Vinzi, V.E., Chatelin, Y.-M., Lauro, C.: PLS path modeling. Comput. Stat. Data Anal. **48**(1), 159–205 (2005)
33. Urbach, N., Ahlemann, F.: Structural equation modeling in information systems research using partial least squares. J. Inf. Technol. Theor. Appl. **11**(2), 5–40 (2010)
34. Vejlgaard, H.: Process knowledge in the innovation-decision period. In: Digital Communication Management. IntechOpen (2018)
35. Venkatesh, V., Bala, H.: Technology acceptance model 3 and a research agenda on interventions. Decis. Sci. **39**(2), 273–315 (2008)
36. Venkatesh, V., Thong, J.Y., Xu, X.: Unified theory of acceptance and use of technology: a synthesis and the road ahead. J. Assoc. Inf. Syst. **17**(5), 328–376 (2016)
37. Wetzels, M., Odekerken-Schroder, G., van Oppen, C.: Using PLS path modeling for assessing hierarchical construct models: guidelines and empirical illustration. MIS Q. **33**(1), 177–196 (2009)

UI-Re-Engineering of a Mobile Documentation Software in the Care Sector

Sergio Staab, Ludger Martin[(✉)], and Anika Degreif

RheinMain University of Applied Sciences, 65195 Wiesbaden, Hesse, Germany
{Sergio.Staab,Ludger.Martin}@hs-rm.de,
Anika.Degreif@student.hs-rm.de

Abstract. A disproportionately growing number of care recipients and the associated avalanche of data in all areas of modern care continuously increases the need for more efficient, higher-quality and at the same time more cost-saving options for care and its networking of relatives, doctors, and nurses. This paper presents a web-based documentation platform for persons with dementia called INFODOQ. INFODOQ is currently used in two dementia residential communities, and the nursing staff requested a mobile application. This was developed in a first step and then evaluated by means of eye tracking. The focus of this paper is the engineering process of the documentation, from a web application to a hybrid mobile application. We discuss the results of the eye-tracking evaluation and new findings about the interaction behaviour of caregivers in dealing with mobile care documentation. This is followed by a re-engineering of mobile care documentation and another eye-tracking evaluation for comparison. This work helps to identify obstacles to the development of mobile nursing documentation at the outset and to highlight the advantages and disadvantages of various design elements.

Keywords: Re-engineering · Interface development · User experience and usability

1 Introduction

This paper describes the transformation of a web-based communication platform for dementia communities called INFODOQ from a pure desktop application to a hybrid mobile application. After the development, the user interfaces were evaluated by means of an eye tracking based system. The focus of this work is the design, evaluation, and re-engineering of the care documentation of persons suffering from dementia.

A communication platform called INFODOQ was developed within the framework of a project for the digitalization of dementia residential communities. According to Staab et al. [12], the system serves as a transparent information and communication platform for various dementia living communities to optimize everyday care and nursing. According to a study [4], around 86% of people in Germany use a smartphone every day. Due to the development of mobile technologies and the widespread use of smartphones, the internet can be accessed regardless of location, which simplifies life in many areas. As more and more people prefer their mobile devices to desktop computers, the interest in simple and intuitively usable mobile applications is increasing. This is exactly the idea behind the hybrid mobile application INFODOQ Mobile. In the future, the application will be used in outpatient dementia residential communities and help caregivers, relatives, and assistants to optimally plan their joint daily routine.

Caregivers often do not have access to a desktop PC within the residential communities, so the mobile use of the application on smartphones is important, according to Springer Pflege [7]. Moreover, since the application is used in a special context, it is necessary to be able to perform tasks easily and quickly.

In order to test usability on mobile devices, an eye tracking-based interaction analysis is carried out. In this process, visual attention patterns of test subjects who will use the application daily in the future are identified and analyzed while they perform representative tasks. When conducting the eye tracking-based usability test, eye and gaze movements of test subjects while operating the mobile application are recorded, which describe both conscious and unconscious activities of the tester. By evaluating this eye tracking data, usage problems can be specifically identified and subsequently eliminated. In the context of this paper, an eye tracking based user test is designed with the aim to identify usability problems of the mobile application INFODOQ, which should be optimized.

This paper contributes:

- the presentation of a mobile information platform developed in the context of the digitalization of dementia living communities
- a possibility to analyze mobile activity documentation by means of eye tracking
- discussion of requirements and problems arising from the interaction of caregivers with digital documentation on the Android operating system
- the comparison of the original and the revised software using an eye tracking analysis method

Following this introduction, Sect. 2 presents related work in the field of health information technologies and UI re-engineering of mobile applications. Section 3 describes the software INFODOQ, as well as its mobile version, and presents the most important functionalities, taking a closer look at nursing documentation. Section 4 deals with the analysis by means of eye tracking, describing the test set-up, subjects, and execution. In Sect. 5, the evaluation of the analysis is presented and then discussed in Sect. 6. In Sect. 7, the different UI re-engineering processes are addressed and the comparison of "old" to "new" is clarified. Section 8 describes the second usability test and argues the users' behaviour in using the new interface. Sect. 9 summarizes the work.

2   Related Work

There are currently over 325,000 mobile apps available in all app stores together, according to Roche [9]. Each app is tailored to a specific use case and is intended to support the user in that specific context. Since this thesis deals with a hybrid app, the different app types will be briefly explained to better classify the mobile application later. There are three different types of apps: Native Apps, Web Apps and Hybrid Apps, which the Nielsen Norman Group [2] discusses in more detail. Native apps are downloaded to the mobile device from application stores. Because they are developed specifically for one platform, native apps can access all the features of the device, such as the camera. Web apps are hardly distinguishable from native apps. As the name suggests, web apps are executed as web pages in a browser. After being called up, they can be added to the start screen of the smartphone and used like a normal application. Hybrid apps are a combination of the previously mentioned app types. Like native apps, they are also made available in application stores and can use many device functions. However, like web apps, they are implemented using HTML, which is rendered in a browser. The difference, however, is that the browser is embedded in the app. Hybrid apps also allow cross-platform development and can therefore be used on different mobile operating systems. Offline use and speed stand out in native and hybrid apps. According to the research paper by Martin [6], special framework conditions apply to mobile devices compared to desktop applications, which at the same time place high demands on good usability. Due to the small screen, there is little space for the presentation of content elements. The available input and output channels as well as the operation of an application on a smartphone also differ in many respects from an application on a desktop computer. A desktop application uses a mouse or keyboard, whereas an app uses a multi-touch screen, voice commands or the navigation buttons on the device itself. Touching the touchscreen is usually done using the thumb, which brings with it the problem of a small interaction radius. This limits the areas within a touchscreen that a user can comfortably reach. In addition, a multi-touch screen can recognize several touch points simultaneously. This so-called gesture control must first be learned by users. Since users do not want to spend a lot of time trying to figure out how to use an app and want it to be simple and intuitive, Lecay [5] has elaborated in his work some components that ensure good app usability. These are tailored to the characteristics of a smartphone mentioned in the previous section and are based on general conventions, best practices, and many years of research. The components of an intuitive app that are important for this work are context, input, output, and responsiveness. Most of these components relate to logical functional areas of the application architecture. Before thinking through the design of an application, the focus is first on application utility. According to Lecay [5], context is the foundation of any application, as it represents the situations and circumstances in which an application is used. For this purpose, it is analyzed where, when, and how the application is to be used. This means that not only the current location plays a role, but also the movement of the user when operating the application, the time of day, lighting, and the noise level around the user. A mobile application that takes the context into account appropriately provides the user with good app usability, as it thus meets the user's needs.

The research article on app usability guidelines by Martin [6] also suggests generally relying on what is already known and learned. Operating principles that a user already recognizes as standardized should continue to be used, as complex multi-touch gestures are difficult to learn.

According to a customer loyalty platform [11], a study found that 56% of users uninstall apps within the first seven days of installation, 23% even within the first 24 h. This result once again underlines the importance of integrating usability tests for mobile apps into the app development process.

According to Wieland [18], particular attention should be paid to the fact that the interview situation can influence the user's gaze behavior when conducting the tests. Accordingly, she recommends using eye tracking with other usability engineering methods, such as the Think Aloud method, during task execution.

Tomlin [17] advises following up by asking follow-up questions to determine certain processes or to reconstruct unclear actions.

This work shows the potential of mobile applications and their growing popularity. The applications in the health sector involve some of the issues raised and underpin further research into eye tracking usability analysis in this area.

3   INFODOQ

INFODOQ is a documentation and communication platform that is used in self-managing, outpatient dementia residential communities. The idea of this platform arose from the desire to optimize the day-to-day care and nursing of various dementia flat-sharing communities, according to Staab et al. [13].

Self-managed housing communities are characterized by private living. This means that a legal representative of a resident concludes his or her own tenancy agreement with the landlord [19]. In the shared flats, the focus is on the organization and design of a common everyday life and household. In the process, the residents are provided with care or nursing services that support them and ensure a "family-like everyday atmosphere". In Hesse (Germany) there are currently about 15 dementia shared flats, two of which are involved in the INFODOQ development process [7].

The nursing staff working in dementia shared flats have successfully completed training as nursing specialists and may also have completed further training in psychiatric nursing. The care workers are partly employed by care services or also self-employed. Since this profession requires flexibility and the willingness to work shifts, nights, and weekends, it can be assumed that the target group already has older children. The user group is therefore made up of experienced caregivers who are between 40 and 55 years old. In addition, they are professionally and humanly qualified for the care of people with dementia. The target group is characterized by a high degree of responsibility, stamina, mental resilience, care, and empathy, according to the Ambulanter Pflegedienst - Aktiv Dahoam [8].

Above all, the nursing services would like to use the application for a prompt and uncomplicated documentation of services to ensure transparent care for the residents' relatives. They want to be able to quickly record any care documentation, which in this case stands for an activity carried out with a resident.

In addition to the functions "news", a display of news including push function. Scheduling", a calendar of appointments across target groups and with the possibility of attachments and filtering. "Tasks", a possibility to distribute tasks individually to people, including description text and due date. The focus of this work is on the most important functionality, the "documentation", which until the implementation of INFODOQ had to be filled out three times a day in analogue form.

Figure 1 shows the care documentation in which different activities were entered by one caregiver (Ben) for several patients.

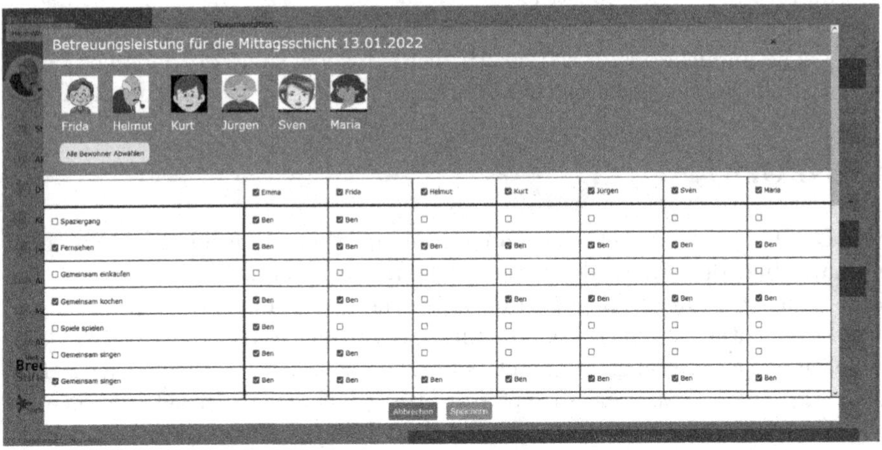

Fig. 1. Desktop view of the care documentation

During the working hours in the residential communities, the target group has neither an office nor a staff room and thus no possibility for digital documentation of the care, which is, however, required by the federal health law [3]. As the target group increasingly works via mobile data collection systems [7], caregivers also benefit from INFODOQ Mobile for more efficient coordination of WG processes. Users do not only want to document care, but also to be able to plan it with relatives and support staff. It is important to them that they can work more productively through digital data collection and thus save time, which can lead to a more intensive connection with the dementia patients. Since a caregiver is allowed to work a maximum of eight hours a day, a quickly recordable exchange between all caregivers is necessary.

INFODOQ is currently only available as a platform for calling up on PCs or laptops. Due to the lack of desktop computers in the residential communities, the idea of INFODOQ Mobile was born. The aim is to integrate the application flexibly into the everyday life of the users and to contribute to more accessibility.

3.1 INFODOQ - Mobile

The new concept of further developing INFODOQ as a hybrid mobile app upgrades the entire system architecture of the website implemented in the INFODOQ project and combines the advantages from the world of mobile apps and web technologies with a hybrid mobile applicable app.

With the help of a smartphone app, a care service can be documented and made centrally accessible with just a few finger movements [7].

The focus here is on easy and intuitive handling for all users of the mobile application. INFODOQ Mobile is implemented as a hybrid application, which makes it platform-independent in relation to the mobile operating system.

Figure 2 shows the nursing documentation as a mobile view.

Fig. 2. Mobile view of the care documentation

The design of the various HTML elements such as the input fields, the colors or the drop-down menus were based on other components of the web application to maintain the uniform design. For example, the expandable fields of already entered activities were designed like in the web application. This increases usability, as users are already familiar with these mechanics and can use them intuitively. Each column of the previous table is mapped individually. The column is selectable via a drop-down menu. In order to minimize the listing of activities, only those activities are displayed that have been carried out. This again saves vertical space and prevents unnecessary scrolling.

4   Eyetracking

In the following, the structure, implementation, and results of the eye-tracking-based user test of the INFODOQ Mobile care documentation are presented.

Difficulties in interaction with the user interface on the part of the users are to be identified, as well as areas that are not optimally designed. In addition, the identification of challenging interaction elements is achieved, which appear intuitive for the app developers, but can lead to difficulties in operation for the target group. The general goal of this user test is to identify problems to improve usability in the long term in line with the target groups and to determine these deficiencies by collecting test data. The following questions are to be clarified:

- Does the order in which users perceive things correspond to the information hierarchy?
- Which areas are only skimmed over, and which are looked at intensively?
- Which areas escape attention?
- How long does the first interaction with an element take on average?
- Is entering data intuitive?
- Is the use of different colors necessary to distinguish target groups?

4.1   Preparation

According to statistics from the German online portal Statistica [1], the global market share in the last 10 years for the Android mobile operating system has increased to 72.4%, which means that in 2021, Android smartphones will be predominantly used for internet usage. Due to this widespread use, INFODOQ Mobile is also tested on an Android smartphone for the interaction analysis carried out in this work. The smartphone used is the Samsung Galaxy S20 FE, which has a screen size of 6.5 in., which corresponds to the dimensions of 159.8×74.5 mm. The screen is in 20:9 format and features a FullVision Infinity-O display, which gives the impression of an edge-to-edge display. The smartphone also has an FHD+ display with a resolution of 1080×2400 pixels, which can be seen in the technical data [10] from Samsung. The Samsung Galaxy S20 FE also supports screen mirroring via USB, which is essential for recording the screen during the eye-tracking-based user test.

This smartphone is attached using a stand, which is available as an accessory for the Tobii Eye-Tracker Pro Nano. Figure 3 shows the hardware used by the manufacturer Tobii AB (publ) [14].

According to the manufacturer [16], this ensures the quality of the eye tracking data because the eye tracker is thus in the optimal position in relation to the mobile device. The eye tracker has a sampling rate of 60 Hz and uses video-based eye tracking with pupil and corneal reflection using the bright and dark pupil techniques. In this process, the camera of the Tobii Eye-Tracker Pro Nano captures images of both eyes of a test person for precise measurement of gaze, eye position in 3D space and pupil diameter. According to the manufacturer, the precision is on average $0.1°$ under optimal conditions, which can be seen in

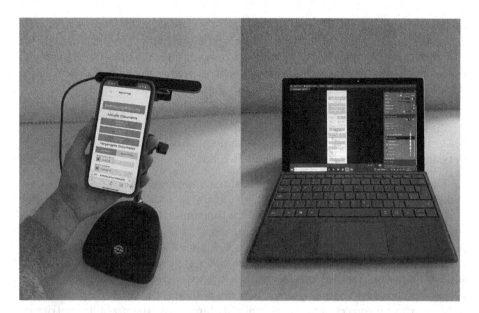

Fig. 3. Example structure of the eye tracker Tobii Pro Nano

the Tobii Eye-Tracker Pro Nano brochure [15]. With the help of the eye tracker, videos are recorded in HD quality of the mobile device screen, which means 60 frames per second with a latency of only 10 milliseconds. The Tobii Pro Lab software can then analyze and evaluate this eye-tracking data and visualize it. This makes for an extremely robust data collection system that acquires data regardless of ethnicity or visual aids and is also tolerant of head movements and different lighting conditions.

4.2 Execution

The eye tracking-based user test is conducted as a summative usability test. Since the basic concept of INFODOQ Mobile already exists and the application is thus in the final phase of realization, this type of usability test is suitable. Here, a controlled execution of the test is aimed at, whereby each test person must solve two tasks with the help of the application.

During the execution of the tasks, there is no interaction between the moderator and the test person, so that the latter cannot be distracted. The tasks are placed in writing directly next to the eye tracker and the smartphone so that the test subjects do not have to leave their seats or move their heads too much. The tasks are processed sequentially. After a task has been read in full, the first glance at the smartphone is considered the start of a task. Reaching the task goal, such as manually or automatically closing a detail page, is considered the end of the task. With the help of the eye-tracker software, the test moderator observes the subjects' gaze trajectories and their interaction with the application. During the performance of each task, abnormalities are noted, and the successful completion of a task is recorded in writing.

For testing the functions of the care documentation, the nurses are to create a care documentation for a given nursing shift, as well as document a short entry of a given resident. The tasks are structured as follows:

- the care documentation for Frida from 01 January until today. to date. When you have finished, close the page again.
- Document a nursing record for the midday shift. You have done memory training with the residents Sven and Helmut.

The eye tracking-based user test measures fixation and visitation metrics as well as patterns of visual attention. These metrics provide information about the dwell time, the number of fixations and the time until the first fixation of certain interaction elements, which are also called Areas of Interests (AoI). In addition, the duration and number of visits to an AoI, time to first visit and sequences are measured. The performance metrics considered in the usability test are Task Success, Time on Task, Errors and Efficiency. By determining how many test subjects successfully complete tasks, how much time is taken to complete a task and how many incorrect actions are made within a task, the usability metrics of effectiveness and efficiency of INFODOQ Mobile can be assessed.

Since the execution of a test takes about 30 to 40 min, all test persons are asked to enter the test room one after the other. A total of five people, all of them female, take part in the usability test. The average age of the test person was 50.

The quantitative data collection in an eye tracking study is always bound to certain areas, the so-called Areas of Interests. For this purpose, the eye tracking recordings are compared with any number of screenshots of the app with the help of the analysis software Tobii Pro Lab in order to transfer any gaze patterns to the screenshots.

Dwell time, duration of fixations, number of fixations and sequence of an AoI are analyzed.

The analysis software measures fixations that lie within an AOI for the fixation-related metrics. Fixations are defined based on a gaze filter, in this case the standard Tobii I-VT filter, which counts every valid eye movement with a minimum fixation duration of 60 milliseconds as a fixation. For a visit, all data between the start of fixation and the end of the last fixation within an AOI's are considered, including saccades, blinks, or invalid gaze data. For the AOI's, important interaction elements of tasks with a low success rate are selected, which ultimately measures the total duration, the average duration, the number, and the time to the first fixation or visit, as well as the minimum and maximum duration of a fixation.

5   First Evaluation

Figure 4 shows the visualization of the heatmaps and the visualization of the gaze trajectories (gaze plots or scan paths) of the care documentation.

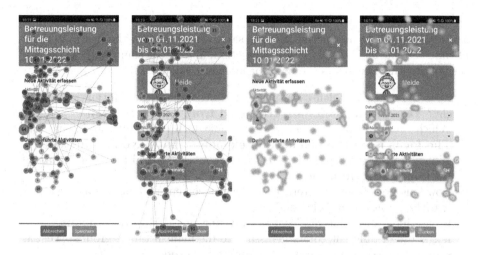

Fig. 4. Mobile care documentation - heatmaps & gauze plots

The average total duration of fixations and the number of fixations is higher than the test moderator. The duration until the heading is perceived for the first time is also two seconds longer on average. The time until the first fixation of the headline took about four times longer for a test person who has difficulty finding his way around the page than for the test moderator. In general, the re-reading of saved care documentation as well as the creation of new care documentation is fraught with errors in execution.

Task Success: The success rate of the nursing staff in creating care documentation was 20%. The success rate of reading past care documentation is 70%. Time on Task: The nurses need on average - 00:03:26 min to create the care documentation, the test moderator needs on average - 00:02:13 min. The nurses need on average - 00:02:44 min to read the care documentation, the test moderator needs on average - 00:01:05 min. Errors: The nurses make an average of two errors per creation of the care documentation, the test moderator makes an average of one error. The nurses make an average of one error when reading the care documentation, the test moderator makes zero errors. Efficiency:

The final performance metric of efficiency is calculated in two ways: counting the number of actions a test taker undertakes per task or combining the success rate against the average time taken. The efficiency of the care service is around 36%.

6   Discussion

The creation of a new care documentation consists of several steps, which were visualized in the Fig. 2 and analyzed by means of eye tracking in Fig. 4.

Selecting a service using the drop-down menu and selecting residents is not intuitive. Confirming the input is also done with complications. The test persons clicked directly on Save and were informed that the data had been successfully saved. However, no new activities were saved. According to the heatmap, a lot of time is spent on elements without function, and at the same time it does not seem clear which elements are used for interaction at all.

- Does the order in which users perceive things match the information hierarchy? **Yes, the elements are traversed from top to bottom**.
- Which areas are only skimmed over, and which are looked at intensively? **The focus is on the header and elements that have no functions**.
- Which areas escape attention? **Little attention is paid to the areas of backup and termination**.
- How long does the first interaction with an element take on average? **Significantly longer than claimed**.
- Is entering data intuitive? **Yes, if they are not dropdown menus**.
- Is the use of different colors necessary to distinguish target groups? **Yes, it seems so - some elements are misinterpreted**.

7 Redesign

The design was completely rebuilt after the alarmingly poor performance of our eye-tracking based user test of the care documentation INFODOQ Mobile.

The optimization for creating a new care documentation is shown in Fig. 5 shown.

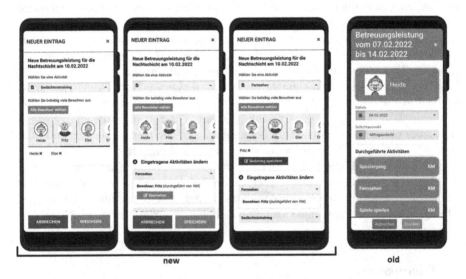

Fig. 5. Mobile - care documentation new version vs. old version

The confirmation of the selected service and the residents is no longer required, as this is very error prone. Thus, only new care documentation can be saved in the new mobile version. The drop-down menu for resident selection is also replaced by a slider, which simplifies selection and editing and does not cover the residents already selected. As soon as a service has been created within the selected shift, it will appear in the lower area of the page when this input mask is opened again. The activities already entered can be expanded and edited as before. All irrelevant buttons are hidden in the edit mode so that the view is directed to the essentials. In addition, the primary color on this page is only used for interaction elements, so that the user's gaze is drawn to these elements. The filter settings for displaying the already saved care documentation are also displayed in a simplified way in the optimized version. However, the old function remains.

As can be seen in Fig. 6, the detailed views of past care documentation are displayed very differently in the previous app version.

Fig. 6. Mobile - care documentation history new version vs. old version

With the app adaptation, these views have been unified so that the user only must learn one way of operating in the saved documentation area. In addition, the user is offered a clear and space-saving display in which it can be directly recorded how many entries are stored per resident.

8 Second Evaluation

This chapter deals with the evaluation of the optimised INFODOQ app. For this purpose, a second eyetracking-based usability test is conducted to test the adapted design for usability. The test from chapter four will be conducted again. Figure 7 shows the visualization of the heatmaps and the visualization of the gaze trajectories (gaze plots or scan paths) of the new care documentation.

In the new design, the attention is clearly more on the operating elements, i.e. precisely on the elements that have a functional task. It can be interpreted

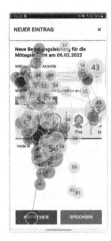 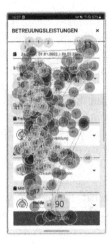

Fig. 7. New mobile care documentation - heatmaps & gauze plots

from this behaviour that the hierarchy and the arrangement of the elements form a clearer unit in the new structure. The performance indicator for the efficiency of the nursing service is 71% (an increase of 35%) in the renewed test, since the operation was clearly perceived as faster and more intuitive.

9   Conclusion

In the scope of this work, a mobile information platform called INFODOQ was presented. The information platform was converted from a web application to a hybrid mobile application and the usability of the care documentation was investigated using an eye-tracking-based interaction analysis with various test subjects from the corresponding target groups according to performance metrics. The integration of eye tracking technology in this usability study offers the possibility to observe actual eye movements of the users and to understand interactions with the application. This allows for a qualitative and quantitative description of the eye movements that can be analyzed. Some interaction difficulties with the user interface were identified, such as elements without a function appearing to be executable, dropdown menus, and no explicit coloring causing confusion. Significantly more time is spent searching for information and the possibilities of the functionalities than on the actual task. These findings contribute to a revised version of the user interface that has been shown to offer significantly improved usability.

References

1. Bolkart, J.: Marktanteile der führenden mobilen betriebssysteme an der internetnutzung mit mobiltelefonen weltweit von september 2010 bis September 2021,

Oktober 2021. https://de.statista.com/statistik/daten/studie/184335/umfrage/marktanteil-der-mobilen-betriebssysteme-weltweit-seit-2009/

2. Budiu, R.: Mobile: native apps, web apps, and hybrid apps. Website, September 2013. https://www.nngroup.com/articles/quant-vs-qual/

3. des Bundes, R.: Gesamte rechtsvorschrift für gesundheits- und krankenpflegegesetz, fassung vom 13 October 2021. https://www.ris.bka.gv.at/GeltendeFassung.wxe?Abfrage=Bundesnormen&Gesetzesnummer=10011026

4. F, T.: Anteil der Smartphone-Nutzer Deutschland in den Jahren 2012 bis 2021, April 2021. https://de.statista.com/statistik/daten/studie/585883/umfrage/anteil-der-smartphone-nutzer-in-deutschland/

5. Lacey, M.: Usability Matters: Mobile-First UX for Developers and other Accidental Designers. Simon and Schuster, New York (2018)

6. Beschnitt, M.: App-usability - herausforderungen und guidelines, Januar 2013. https://www.eresult.de/ux-wissen/forschungsbeitraege/einzelansicht/news/app-usability-herausforderungen-und-guidelines/

7. Pflege, S.: Kommunikationsplattform für demenz-wgs. https://www.springerpflege.de/demenz/kommunikationsplattform-fuer-demenz-wgs/18669178

8. Pflegedienst, A., Dahoam, A.: Die pflegeausbildung und ihre voraussetzungen. https://www.aktiv-dahoam.de/pflegeausbildung-voraussetzungen/

9. Roche, D.: mHealth App Economics Current Status and Future Trends in Mobile Health. techreport 1, The Digital Health Strategy Company (2017)

10. Samsung: Technische daten. https://www.samsung.com/de/smartphones/galaxy-s20/specs/

11. Chengappa, S.: 56% of users uninstall apps within 7 days of installation, März 2020. https://www.thehindubusinessline.com/info-tech/56-of-app-users-uninstall-it-them-apps-within-the-first-7-days-ofinstallation/article31098697.ece

12. Staab, S.: Eine Informationsplattform für den Einsatz betreuter Wohn und Pflegegruppen. In: 18. Deutschen Kongress für Versorgungsforschung. Berlin, Germany, October 2019. https://doi.org/10.3205/19dkvf017, dKVF

13. Staab, S., Luderschmidt, J., Martin, L.: Evaluation of the Results of UI-Re-Engineering. In: Mobile Web and Intelligent Information Systems. vol. 1. Roma Italy, August 2021, mobiWis

14. TobiiPro: Analyzing recordings made with the mobile device stand. https://www.tobiipro.com/learn-and-support/learn/steps-in-an-eye-tracking-study/data/how-do-i-analyse-my-study/

15. TobiiPro: What do we study when we use eye tracking data? https://www.tobiipro.com/learn-and-support/learn/eye-tracking-essentials/what-do-we-study-when-we-use-eye-tracking-data/

16. TobiiPro: Zubehör für mobiles testen. https://www.tobiipro.com/de/produkte/mobile-testing-accessory/

17. Tomlin, W.C.: UX Optimization, Combining Behavioral UX and Usability Testing Data to Optimize Websites. Apress, New York (2018)

18. Wieland, M.: Eye tracking Ein Überblick, May 2016. https://www.eresult.de/ux-wissen/forschungsbeitraege/einzelansicht/news/eye-tracking-ein-ueberblick/

19. Wohngemeinschaften, H.F.D.: Was macht eine selbstverwaltete demenz-wg aus? https://demenz-wg-hessen.de/grundsaetze-selbstverwalteter-demenz-wgs/

GUI Element Detection from Mobile UI Images Using YOLOv5

Mehmet Dogan Altinbas(✉) ⓘ and Tacha Serif(✉) ⓘ

Yeditepe University, 34755 Atasehir Istanbul, Turkey
{daltinbas,tserif}@cse.yeditepe.edu.tr

Abstract. In mobile application development, building a consistent user interface (UI) might be a costly and time-consuming process. This is especially the case if an organization has a separate team for each mobile platform such as iOS and Android. In this regard, the companies that choose the native mobile app development path end up going through do-overs as the UI work done on one platform needs to be repeated for other platforms too. One of the tedious parts of UI design tasks is creating a graphical user interface (GUI). There are numerous tools and prototypes in the literature that aim to create feasible GUI automation solutions to speed up this process and reduce the labor workload. However, as the technologies evolve and improve new versions of existing algorithms are created and offered. Accordingly, this study aims to employ the latest version of YOLO, which is YOLOv5, to create a custom object detection model that recognizes GUI elements in a given UI image. In order to benchmark the newly trained YOLOv5 GUI element detection model, existing work from the literature and their data set is considered and used for comparison purposes. Therefore, this study makes use of 450 UI samples of the VINS dataset for testing, a similar amount for validation and the rest for model training. Then the findings of this work are compared with another study that has used the SSD algorithm and VINS dataset to train, validate and test its model, which showed that proposed algorithm outperformed SSD's mean average precision (mAP) by 15.69%.

Keywords: Object detection · Graphical user interface · Deep learning

1 Introduction

Nowadays smartphones are much more capable than the computer that guided the first man to the moon [1]. Indeed, smartphones these days have powerful processors, advanced cameras, precise sensors, and user-friendly operating systems. Currently, there are more than 6 million mobile apps available in leading app markets for smartphones, tablets, and other devices running on different operating systems [2]. The revenue generated by these mobile apps is expected to be more than $935 billion by 2023. That is almost double the revenue generated in 2020 [3].

One of the most cumbersome parts of mobile application development is the design of its UI. There are multiple steps that need to be undertaken to build and design a user-centered and user-friendly interface that would be easy to use by its target audience.

I. Awan et al. (Eds.): MobiWIS 2022, LNCS 13475, pp. 32–45, 2022.
https://doi.org/10.1007/978-3-031-14391-5_3

Hence, depending on the target group - e.g. young children, teenagers, professionals, elderly etc. - of the user base, the UI is created with different GUI element sizes, color schemes and haptics. Developing a GUI is one of those repetitive tasks since every mobile platform has its own UI design editor, programming, or markup language. There are several techniques - such as native development and cross-platform development - to implement mobile applications and their UI. Cross-platform applications are the ones that can run on multiple platforms with little or no modification. On the other hand, native apps are built specifically for a particular platform or operating system. Essentially, when these kinds of apps are built, they are designed to run on one specific platform. So, if an app is made for Android, it will not work on iOS or vice versa. Therefore, work done for one platform is required to be duplicated for another. There are a considerable number of studies in the literature that have proposed tools and frameworks to improve GUI development processes by addressing GUI element detection and automated GUI generation. These studies utilize current or newly emerged algorithms or models to achieve this automation. Bearing in mind that, GUI element detection in mobile UI images is a domain-specific object detection task, there is still room for improvement based on the cutting-edge improvements in the area of object detection. To the best of our knowledge, no work has utilized the YOLOv5 object detection algorithm for mobile GUI element detection. Therefore, this study aims to create and train a model that identifies a set of known GUI elements and detects their location within a UI image.

Accordingly, this paper is structured as follows; Sect. 2 provides a brief introduction to GUI element detection and elaborates on its common use cases. Section 3 details the tools, algorithms, UI image datasets, and performance evaluation metrics for object detection tasks. Section 4 describes the requirements and system design. Section 5 depicts the implementation of the prototype, and Sect. 6 provides the results in detail and elaborates on the findings. Finally, Sect. 7 summarizes the outcomes and discusses future development areas.

2   Background

By making use of 50000 GUI images, Chen et al. [4] attempted to undertake an empirical comparative study using the seven most popular GUI detection methods to evaluate their capabilities, limitations, and effectiveness. The findings of this study point out that existing computer vision (CV) techniques are inadequate in extracting the unique characteristics of GUI elements and detecting their location with high accuracy. So, the authors propose and implement a hybrid prototype, where they combine both the CV methods and deep learning models to test the hybrid method's extraction and location accuracy. The newly proposed prototype uses CV methods to detect non-text GUI elements and deep learning models for text-based GUI elements. As a result, their findings indicated that the proposed system performed 86% better in accuracy of region classification for non-textual GUI elements; whereas 91% accuracy in region classification of all elements.

Similarly, Xie et al. [5] suggested a tool that utilizes CV and object detection methods to provide accurate positioning of GUI elements along with their types. This tool is designed to assist GUI reverse engineering or GUI testing operations. Accordingly, in their work, they take the advantage of CV algorithms to detect the position and frame of non-text GUI elements. Algorithms such as flood-filling, Sklansky's, and shape recognition are used to obtain layout blocks and as a follow up; the connected component labeling technique is applied to identify the region of the GUI components. Following that, the ResNet50 classifier, trained with 90000 GUI elements, is then used to recognize and group each GUI element in predefined regions into 15 categories. On the other hand, in order to detect and expose text-based GUI elements, they utilize the EAST text detector. Consequently, it has been determined that the suggested tool produces more accurate identification results than the similar studies in the literature.

Bunian et al. [6] proposed a visual search framework that takes a UI design as an input and returns design samples that resemble visually. A part of this study includes creating a custom GUI element detection model. This model is generated by using a custom dataset of 4543 UI images and adopting the SSD (Single Shot MultiBox Detector) high-accuracy object detection algorithm. It is used to find types of GUI components and their positions in the input image. The GUI element detection model is tested using 450 images from their custom dataset and it has achieved a mean average precision (mAP) of 76.39%.

On the other hand, Nguyen et al. [7] proposed a system that automatically identifies UI components from iOS or Android app screenshots and generates user interfaces that closely resemble the original screenshots. The authors of this study intend to automate the UI code generation based on existing app screenshots. Accordingly, the proposed system applies CV and optical character recognition (OCR) algorithms on a given screenshot image. After that, overlapping areas and text blocks are rearranged by adhering a set of rules that were defined by the authors. This rearrangement step is followed by UI element classification and app generation. Their evaluations showed that the proposed system produces very similar UIs to the original input image. Also, despite its high precision, the prototype system was able to generate UI code for each given screenshot in 9 s on average, which is an admirable performance.

Last but not least, Chen et al. [8] proposed a framework that takes a UI image as input and generates GUI code for the requested target platform. This study aimed at lowering the development and maintenance cost of GUI code generation for both Android and iOS platforms. The implemented prototype has three sub-processes. The first process entails the component detection task, which is performed using CV algorithms such as Canny edge and Edge-dilation. Additionally, a convolutional neural network (CNN) is used to train two classification models based on iOS and Android platforms to identify the types of the detected GUI components. The second process involves the type mapping of the detected GUI components for iOS and Android platforms. And lastly, the final process encompasses the GUI file generation, which is accomplished by using individual GUI code templates for Android and iOS apps. The test results of the prototype system showed that it achieved 85% accuracy in GUI element classification and managed to create UI designs that are 60%–70% compatible and similar to the original UI image.

3 Methodology

In line with the literature detailed above, this section discusses the tools, algorithms, datasets, and evaluation metrics that are used for GUI element detection.

3.1 Tools

There are numerous approaches to implementing a GUI element detection model. Accordingly, there are many development environments and an extensive set of libraries that are built upon various programming languages. For example, OpenCV (Open-Source Computer Vision Library) [9] is a free and open-source software library for computer vision and machine learning. OpenCV provides a common infrastructure for computer vision applications. It supports several programming languages and platforms. Additionally, Apple has recently launched its CV framework called Vision [10], which enables developers to utilize computer vision algorithms. Also, Google Colab [11] has been developed as an open-source project to provide researchers with a fully functional computing environment, where they can write and execute arbitrary Python code for machine learning tasks without needing to set up a whole computing infrastructure.

3.2 Algorithms

It is undoubtedly true that object detection tasks can take advantage of image processing algorithms. These algorithms can be used to filter out redundant or less relevant information and highlight the desired parts and important features of the image, which can be an invaluable asset in GUI element detection. Accordingly, an image in hand can be sharpened or its contrast can be increased using these algorithms, which as a result end up in a much clearer form with highlighted edges, finer details, and more explicit regions. Also, image processing algorithms can be used to flip, rotate, scale, or crop images to achieve data augmentation and increase the amount of data that can be used while an object detection model is trained. Image processing techniques can be considered as an intermediary step in the preparation and enhancement of a raw input image before it is processed with object detection algorithms to derive some meaningful information.

Even though numerous studies have combined and utilized the aforementioned algorithms successfully, deep learning techniques also produce promising results when used for GUI element detection. Deep learning, which is a subdomain of machine learning, introduces a more accurate way of computer vision as it uses a more sophisticated algorithm called artificial neural network (ANN). An ANN mimics the human brain as it consists of millions of interconnected processing nodes that correspond to similar behavior to neurons in the brain. Therefore, ANNs are broadly used to make generalizations and inferences. Also, it is one of the best techniques to find patterns, make predictions and reveal the relationships between the input and the output of any given problem.

There are several types of neural networks depending on the context of their use; however, convolutional neural networks (CNNs) [12] are the ones that are most utilized in object detection. CNNs vary based on the procedure they follow. For instance, in region-based convolutional neural networks (R-CNN), an image is divided into region proposals and then CNN is applied for each region to extract the most fundamental features. Although this approach produces good results, the training phase is long and time-consuming since it applies CNN to each one of the regions one by one. On the other hand, Fast R-CNN [13], which is proposed to solve the aforementioned drawbacks of R-CNN, performs faster object detection by feeding input images to CNN rather than feeding the region proposals individually. However, You Only Look Once (YOLO) [14] is one the most popular algorithms for object detection. YOLO stands out from the above-mentioned algorithms as it seeks parts of the image rather than complete image and predicts the bounding boxes of objects and their class probabilities.

3.3 Datasets

There are several datasets in the literature that are used in various GUI-related studies. The Rico dataset [15] is a collection of design data that reveals the graphical, textual, structural, and interactive design attributes of Android apps. These attributes can be convenient to support data-driven applications in various ways such as design searching and UI layout generation. This dataset consists of 72000 individual UI screens from more than 9700 Android applications, which are created based on 27 different app categories.

Last but not least, the VINS dataset [6] is a collection of annotated UI images and it consists of wireframe images, screenshots from iPhone and Android apps. The UI designs in the dataset are from the Uplabs [16], and UI screens from the Rico dataset. It comprises 4800 pairings of UI design images with their matching XML files in Pascal-VOC format. The original study [6] where the VINS dataset was first introduced aimed at building an object detection-based visual search framework for a given mobile UI image. The evaluation result of the framework produced promising results in terms of GUI element detection accuracy and visual search precision.

3.4 Object Detection Evaluation Metrics

Object detection evaluation metrics reveal how well the object detection model is performing. Accordingly, precision is the ratio of correctly detected elements to all the elements detected by the model. It is a measure of how accurate a model is at predicting positive samples. As it is depicted in Eq. 1, it is calculated by dividing the true positives by the total number of positive predictions. Also, recall is a measure of how many relevant objects are detected, which is calculated by dividing the true positive elements by the total number of true positives and false negatives - see Eq. 2.

$$Precision = \frac{True\ Positive}{True\ Positive + False\ Positive} \tag{1}$$

$$Recall = \frac{True\ Positive}{True\ Positive + False\ Negative} \tag{2}$$

On the other hand, the intersection over union (IoU) (Fig. 1) is the ratio that is obtained by dividing the number of pixels in the intersection between a ground-truth object and a predicted object, with the the number of pixels in the union. It is mostly used as an evaluation metric for tasks such as object detection and segmentation. Also, the average precision (AP) metric is often used to assess the accuracy of object detectors such as the Faster R-CNN and YOLOv5. AP is calculated as the area under the precision-recall curve.

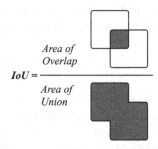

Fig. 1. Intersection over union formula

4   Analysis and Design

In order to create a custom GUI detection model, a collection of mobile UI images must be either newly generated or an existing dataset should be used. Furthermore, these images should be grouped in a way that they contain predominantly a specific GUI element - where each image group becomes a training class for the specific GUI element. These classes can be seen as the objects that are intended to be discovered by the object detector.

Considering that this study aims to evaluate accuracy and the average precision of the new YOLOv5 model, there was a need for a similar study where the same classes and evaluation phases can be followed. Accordingly, the training image dataset and the algorithm that was suitable for our study was the work of Bunian et al. [6]. Therefore, all the image classes that need to be generated for this study, required to follow suit the structure of Bunian et al.'s work. For the very same reason, instead of creating our own dataset of UI images, the VINS dataset which was used in Bunian et al.'s study is obtained and split into multiple subsets - i.e. training images, validation images and testing images. In order to keep the consistency of the comparative work, this model was also to be trained, validated and tested with the very same number of UI images of the same image dataset. In the comparative study [6], the authors make use of 4543 out of 4800 VINS UI images; where the total 4543 is split into three smaller groups as 3643 for training, 450 for validation and 450 for testing.

Taking into consideration the above image numbers, the system that would be training the model should at least have a decent amount of CPU and GPU resources. There are multiple paths that could be taken to train this model - such as local PC-based or cloud-based training approaches. Each one of these options do contain their own advantages, such as for the prior, all the data is stored locally and training could last as long as required. The latter does not involve running a local server or inhouse PC, which can be distracted by hardware failure or power outage. However, if the training process is conducted on cloud, then the researcher is limited with the amount of service time that is given by the cloud provider, which can be a cumbersome task if the training phases take long periods of time and require re-setup/reconfigure every time.

5   Implementation

The following section details the preparation and development steps taken to achieve the proposed GUI element detection model. Accordingly, to train the prototype model, a Mac mini, with 3 GHz 6-Core 8th generation Intel core i5 and 32 GB memory, is used to carry out all the operational steps necessary - such as data preparation and model training. As mentioned in the previous section, the same training can be conducted on Google's Colab cloud solution, however, when this option was tried initially, the time required to train the model increased substantially, since the Colab virtual machine lifetime is limited to 12 h and required reconfiguration to continue from the last checkpoint. Hence, the implementation of the prototype proceeded with an inhouse Mac mini.

First and foremost, the implementation started with data preparation, which involved the conversion of the Pascal VOC annotation files to a YOLOv5 compatible format. Thereafter, the GUI element detection model training phase is performed.

5.1   Preparing the Dataset

The work by Bunian et al. [6] has two phases: (a) to identify and locate UI elements in any given screen capture image using a trained model by the SSD algorithm; (b) to use the initially created VINS image dataset to compare with the given screen capture image and identify the most similar images based on UI element hierarchies. Since this work only aims to evaluate and compare the precision of UI element identification and location using a YOLOv5 trained model, it will try to faithfully follow the steps of the first phase (a) of Bunian et al. Therefore, all class sizes and names used in the implementation will comply with the existing study.

In line with the Bunian et al. study, the total number of UI images in the dataset is reduced from 4800 to 4543. This reduction is achieved by removing the existing wireframe images in the original dataset. Also, to match the dataset structure with the existing study, 4543 UI images are split into three sets for training, validation and testing - respectively having the ratio of 80%, 10% and 10%. Furthermore, the naming convention of the classes that are used for training were kept in compliance with the existing study so that the results of the new model can be compared directly. Accordingly, the names of the classes generated are *Background Image, Checked View, Icon, Input Field, Image,*

Text, Text Button, Sliding Menu, Page Indicator, Pop-Up Window, Switch and *Upper Task Bar.*

The VINS dataset contains annotation files along with the mobile UI images. The annotations are stored in XML files using Pascal VOC format. However, YOLOv5 demands annotations for each image in the form of a TXT file, with each line describing a bounding box. Therefore, a Python script is run in the directory where the dataset is located, to find each of the XML files (Fig. 2a) and convert them to TXT format (Fig. 2b).

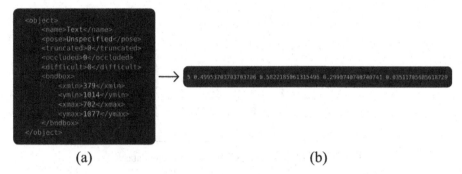

(a)   (b)

Fig. 2. An example of conversion from Pascal VOC XML to YOLO TXT

5.2 GUI Element Detection Model

The YOLOv5 algorithm is employed to create a custom GUI element detection model. It is deemed appropriate since YOLO family algorithms tend to be fastly deployable - requiring limited number of library and dependency setup; but on the other hand, resulting with a swift and accurate real-time object detection architecture.

Accordingly, initially the YOLOv5 repository, which includes its open-source implementation, is cloned to the computer. Then, the YOLOv5 libraries and dependencies are installed. The YOLOv5 algorithm takes the required configuration data from two *yaml* text files - namely *train.yaml* and *data.yaml*. The *train.yaml* includes parameters that describe the model architecture. In order to speed up the training process, there are a couple of pre-trained models (*YOLOv5n, YOLOv5s, YOLOv5m, YOLOv5l* and *YOLOv5x*) within the repositories. For the purpose of UI image training, in our study *YOLOv5s*, which is the smallest and fastest model available, is used as the reference starting point. Hence, the pretrained weights of *YOLOv5s* are used as the beginning of the training process to avoid an overfitting of the model. In the second configuration file - *data.yaml* - the training, validation, and test set paths on the local PC are provided. Also a parameter called *nc* is set, which declares the number of classes in the dataset in both of the *train.yaml* and *data.yaml* files. Considering the total number of classes - GUI element types - that is utilized as part of this training process, the *nc* value is set to 12.

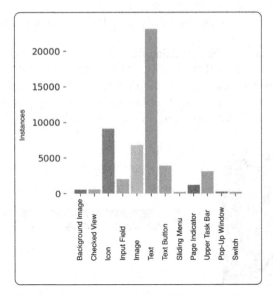

Fig. 3. Distribution of class labels in training dataset

After the *yaml* files are configured, the model training phase is initiated. The above figure (Fig. 3) shows the distribution of the total 50413 annotated GUI instances in 3643 training images, which are split into 12 classes. The new model is trained (Fig. 4) for 100 epochs and with a batch size of 16 training images; and as a result, it took 38 h and 33 min to fully train the GUI element detection model.

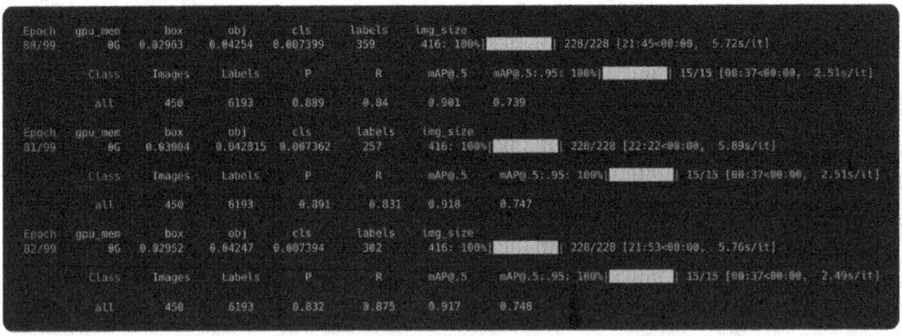

Fig. 4. A snapshot from the training phase

After the training phase is completed, the resulting model is used to detect GUI elements in a given image. This process is achieved by invoking the Python detector script, which is provided as part of the YOLOv5 repository. The detector script is fed with an UI image (Fig. 5a) and after running the trained model, it inferences the relevant UI items and their location on images and saves the annotated image (Fig. 5b) to a specified destination folder.

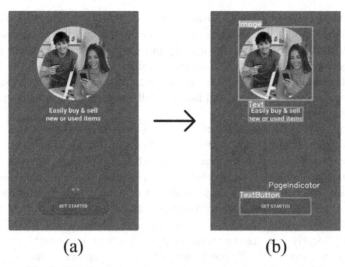

(a)   (b)

Fig. 5. Running inference on an image using the trained model

6 Evaluation

Since one of the main objectives of this study is to train and evaluate a newly released object detection model, which in this case is used to detect and classify GUI elements in UI images, this section initially draws plots using PASCAL VOC (IoU = 0.5) and MS COCO [17] (AP@[0.5:0.05:0.95]) evaluation metrics. The rest of the section presents the class base average precision findings and compares with the benchmark study.

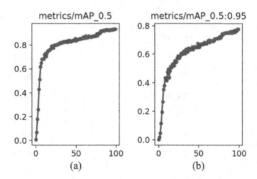

Fig. 6. Accuracy results of model training on the validation set

After each epoch during the training process, the validation set is used to evaluate the model. This evaluation is specifically observed to optimize and fine-tune the model hyperparameters for the subsequent epoch of training. Thus, it is ensured that the training proceeds in the right direction without any issues. Accordingly, the total of 450 UI images that are selected as the validation set are utilized to calculate the mAP values at specific IoU thresholds. As a result, the validation findings show that the model has achieved an mAP (IoU = 0.5) of 93.3% at the last epoch of the training process (Fig. 6a). Considering the MS COCO dataset challenge, which introduces a new evaluation metric (AP@[0.5:0.05:0.95]), during the training process APs were calculated at 10 IoU thresholds between 0.5 and 0.95 with a step size of 0.05. The average of the 10 calculated APs achieved the mAP of 77.6%. The two calculated mAP results conducted on the validation set show that the model incrementally gives better results in classifying the GUI elements by each epoch.

The second part of the evaluation entails the comparison of this newly trained model with the existing benchmark study's results. Therefore, after the model training has ended, the Python script, which is provided as part of the YOLOv5 repository, has been deployed on the selected 450 testing UI image dataset. After this process, an AP value is generated per input class, which then their average is calculated to obtain the overall mAP.

Based on the calculations described above, Table 1 depicts the average precision findings for each one of the classes in our prototype and the benchmark study by Bunian et al. As can be clearly seen, the superiority of the model that is trained with the YOLOv5 is apparent to the naked eye. To put in numbers, the average precision of 10 out 12 classes has yielded better results compared to the Bunian et al. [6] model. Even though the YOLOv5 model has achieved slightly lower AP score in the *Background Image* and *Sliding Menu* classes than the Bunian et al. [6], it successfully has achieved higher average precision rates in smaller GUI elements, such as *Icon, Checked View* and *Page Indicator*. Overall, it is calculated that the proposed YOLOv5 model has outperformed the Bunian et al. [6] model's mAP by 15.69%.

Table 1. Average precision (AP) at IoU of 0.5 for each of the 12 class labels on the test set

Class label	AP (%) at IoU = 0.5	
	Bunian et al. [6]	YOLOv5
Background image	89.33	84.62
Checked view	44.48	67.59
Icon	50.5	89.58
Input field	78.24	94.57
Image	79.24	83.87
Text	63.99	96.3
Text button	87.37	98.83
Sliding menu	100	99.5
Page indicator	59.37	97.96
Pop-Up window	93.75	95.52
Switch	80	97.16
Upper task bar	90.4	99.49
Overall mAP (%)	**76.39**	**92.08**

The findings have been further explored through the confusion matrix (at IoU = 0.5) to evaluate the matching success of the test UI images to the corresponding 12 classes - see Fig. 7. The figure indicates that all the *Sliding Menu* and *Upper Task Bar* containing images have success matched with the correct class. Following this, the second best performance of matching with the relevant classes have been achieved by the test UI images that contain *Text*, *Text Button*, and *Page Indicator* instances. However, UI images that contain *Checked View* and *Switch* instances have not performed as well. This problem is believed to be related to the size of these UI elements in relation to the image in general. Hence, it can be said that smaller UI elements tend to be harder to detect and locate. Lastly, it has been observed that some akin and look-alike UI types such *Icon* and *Image* can be falsely predicted. As a result, the newly generated model falsely predicted %18 of *Icon*s as *Image*s; similarly, falsely predicted %9 of *Image*s as *Icon*s.

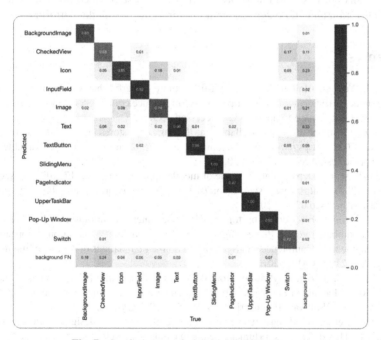

Fig. 7. Confusion matrix based on 450 test images

7   Conclusion and Future Work

Overall, this study proposes, trains and develops a GUI element detection model that is making use of the YOLOv5 algorithm and VINS dataset. The original dataset contains 4800 UI images and their annotation files, which is later reduced to 4543 images to make it comparable with the Bunian et al. [6] study. Accordingly, a total of 4543 images are split into 3 subsets for training, validation, and testing purposes. Furthermore, the accompanying VINS dataset annotation files are converted to YOLO TXT format. The model is trained using the newly proposed YOLOv5 algorithm that employs the pre-selected training dataset. Then in line with the benchmark study, 450 images are used for validation and the same number of images for testing. Accordingly, it is observed that the model has given 15.69% better mAP than the model used in the Bunian et al. [6] study. Overall, the comparison showed that the newly created model has performed better than the benchmark study in 10 out of 12 classes.

Based on the experience gained throughout the evaluations, it is foreseen that if the classes used for training were more evenly distributed the final results could have been much more accurate. Even though the newly generated model outperforms the set benchmark study findings, there is still room for improvement in the detection of small GUI elements. It is believed that this could be achieved by tiling the dataset [18] or using a different YOLO-based algorithm specifically developed for small object detection. The success of this phase would inevitably lead to the next step which involves automated UI file generation and UI design regeneration for multiple mobile platforms.

References

1. Puiu, T.: Your smartphone is millions of times more powerful than the Apollo 11 guidance computers. ZME Science (2021). https://www.zmescience.com/science/news-science/smartphone-power-compared-to-apollo-432/. Accessed 15 Jan 2022
2. Ceci, L.: Number of apps available in leading app stores as of 1st quarter 2021. Statista (2022). https://www.statista.com/statistics/276623/number-of-apps-available-in-leading-app-stores/. Accessed 30 Jan 2022
3. Statista Research Department: Revenue of mobile apps worldwide 2017–2025, by segment. Statista (2021). https://www.statista.com/statistics/269025/worldwide-mobile-app-revenue-forecast/. Accessed 02 Feb 2022
4. Chen, J., et al.: Object detection for graphical user interface: old fashioned or deep learning or a combination? In: Proceedings of the 28th ACM Joint Meeting on European Software Engineering Conference and Symposium on the Foundations of Software Engineering, pp. 1202–1214. ACM (2020)
5. Xie, M., et al.: UIED: a hybrid tool for GUI element detection. In: Proceedings of the 28th ACM Joint Meeting on European Software Engineering Conference and Symposium on the Foundations of Software Engineering, pp. 1655–1659. ACM (2020)
6. Bunian, S., et al.: VINS: visual search for mobile user interface design. In: Proceedings of the 2021 CHI Conference on Human Factors in Computing Systems, pp. 1–14. ACM (2021)
7. Nguyen, T.A., Csallner, C.: Reverse engineering mobile application user interfaces with REMAUI (T). In: Proceedings of the 30th IEEE/ACM International Conference on Automated Software Engineering, pp. 248–259. ACM (2015)
8. Chen, S., et al.: Automated cross-platform GUI code generation for mobile apps. In: IEEE 1st International Workshop on Artificial Intelligence for Mobile, pp. 13–16. IEEE (2019)
9. OpenCV About. https://opencv.org/about/. Accessed 13 Feb 2022
10. Apple Developer Vision. https://developer.apple.com/documentation/vision. Accessed 16 Feb 2022
11. Google Colab. https://colab.research.google.com. Accessed 1 Jan 2022
12. Zhiqiang, W., Jun, L.: A review of object detection based on convolutional neural network. In: Proceedings of the 36th Chinese Control Conference, pp. 85–112. IEEE (2017)

13. Girshick, R.: Fast R-CNN. In: Proceedings of the IEEE International Conference on Computer Vision, pp. 1440–1448. IEEE (2015)
14. Redmon, J., et al.: You only look once: unified, real-time object detection. In: Proceedings of the IEEE Conference on Computer Vision and Pattern Recognition, pp. 779–788. IEEE (2016)
15. Deka, B., et al.: Rico: a mobile app dataset for building data-driven design applications. In: Proceedings of the 30th Annual ACM Symposium on User Interface Software and Technology, pp. 845–854. ACM (2017)
16. What is Uplabs? https://www.uplabs.com/faq. Accessed 18 Feb 2022
17. Lin, T..-Y.., et al.: Microsoft coco: common objects in context. In: Fleet, D., Pajdla, T., Schiele, B., Tuytelaars, T. (eds.) ECCV 2014. LNCS, vol. 8693, pp. 740–755. Springer, Cham (2014). https://doi.org/10.1007/978-3-319-10602-1_48
18. Unel, F.O., et al.: The power of tiling for small object detection. In: Proceeding of the IEEE/CVF Conference on Computer Vision and Pattern Recognition, pp. 582–591. IEEE (2019)

Mobile Devices and Autonomous Vehicles

Active Federated YOLOR Model for Enhancing Autonomous Vehicles Safety

Gaith Rjoub[ID], Jamal Bentahar[✉][ID], and Y. A. Joarder

Concordia Institute for Information Systems Engineering, Concordia University,
Montreal, Canada
{g_rjoub,bentahar,y_joarde}@encs.concordia.ca

Abstract. A precise and real-time object detection system is crucial to ensuring the safety, smoothness, and trust of Autonomous Vehicles (AVs). Several machine learning techniques have been designed to improve vehicle detection capabilities and reduce the shortcomings caused by limited data and by transferring these data to a central server, which has shown poor performance under different conditions. In this paper, we propose an active federated learning-integrated solution over AVs that capitalizes on the You Only Learn One Representation (YOLOR) approach, a Convolutional Neural Network (CNN) specifically designed for real-time object detection. Our approach combines implicit and explicit knowledge, together with active learning and federated learning with the aim of improving the detection accuracy. Experiments show that our solution achieves better performance than traditional solutions (i.e., Gossip decentralized model and Centralized model).

Keywords: Autonomous vehicles · Active Learning · Federated Learning · YOLOR · Object detection · Edge computing

1 Introduction

Autonomous vehicles (AVs) are playing a crucial role in our modern world. The World Health Organization (WHO) estimates that 1.35 million people die and 50 million people are injured on the roads each year, and the cost of road traffic crashes to the global economy is estimated at 2.7$ trillion per year. Most of these crashes are caused by human errors, and autonomous vehicles promise to reduce their number and the number of people injured and killed on our roads. The promise of AVs and Internet of Vehicles (IoVs) has captured the imagination of many researchers [14,24,26] and the technology is advancing quickly. IoVs are being used to enable dynamic rerouting of road traffic to more efficient routes, for example, in response to incidents or delays. The IoVs will also require vehicle-to-vehicle (V2V) and vehicle-to-infrastructure (V2I) communications to enable vehicles to communicate with each other and with roadside infrastructure, such

© The Author(s), under exclusive license to Springer Nature Switzerland AG 2022
I. Awan et al. (Eds.): MobiWIS 2022, LNCS 13475, pp. 49–64, 2022.
https://doi.org/10.1007/978-3-031-14391-5_4

as traffic lights and signs. These communications allow vehicles to exchange valuable information, such as the presence of obstacles, potholes, or pedestrians, as well as other vehicles' speed and direction.

In the areas of vehicle automation, the incorporation of machine learning into vehicles is highly promising [25, 30, 31]. The ability to incorporate these powerful algorithms into vehicles allows for more informed and real-time driving decisions such as pedestrians and cyclists detection. Instead of vehicles being driven by rules, they can be driven by data and algorithms, creating a much safer and more efficient roadway environment for all road users. Machine learning algorithms are becoming increasingly sophisticated and are finding their way into a variety of automotive applications. These algorithms can be trained on data from multiple sources such as radar, lidar, and on-board sensors to detect and classify objects such as pedestrians and vehicles, and calculate their trajectory and distance traveled. The result is a much more accurate and real-time determination of the position and movement of these objects, which helps the vehicle determine the best evasive action to take, such as reducing speed or changing lanes. Road users and vehicles can also be classified based on characteristics such as their speed, size, and trajectory to determine if they are likely to be a threat.

While most of the current state-of-the-art object detection models are trained and benchmarked on labeled datasets, which are unrealistically small and contain only a few hundred images of each class, the latest research has focused on real-world applications where millions of images are being captured by cameras and other sensors. For these applications, it becomes crucial to build large-scale models which can process large amounts of unlabeled data and generalize well to real world scenarios. In order to address the limited amount of labeled data, we employ in this work Active Learning (AL) with the YOLOR (You Only Learn One Representation) method, which allow us to use a large amount of unlabeled data to learn representations similar to the ones learned from labeled data. YOLOR is based on the idea that a deep learning model is most effective when it is trained on a large set of samples, each of which is representative of the general population. However, because we only have a small number of labeled data, the model will not be as effective when it is used to make decisions. Therefore, AL combined with YOLOR trains the model on the small number of labeled data and uses the resulting representation to generate predictions for the large number of unlabeled data.

Another challenge of AVs object detection is the high communication cost and delay needed to transfer the data between vehicles, given the high number of data instances that can be collected and the long-distance communications. We address this challenge by the use of Federated Learning (FL), which enables the training of a model across multiple vehicles without having to share the data among them, but only the model parameters. This enables the vehicles to collaborate and learn from each other [18, 22]. Technically speaking, multiple rounds of FL are orchestrated by a central server. The server forwards the global model to the participating AVs at the beginning of each round. Each AV trains the model on its local data and then send back model updates to the server.

The server combines all the obtained updates in the local computation process to build a global machine learning model, thereby concluding the round.

1.1 Contributions

The main contributions of the paper can be summarized as follows:

- We propose a novel FL model to enable AVs to perform object detection and reduce the amount of data transferred during training by using object detection models trained on different local datasets.
- We employ the AL locally on the AVs and create a set of labelled images which can be used for training the YOLOR object detection model with FL.
- We study the performance of the proposed solution experimentally on the SODA10M[1] Dataset. The experimental results reveal that our proposed method achieves a better performance compared to the gossip and centralized models for object detection.

1.2 Organization

The rest of the paper is organized as follows. Section 2 describes the existing literature on object detection and image recognition techniques for AVs, FL, and AL techniques. Section 3 presents the methodology. Section 4 provides the details of the experimental setup, conducted experiments and results. Finally Sect. 5 provides some concluding remarks and future research directions.

2 Related Work

2.1 Object Detection over Autonomous Vehicles

By combining complementary information from multiple types of sensors, the authors in [36] present a novel method for detecting and identifying objects. They begin by generating accurate object-region proposals using 3D LIDAR data. Thereafter, these candidates are mapped onto the image space for selection of regions of interest (ROIs) for further object recognition in a convolutional neural network (CNN). Using the features of the last three layers of the CNN, they extract multi-scale features from each ROI to accurately identify each object's size. A cooperative spatial feature fusion (CoFF) method for AVs has been proposed in [11], which will allow AVs to effectively fuse feature maps for a higher and more accurate 3-D object detection capability. In particular, CoFF provides a powerful way to guide fusion by using weighted feature maps that are differentiated based on how much new semantic information they provide. Moreover, this method allows AVs to improve their detection precision and enhance the inconspicuous features associated with far/occluded objects.

---

[1] https://soda-2d.github.io/.

The authors in [15], propose a framework for real-time object detection (EODF) that exploits edge networks. EODFs allow AVs to detect objects based on regions of interest (RoIs) of the captured image when the channel quality is insufficient for supporting real-time object detection. After AVs have compressed the image data according to RoIs, they transmit the compressed version to the edge cloud. Thus, real-time object detection can be achieved due to a reduced transmission latency. In [29], the authors suggest three enhancements for CNN-based visual object detection for advanced driving assistance systems (ADAS). In order to address the large-scale variation challenge, a CNN deconvolution and fusion method is proposed to add context and deeper features for better object detection at small scales. The object occlusion challenge is addressed by implementing soft non-maximal suppression at different feature scales across object proposals. Because the vehicles have a distinct aspect ratio, they measure and utilize their aspect ratio statistics for more accurate object matching and localization.

According to [13], the authors propose a solution to improve vehicles' handling capabilities and performance by using a closed-loop steering controller with CNN feedback as opposed to previous techniques that used pure CNN. With the help of images taken from the vehicle's camera, this study shows that DAVE-2SKY, a neural network that learns how to steer lateral control using images from a camera mounted on the vehicle, can discern steering wheel angles for self-driving vehicles. In [7], the authors present a perspective-aware methodology that divides the image into key regions using clustering and uses evolutionary algorithms to specify the base anchors for each region. Additionally, they also add a module that increases the precision of the second-stage header network by including spatial information from the first-stage candidate regions. Researchers have also explored different reweighting strategies to solve the foreground-foreground imbalance, showing that a reduced form of focal loss can improve the detection of difficult and underrepresented targets in two-stage detectors. The researchers then design an ensemble model that combines the strengths of the different learning strategies.

2.2   Federated Learning over Autonomous Vehicles

According to [35], the authors present a FedMEC, FL architecture that combines partition technique with differential privacy. By splitting a DNN model into two parts, FedMEC proposes to leave the complex computations to the edge servers. Additionally, the authors employ a differential private data perturbation process to prevent privacy leakage that occurs when Laplace noise prevents updates from the edge server to the local devices. The authors of [33] propose a modern mobility-aware proactive edge cache model (MPCF) for FL that increases cache efficiency and preserves vehicle privacy. The MPCF uses a context-conscious auto encoder model to approximate popularity of content, and then places common content, which will decrease latency at the edge of the vehicle network. Furthermore, MPCF incorporates a cache replacement policy that allows network edges to add or evict contents based on mobility patterns and vehicles' preferences.

A real-time object detection system using CNNs and a FL framework is proposed in [23] to enhance the detection accuracy in adverse weather conditions utilizing You Only Look Once (YOLO) in conjunction with AVs. The YOLO CNN model is used to simultaneously estimate multiple bounding boxes and class probabilities for those boxes based on a FL based object detection model utilizing edge computing technology. In [16], the authors introduce FL into autonomous driving with the intention of preserving vehicular privacy by retaining original data within the vehicle and sharing training model parameters only through the MEC server. The study takes into account malicious MEC servers and malicious vehicles, rather than the common assumption of honest servers and honest vehicles in previous studies. The authors also propose a blockchain-based Reputation-based Incentive Autonomous Driving Mechanism (RIADM) based on reputation incentives to protect the privacy of vehicular messages where the honorary but curious MEC server is distinguished from malicious vehicles. Additionally, they propose to protect the identity privacy of vehicles with Zero-Knowledge Proof (ZKP), an anonymous identity-based privacy maintaining scheme when both parties are not trusted.

In [17], the researchers examine a novel form of vehicular network model, namely the Federated Vehicle Network (FVN). Based on this model, a high-database application such as computer distribution and FL can be supported by a robust distributed vehicular network. The authors leverage blockchain-dependent auxiliary systems to facilitate the transfers and prevent malicious behavior. According to [32], a selective aggregation method is presented where "fine" local DNN models are selected and submitted by local computer capabilities and image quality assessment to the central server. In order to promote the connections between central servers and vehicles, the authors take advantage of two-dimensional contract theory as a distributed paradigm to overcome knowledge asymmetry. Overall, the existing object detection approaches over AVs are still far from perfect. The major shortcoming of these algorithms is that they cannot handle the huge amount of unlabeled data they are confronted with in real-world scenarios and work with limited data. In this work, we aim to further improve the object detection over AVs through proposing a multi-faceted approach which integrates state-of-the-art approaches, namely federated learning, active Learning and YOLOR. To the best of our knowledge, no existing approach has yet considered the integration and interconnection between these approaches for object detection over AV environments.

3 Methodology

Our methodology is composed of two main parts: Part A: AL workflow; and Part B: Active and FL-integrated with YOLOR chains. These parts are inspired by the steps discussed in [5] and [23].

3.1 Active Learning Workflow

Sampling Process. Sampling is the 1st step of the AL workflow of our system. AL is used to selectively label images in FL to overcome the labeling challenge. Each of the devices involved in FL has a pool of unlabeled data from where a sample will be chosen for annotation. Many criteria have been devised for selecting such a sample. We concentrate on the widely utilized uncertainty sampling. To calculate the uncertainty (γ), we use the least confidence approach. According to [8], we can estimate for an image e the difference between the most confident forecast and a 100% confidence, denoted by $\gamma_r(e)$ as follows:

$$\gamma_r(e) = 1 - \max_{u_1,\ldots,u_n} P(u_1,\ldots,u_n \mid e) \tag{1}$$

where u_i = the prediction of a label i.

Aggregation Process. In our system, aggregation is the 2nd step of the AL workflow. According to [6], there are three basic and efficient aggregation strategies: sum, average, and maximum. These approaches produce an aggregated least confidence metric for each of the detections (j) in an image (e). Images with many uncertain detections are preferred by the sum aggregation approach that is used to compute the value for e using the detection (j) as follows [5]:

$$\gamma_{sum}(e) = \sum_{j \in e} \gamma_r(j) \tag{2}$$

The least confidence metric can also be made comparable between images by averaging over the amount of detections per image. The average aggregation method is as follows [5]:

$$\gamma_{avg}(e) = \frac{1}{|e|} \sum_{j \in e} \gamma_r(j) \tag{3}$$

Finally, the maximally uncertain value, $\gamma_r(j)$ is used for an image (e), containing (j) detections. This helps when there are many noise detections per image, but it also causes some information loss. It is expressed as follows [5]:

$$\gamma_{max}(e) = \max_{j \in \theta} \gamma_r(j) \tag{4}$$

YOLOR's Confidence. YOLOR's confidence finding is the 3rd step of the AL workflow of our system. The purpose is to get a certain type of confidence measure out of the YOLOR model. Regular CNNs use a softmax layer to produce a probability distribution over class confidences. YOLOR uses a unified network of explicit and implicit knowledge together. it can accurately and quickly identifies the object as well as provides output on what the object is or what type of object it is known by. The AL workflow of our system is illustrated in Fig. 1.

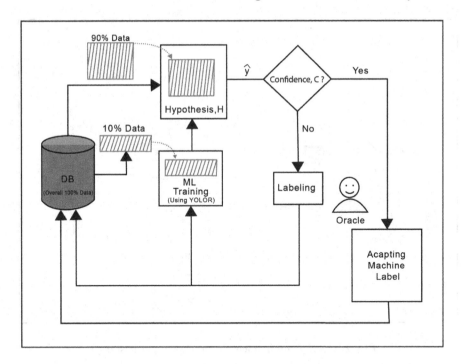

Fig. 1. The active learning workflow of our system

3.2 Integrating Active and Federated Learning with YOLOR

Integrating AL and FL is a useful approach for enabling distributed training of the YOLOR model by involving AVs with edge cloud servers in a functional communication network. This type of collaborative learning aids the vehicles in producing fast and accurate real-time decisions. As depicted in to Fig. 2, AVs are commonly equipped with embedded sensors like 3D cameras, GPS, tachographs, wheel encoder, lider, radar, ultrasonic sensors and lateral acceleration sensors, as well as computational and networking tools like memory, CPU and data communication [34].

Suppose there are n AVs responsible for object detection, $AV = \{av_1, av_2, \ldots, av_n\}$ and a set of n datasets, $DP = \{DP_1, DP_2, \ldots, DP_n\}$. Each DP_i is the dataset stored in the vehicle av_i. Figure 2 shows how AL works with FL together with YOLOR for labeling the unlabeled data. The figure illustrates our system's whole communication process.

A global YOLOR CNN model is trained in the edge server on the publicly available dataset and sends the initial parameters to all the AVs. Then, the AVs use the parameters to perform local training on their own data. Thereafter, AL works with the local model by labeling the unlabelled dataset that is received by a specific vehicle from the environment. Afterwards, the edge server collects the weights of the AL featured local models z^{av}_{g+1} for each vehicle (av) at the next

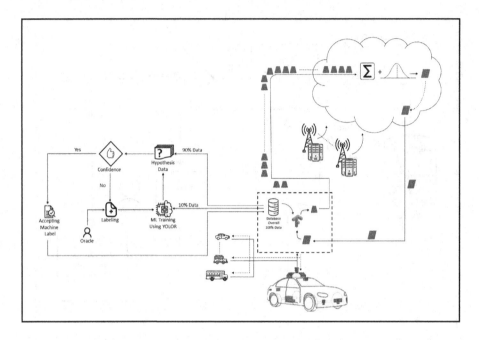

Fig. 2. Overall communication process of our system

communication round $g + 1$ from different AVs and aggregates them using the FedSGD method [1] as shown in Eq. 5.

$$z_{g+1} = \sum_{av=1}^{n} \frac{d_{av}}{d} z_{g+1}^{av} \tag{5}$$

where z, d_{av} and d represent the weight, the volume of local data at the av-th vehicle and the size of the whole data across the selected vehicles respectively. The edge server always gives global model aggregation feedback to the AVs about YOLOR model updates. The aimed of the learning model is to reduce global loss function using [23] as shown in Eq. 6.

$$\min_{z \in \mathbb{R}} E(z) = \frac{1}{n} \sum_{av=1}^{n} \frac{d_{av}}{d} E_{av}(z) \tag{6}$$

where $E_{av}(z)$ represents the loss function of each vehicle (av) on its own data.

The local models are trained to predict objects using images captured using built-in sensors. The AVs connect to the edge server to get the starting and aggregated model parameters, then train their own YOLOR CNN models with their own image data to get an updated set of parameters. AVs submit updated local versions to the edge server according to Eq. 7.

$$z_{g+1}^{av} = z_g^{av} - \lambda \nabla E_{av}(z) \tag{7}$$

where ∇ and λ represent the gradient operation and the fixed learning rate successively. The edge server compiles then these versions into a new one. The whole workflow of our active and federated learning-integrated with YOLOR chains is illustared in Fig. 3.

4 Implementation and Experiments

4.1 Experimental Setup

To carry out our experiments, we capitalize on a Large-Scale 2D Self/semi-supervised Object Detection dataset for Autonomous driving (SODA10M) [12]. The dataset consists of 10 million unlabeled images and 20000 labeled images with 6 sample object categories. The images are taken every 10 seconds per frame over the course of 27833 driving hours in various weather conditions, times, and location scenarios in 32 distinct cities to increase diversity. To perform machine learning and computations on decentralized data, we use the TensorFlow Federated (TFF) framework. TFF facilitates open experimentation and research with FL. We train the YOLOR CNN model integrated to our active federated model on the dataset to determine our algorithm's efficiency and effectiveness. We evaluated our proposed model against 1) the centralized model, that is the most prevalent technique, in which a significant quantity of training data is gathered centrally and used to train models across a set of AVs in a sequential manner; and 2) the decentralized gossip model, which does not require any central component or an aggregation server.

4.2 Experimental Results

In Fig. 4, we measure the training and test accuracy in terms of detection objects of our approach against FL that does not include the AL component, and

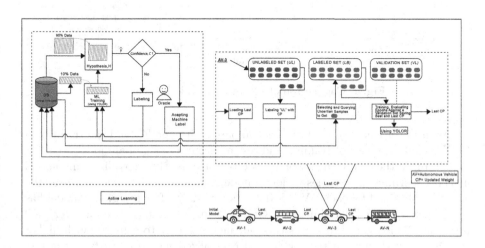

Fig. 3. Full workflow of our model

against traditional CNN that does not include the FL component. We run the experiments over 1500 iterations. In particular, the average training and test accuracy obtained by our model, FL, and the traditional CNN approaches are 97.2%, 95.4%, 92.3%, 90.1%, and 86.5%, 84.6% respectively. We observe from this figure that our proposed solution achieves the highest training and test accuracy level compared to the FL and traditional CNN approaches and exhibits a better scalability and a faster convergence. The reason for this can be traced to the fact that our solution uses YOLOR, which has been designed to be quick and contains both AL and FL components to compensate for any data shortages on certain edge servers and then train the model on the local data of each AV.

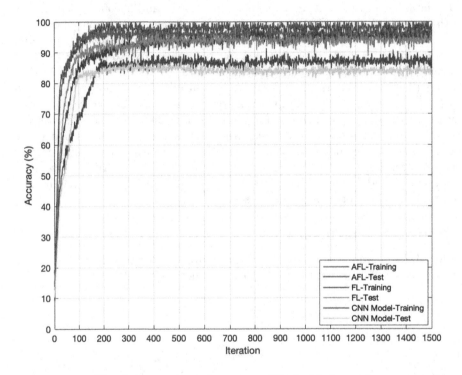

Fig. 4. Comparison of accuracy of final global model

As in Fig. 4 where our solution is compared with the FL and the traditional CNN models in terms of training and testing accuracy of global model, we compare in Fig. 5 the test accuracy of our solution against the centralized and gossip machine learning approaches of local models. The test accuracy measures the accuracy obtained by each AV based on its own data after the global model has been trained in a federated manner. Our experiments were carried out over 1400 iterations. This figure illustrates that our model is able to achieve much higher test accuracy than both the gossip and centralized methods. In fact, the test accuracy obtained by our model, gossip, and centralized approaches are 96.4%,

91.7%, and 87.2%, respectively. This mean that our model enables the AVs to better learn and detect objects.

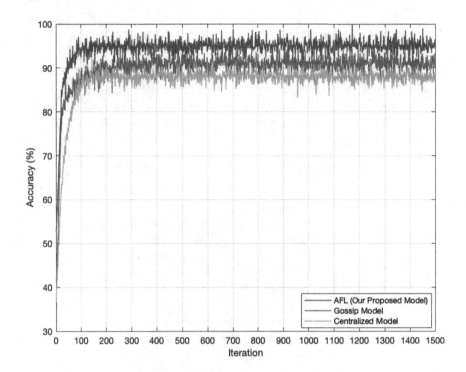

Fig. 5. Comparison of prediction accuracy

The comparison of confusion matrices is presented in Fig. 6 in order to further demonstrate the performance of our integrated active federated learning, gossip, and centralized models in Fig. 6a, Fig. 6b, and Fig. 6c respectively. The column on the far right of the plot shows the percentages of all the examples predicted to belong to each class that are correctly and incorrectly classified. These matrices are known as precision (or positive predictive value) and false discovery rate, respectively. The bottom row of the plot shows the percent of all examples within each class that were classified correctly or incorrectly. These matrices are often called the recall (or true positive rate) and false negative rate, respectively. The bottom right cell of the plot shows the overall accuracy. This figure reveals that our model is able to achieve much higher overall accuracy than both the gossip and centralized models. In particular, the overall accuracy obtained by our model, gossip, and centralized approaches are 93.8%, 85.2%, and 80.6%, respectively.

In Fig. 7, by varying the number of AVs from 10 to 100, we measure the learning time of different approaches. Based on this figure, we can infer that, as the number of AVs increases, the learning time in the different studied solutions

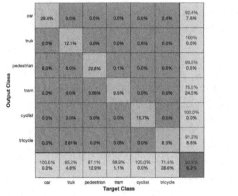

(a) AFL (Our proposed model)

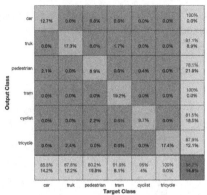

(b) Gossip Model

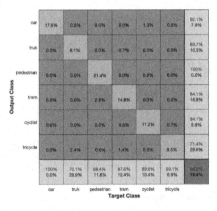

(c) Centralized Mode

Fig. 6. Comparison of confusion matrices for classification results

increases modestly. In addition, the figure shows that our proposed model has the lowest learning time. This is justified by the fact that in contrast to the gossip model, which exchanges models directly between AVs with limited resources, and the centralized model, which gathers the training data and trains the model on one of the AVs before distributing it across a set of AVs, our proposed model distributes the training across multiple AVs and aggregates the global model on the server.

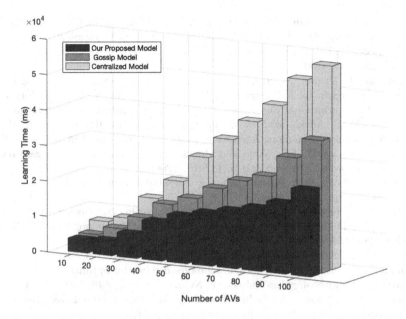

Fig. 7. Learning time versus the number of AVs

5   Conclusion

In this work, we proposed an integrated active federated learning with YOLOR approach to improve the real-time object detection over AVs and reduce the shortcomings caused by the limited data. The experiments demonstrated the effectiveness of our approach by achieving an average training and test accuracy of 97.2%, 90.4% compared with 85.3%, 80.1%, and 76.5%, 71.6% obtained by FL, and the traditional CNN approaches respectively. Finally, the results revealed that the accuracy obtained by our proposed solution (96.7%) is higher than the one obtained by gossip (92.6%), and centralized approaches (91.4%). In the future, we plan to extend this work considering business scenarios over the cloud [2] and investigate federated learning scheduling by combining reinforcement learning and trust models [9,18–21,27,28] to further reduce the training time and cost by avoiding unnecessary computations on untrusted AVs. Extending model checking approaches [3,4,10] to these systems is another plan for future work.

References

1. Amiri, M.M., Gunduz, D.: Machine learning at the wireless edge: distributed stochastic gradient descent over-the-air. IEEE Trans. Sig. Process. **68**, 2155–2169 (2020)

2. Bataineh, A.S., Bentahar, J., Mizouni, R., Wahab, O.A., Rjoub, G., El Barachi, M.: Cloud computing as a platform for monetizing data services: a two-sided game business model. IEEE Trans. Netw. Serv. Manage. (2021). https://doi.org/10.1109/TNSM.2021.3128160

3. Bentahar, J., Drawel, N., Sadiki, A.: Quantitative group trust: a two-stage verification approach. In: Faliszewski, P., Mascardi, V., Pelachaud, C., Taylor, M.E. (eds.) 21st International Conference on Autonomous Agents and Multiagent Systems, AAMAS, Auckland, New Zewland, 9–13 May, pp. 100–108. International Foundation for Autonomous Agents and Multiagent Systems (IFAAMAS) (2022)

4. Bentahar, J., Meyer, J.C., Wan, W.: Model checking communicative agent-based systems. Knowl. Based Syst. **22**(3), 142–159 (2009)

5. Bommel, J.R.V.: Active learning during federated learning for object detection, July 2021. http://essay.utwente.nl/86855/

6. Brust, C.A., Käding, C., Denzler, J.: Active Learning for Deep Object Detection. arXiv:1809.09875 [cs], September 2018. http://arxiv.org/abs/1809.09875, arXiv: 1809.09875

7. Carranza-García, M., Lara-Benítez, P., García-Gutiérrez, J., Riquelme, J.C.: Enhancing object detection for autonomous driving by optimizing anchor generation and addressing class imbalance. Neurocomputing **449**, 229–244 (2021)

8. Culotta, A., McCallum, A.: Reducing labeling effort for structured prediction tasks. In: Proceedings of the 20th national conference on Artificial intelligence, vol. 2, pp. 746–751. AAAI 2005, AAAI Press, Pittsburgh, Pennsylvania, July 2005

9. Drawel, N., Bentahar, J., Laarej, A., Rjoub, G.: Formal verification of group and propagated trust in multi-agent systems. Auton. Agent. Multi-Agent Syst. **36**(1), 1–31 (2022)

10. El-Menshawy, M., Bentahar, J., Dssouli, R.: Symbolic model checking commitment protocols using reduction. In: Omicini, A., Sardina, S., Vasconcelos, W. (eds.) DALT 2010. LNCS (LNAI), vol. 6619, pp. 185–203. Springer, Heidelberg (2011). https://doi.org/10.1007/978-3-642-20715-0_11

11. Guo, J., Carrillo, D., Tang, S., Chen, Q., Yang, Q., Fu, S., Wang, X., Wang, N., Palacharla, P.: Coff: cooperative spatial feature fusion for 3-d object detection on autonomous vehicles. IEEE Internet Things J. **8**(14), 11078–11087 (2021)

12. Han, J., et al.: SODA10M: a large-scale 2D self/Semi-supervised object detection dataset for autonomous driving. arXiv:2106.11118 [cs], November 2021. http://arxiv.org/abs/2106.11118, arXiv: 2106.11118

13. Jhung, J., Bae, I., Moon, J., Kim, T., Kim, J., Kim, S.: End-to-end steering controller with CNN-based closed-loop feedback for autonomous vehicles. In: 2018 IEEE intelligent vehicles symposium (IV), pp. 617–622. IEEE (2018)

14. Jiang, T., Fang, H., Wang, H.: Blockchain-based internet of vehicles: distributed network architecture and performance analysis. IEEE Internet Things J. **6**(3), 4640–4649 (2018)

15. Kim, S.W., Ko, K., Ko, H., Leung, V.C.: Edge-network-assisted real-time object detection framework for autonomous driving. IEEE Network **35**(1), 177–183 (2021)

16. Li, Y., Tao, X., Zhang, X., Liu, J., Xu, J.: Privacy-preserved federated learning for autonomous driving. IEEE Trans. Intell. Transp. Syst. **23**(7), 8423–8434 (2022)

17. Posner, J., Tseng, L., Aloqaily, M., Jararweh, Y.: Federated learning in vehicular networks: opportunities and solutions. IEEE Network **35**(2), 152–159 (2021)

18. Rjoub, G., Abdel Wahab, O., Bentahar, J., Bataineh, A.: A trust and energy-aware double deep reinforcement learning scheduling strategy for federated learning on IoT devices. In: Kafeza, E., Benatallah, B., Martinelli, F., Hacid, H., Bouguettaya,

A., Motahari, H. (eds.) ICSOC 2020. LNCS, vol. 12571, pp. 319–333. Springer, Cham (2020). https://doi.org/10.1007/978-3-030-65310-1_23

19. Rjoub, G., Bentahar, J., Abdel Wahab, O., Saleh Bataineh, A.: Deep and reinforcement learning for automated task scheduling in large-scale cloud computing systems. Concurrency Comput. Pract. Experience 33(23), e5919 (2021)

20. Rjoub, G., Bentahar, J., Wahab, O.A.: Bigtrustscheduling: trust-aware big data task scheduling approach in cloud computing environments. Future Gener. Comput. Syst. 110, 1079–1097 (2020)

21. Rjoub, G., Bentahar, J., Wahab, O.A., Bataineh, A.: Deep smart scheduling: a deep learning approach for automated big data scheduling over the cloud. In: 2019 7th International Conference on Future Internet of Things and Cloud (FiCloud), pp. 189–196. IEEE (2019)

22. Rjoub, G., Wahab, O.A., Bentahar, J., Bataineh, A.: Trust-driven reinforcement selection strategy for federated learning on IoT devices. Computing (2022). https://doi.org/10.1007/s00607-022-01078-1

23. Rjoub, G., Wahab, O.A., Bentahar, J., Bataineh, A.S.: Improving autonomous vehicles safety in snow weather using federated YOLO CNN learning. In: Bentahar, J., Awan, I., Younas, M., Grønli, T.-M. (eds.) MobiWIS 2021. LNCS, vol. 12814, pp. 121–134. Springer, Cham (2021). https://doi.org/10.1007/978-3-030-83164-6_10

24. Tian, Z., Gao, X., Su, S., Qiu, J., Du, X., Guizani, M.: Evaluating reputation management schemes of internet of vehicles based on evolutionary game theory. IEEE Trans. Veh. Technol. 68(6), 5971–5980 (2019)

25. Vanitha, V., Resmi, R., Reddy, K.N.S.V.: Machine learning-based charge scheduling of electric vehicles with minimum waiting time. Comput. Intell. 37(3), 1047–1055 (2021)

26. Wahab, O.A., Cohen, R., Bentahar, J., Otrok, H., Mourad, A., Rjoub, G.: An endorsement-based trust bootstrapping approach for newcomer cloud services. Inf. Sci. 527, 159–175 (2020)

27. Wahab, O.A., Mourad, A., Otrok, H., Taleb, T.: Federated machine learning: Survey, multi-level classification, desirable criteria and future directions in communication and networking systems. IEEE Commun. Surv. Tutorials 23(2), 1342–1397 (2021)

28. Wahab, O.A., Rjoub, G., Bentahar, J., Cohen, R.: Federated against the cold: a trust-based federated learning approach to counter the cold start problem in recommendation systems. Inf. Sci. 601, 189–206 (2022)

29. Wei, J., He, J., Zhou, Y., Chen, K., Tang, Z., Xiong, Z.: Enhanced object detection with deep convolutional neural networks for advanced driving assistance. IEEE Trans. intell. Transp. Syst. 21(4), 1572–1583 (2019)

30. Xu, Y., Lin, J., Gao, H., Li, R., Jiang, Z., Yin, Y., Wu, Y.: Machine learning-driven apps recommendation for energy optimization in green communication and networking for connected and autonomous vehicles. IEEE Trans. Green Commun. Networking (2022). https://doi.org/10.1109/TGCN.2022.3165262

31. Yang, Q., Fu, S., Wang, H., Fang, H.: Machine-learning-enabled cooperative perception for connected autonomous vehicles: Challenges and opportunities. IEEE Network 35(3), 96–101 (2021)

32. Ye, D., Yu, R., Pan, M., Han, Z.: Federated learning in vehicular edge computing: a selective model aggregation approach. IEEE Access 8, 23920–23935 (2020)

33. Yu, Z., Hu, J., Min, G., Zhao, Z., Miao, W., Hossain, M.S.: Mobility-aware proactive edge caching for connected vehicles using federated learning. IEEE Trans. Intell. Transp. Syst. 22(8), 5341–5351 (2020)

34. Yu, Z., Hu, J., Min, G., Zhao, Z., Miao, W., Hossain, M.S.: Mobility-aware proactive edge caching for connected vehicles using federated learning. IEEE Trans. Intell. Transp. Syst. **22**(8), 5341–5351 (2021). https://doi.org/10.1109/TITS.2020. 3017474
35. Zhang, J., Zhao, Y., Wang, J., Chen, B.: FedMEC: improving efficiency of differentially private federated learning via mobile edge computing. Mob. Netw. Appl. **25**(6), 2421–2433 (2020). https://doi.org/10.1007/s11036-020-01586-4, https:// doi.org/10.1007/s11036-020-01586-4
36. Zhao, X., Sun, P., Xu, Z., Min, H., Yu, H.: Fusion of 3d lidar and camera data for object detection in autonomous vehicle applications. IEEE Sens. J. **20**(9), 4901– 4913 (2020)

Neural Network for Public Transport Mode Inference on Mobile Devices

Anders Skretting[✉] and Tor-Morten Grønli

School of Economics, Innovation, and Technology, Mobile Technology Lab,
Kristiania University College, Oslo, Norway
{anders.skretting,Tor-Morten.Gronli}@kristiania.no

Abstract. Digital solutions are evolving and a general trend is to reduce
the amount of user interactions needed while moving towards a more
automatic and seamless paradigm. Public transportation solutions are
no exception and in recent years the concept of Be-In/Be-Out solutions,
where no explicit interactions are needed, have gained enhanced research
focus. These solutions need to automatically detect travelers on board
the different public transport vehicles so that the system is able to issue
tickets in a seamless manner. Various on-board equipment has been suggested for this purpose, however, mounting additional equipment in vehicles both reduce scalability and increase cost. In this paper, we instead
suggest an approach, completely void of any additional equipment, using
only the smartphone of the given traveler. We propose a machine learning approach, where we take advantage of real sensor data, collected
by actual travelers. We present a model which is ready to be deployed
on-device through off-the-shelf technology, that determine the mode of
transport with high accuracy for any given traveler using their smartphone.

Keywords: Machine learning · Neural network · Mobile · Intelligent
transportation

1 Introduction

Today, digital solutions permeate almost every aspect of our daily lives and
public transport is no exception. Public transportation solutions have been on
a journey. This journey spans from checking in and out with paper tickets and
tokens, the use of smart cards and other radio frequency technologies, to the use
of a variety of mobile applications for issuing tickets and collecting fares. Public
transport solutions today can be very complex and may provide a plethora of
digital functionalities that may improve both the safety and travel experience for
passengers. These functionalities range from driver drowsiness detection [4] to
passenger counting [18] and crowd-aware route recommendations [8]. However,
regardless of how technological and modern the solution is, travelers still need
to interact with the system in order to either check-in -or out, obtain a monthly

© The Author(s), under exclusive license to Springer Nature Switzerland AG 2022
I. Awan et al. (Eds.): MobiWIS 2022, LNCS 13475, pp. 65–78, 2022.
https://doi.org/10.1007/978-3-031-14391-5_5

ticket or similar. Thus, public transport solutions have not reached its destination and so the journey continues. Recently, researchers have been looking into the concept of Be-In/Be-Out (BIBO) solutions where explicit interaction is no longer needed [2,17,19]. The idea is that travelers can embark or disembark any public transport vehicle and the system would automatically know which passenger traveled what distance with which public transport vehicle. As such, the system can automatically issue a ticket, or withdraw the required amount from the traveler's digital wallet or bank card. Employing a BIBO solution comes with many benefits. First and foremost, traveling using public transport will be seamless and effortless in terms of ticket purchase which can be a challenging task, especially when maneuvering in large, complicated networks with different zones and pricing schemes. Additionally, if the system knows the exact point of embarking and disembarking, new, more dynamic business models can be taken advantage of such as distance-based or duration-based pricing schemes. This can lead to fairer pricing, especially for people living close to bordering zones. Moreover, the information collected through this kind of solution can contribute to ease the decision-making process and lead to better decisions which may benefit more people when planning new roads, routes and so on. The benefits of BIBO solutions stands for themselves, however, in order to reach the next step of the journey of public transport solutions and reap the benefits of BIBO, one particular challenge remain—the challenge of accurate in-vehicle presence detection.

BIBO solutions stand in contrasts to other public transport ticketing paradigms where passengers are required to explicitly check in or check out using either physical or digital tickets. BIBO, on the other hand, does not require any explicit interaction. BIBO solutions, however, needs to be able to accurately locate a traveler within a given public transport vehicle and this is a non-trivial process. In this paper we suggest a novel approach to solve the issue of accurate in-vehicle presence detection using a pre-trained machine learning model deployed on a smartphone. The model is able to infer which type of public transport vehicle the traveler is on based solely on on-device smartphone data collected in real-time.

The next section reviews past and ongoing efforts for solving this particular problem, while Sect. 3 entails details regarding the approach taken and how the training data was collected. Section 4 presents the preprocessing and analysis of the raw data, in addition to the feature selection approach taken and its results. In Sect. 5 we present the model, its configurations and the classification results, while in Sect. 6 we discuss our findings. In Sect. 7 we conclude this paper with pointers towards future work.

2   Background

A variety of equipment and sensors have been employed to solve the problem of accurate in-vehicle presence detection for BIBO solutions. The simplest approach is to mount hardware for sensing or scanning passengers within the public transport vehicles. The authors of [11] installed a Bluetooth scanner on the roof,

inside the bus in order to detect passengers. This scanner detected discoverable
Bluetooth devices of passengers embarking or disembarking. The authors argue
that Bluetooth data in combination with GPS data, received from the bus, can
provide travel information about passengers. However, the authors stress that
Bluetooth cannot be switched on or off during transit for this solution to work.
In addition, using this technique, it was not possible to identify which passenger embarked or disembarked. Bluetooth is a popular technology when trying
to solve the in-vehicle presence detection problem of BIBO and has been identified as an enabling technology [16]. A similar approach has been suggested in
[15] where they install an on-board device that is able to detect nearby Bluetooth devices, either smartphones or beacons carried by passengers. Narzt et al.
[15] emphasize that they did not evaluate the consequences of people standing
outside the public transport vehicle, within the signal range of the on-board
device. On the other hand, instead of the passengers having to carry a beacon
that interacts with an on-board device, the authors of [21] turns it around and
suggest instead to mount the beacon inside the public transport vehicle and let
the passengers smartphone do the work. In their approach the authors tries to
mitigate the issue of a passenger being outside the vehicle but within reach of
the Bluetooth signal by suggesting the use of an artificial neural network.

Other authors have embraced the idea of using machine learning in the
context of public transportation [1,13,17,19]. Machine learning has been taken
advantage of, in particular, to increase the accuracy of detecting the mode of
transportation or to detect whether a traveler is actually inside the public transport vehicle and not outside of it. Oplenskedal et al. [17] suggest a framework
comprised of an on-board reference unit and a neural network residing in the
cloud. In their approach, the sensor data, such as acceleration, air pressure,
magnetic field and gyroscope is collected from the passengers smartphones. This
sensor data is then compared with that of an on-board reference unit. The data
from both devices is sent to a cloud solution which is running the neural network
in order to estimate whether or not the passenger is actually inside a given vehicle. In [13] the authors collected smartphone sensor data and used this to train a
model for classifying vehicle types. Servizi et al. [19], on the other hand, trained
two different models and compared classifiers based on Bluetooth to classifiers
based on smartphone sensor data.

Most suggested solutions today require a combination of technologies, such
as smartphone sensors and Bluetooth, in combination with machine learning
techniques in order to reach high precision when it comes to in-vehicle presence
detection. Although a solution seems close at hand, issues related to scalability
and resource utilization still persist.

3   Approach

In order to make this kind of solution scalable it is desirable to omit any kind
of on-board devices. This will reduce cost related to both installation and maintenance, in addition to enable a faster on-boarding for public transportation

companies that want to utilize such a solution. Therefore, we suggest an approach completely void of any on-board equipment. Moreover, since our solution resides solely on the passenger's smartphone, significantly less network calls are needed which in turn can reduce cost both for the service provider and the passenger.

3.1 Data Collection

Our approach takes advantage of a pre-trained machine learning model, deployed on device. In order to collect the data needed for training the model, we recruited regular travelers from two cities in Norway, which installed a custom mobile application on their personal smartphone which collected contextual data whenever the travelers were on a journey. We enlisted a total of 101 participants which were instructed to activate the data collection application whenever they were traveling. We defined ten different modes of transportation. Namely, bus, metro, train, tram, boat, bicycle, car, e-scooter, inside and outside.

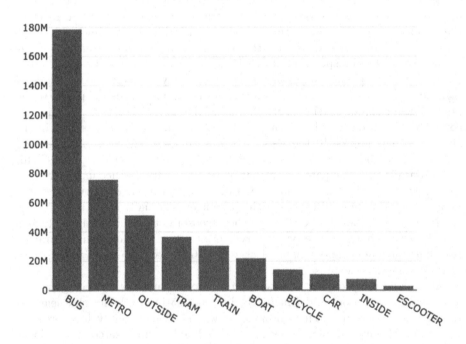

Fig. 1. Transport mode distribution

Figure 1 shows the distribution of sensor events for each mode of transportation. The 101 participants collected sensor data on a total of 1961 trips where a total of 429 558 934 single sensor event were collected.

3.2   Custom Mobile Application

The custom mobile application that we developed was a native android app which the travelers installed on their own smartphones. The user had to manually start the collection when they were situated within a given mode of transport. That is to say, when a user entered a bus they would choose where they would put their phone and then start the data collection. Before disembarking, they would turn off the data collection and at a later time, upload the data. Once started, the application checks for available sensors and activates all of them. This includes both base sensors, which are hardware sensors such as accelerometer or magnetometer, and composite sensors, which is data derived from processing or fusing different base sensors, such as linear acceleration or rotation vector. Some devices also have their own device-specific sensors which means that there was a large variety of different sensor data being collected dependant on the traveler's smartphone. Each sensor event was placed within an object and metadata such as timestamp, transport type, journey and trip number were appended to it. These objects were stored on the traveler's smartphone until the traveler chose to uploaded them. By storing the data on-device rather than just uploading it directly, we gave the travelers the opportunity to verify that the timestamps of start and stop was correct, in addition to having selected the correct mode of transport. If the traveler had mistakenly started the collection before entering, or stopped it after exiting the given mode, the traveler would then delete the data. On-device storage also mitigated the risk of losing data due to poor network conditions. Every traveler was instructed, in person, on how they should use the application in order to mitigate the risk of data being collected in the wrong mode of transport and thus contaminating the dataset.

4   Analysis

Once the data was collected, various steps of preprocessing were conducted in order to select the most appropriate features to be able to infer mode of transportation.

4.1   Sensor Removal and Aggregation Function

From the collected data, we first removed trips with a duration less than 30 s or more than an hour. Trips shorter than thirty seconds were not likely to be an actual trip but rather an accidental data collection. Trips exceeding 1 h, on the other hand, could be the result of a traveler forgetting to stop the data collection when leaving the transport vehicle. We then removed all device-specific sensors which were not part of the Android operating system. After that we also removed sensors which were unlikely to yield any results based on previous research and intuition. For instance, most Android devices has a light sensor, however, light levels may vary based on the time of the day or where the device is placed (e.g. in a backpack) and as such, data relating to the light sensor were omitted. After removing sensors with a low likelihood of having a correlation with the mode of transport we were left with the following sensors: accelerometer, magnetic field, gyroscope, pressure, rotation vector and game rotation vector. Many of these sensors corresponds to sensors other authors has deemed useful in previous work [13,17] Each of the chosen sensors sense across three axis, x, y and z. This in turn leaves us with a total of 18 unique sensor values. In order to investigate any particular patterns related to the movement and the environment of a particular public transport vehicle we needed to analyze the data over a period of time. We tested time windows of 10, 20 and 30 s. The different time windows yielded no significant difference in terms of inference accuracy and we therefore chose the shortest window of 10 s with a five second overlap. The smaller the window size, the faster will the on-device inference be. However, with a too small window size it may be difficult to distinguish patterns related to the environment and movement of the given transport mode. With a window size of 10 s we calculated the mean, standard deviation and quantiles for each value during the 10 s window. All the aforementioned steps resulted in a total of 80 different features.

4.2   Feature Selection

From the literature we identified 5 different techniques for assessing the importance of the 80 features; Classification and Regression Trees (CART) [5], Random Forest [12], XGBoost [3], ANOVA f-test [22] and Mutual Information [6]. There are no standard techniques for selecting features for a deep neural network and thus, we instead explored the results of a variety of feature selection techniques in order to identify which of these 80 features were best suited for training our particular model.

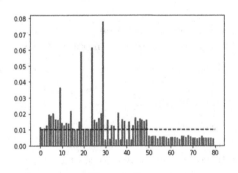

Fig. 2. CART

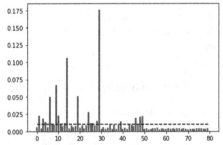

Fig. 3. Random forest

The results of the feature selection using the 5 different techniques are shown in the Figs. 2, 3, 4, 5 and 6. The x axis shows the different features from the first to the 80th while the y axis shows the classification score the given feature

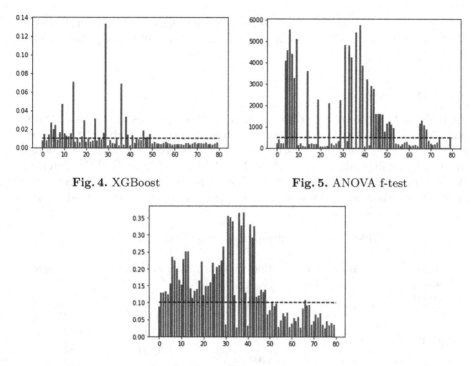

Fig. 4. XGBoost   **Fig. 5.** ANOVA f-test

Fig. 6. Mutual information

was assigned using each particular technique. We established a threshold for each technique in order to select the most promising features. This threshold is visualized as the dotted line separating the red bars and the green bars on the charts. Even though the most important features varied significantly for the different techniques, some commonalities were apparent. We therefore, took the intersection of the 5 techniques and selected the features above the score threshold which were common to all of the techniques. This resulted in a total of 6 different sets of important features which we used for training different models.

5   Classification

We wanted our model to be easily deployable to devices using off-the-shelf technology. The most well-known machine learning framework for on-device machine learning is TensorFlow Lite [7] which is a open-source framework delivered by Google, which makes it the standard for machine learning on Android devices as well. As such, we based the choice of model on that it needed to be supported through TensorFlow Lite for easy, large-scale deployment. To our knowledge, there is no overview over supported algorithms for TensorFlow Lite, however, from the documentation and the literature, it is apparent that neural networks are supported. Multilayer Perceptron (MLP) is such a technique and has shown promising results in terms of classifying sensor data [9,13,14]. Based on the afore-mentioned criterion we chose to take advantage of the multilayer perceptron for this work.

5.1 Multiclass

From the dataset we chose to focus on the 4 most promising modes of transport. Namely, bus, metro, tram and train. In addition, we re-labeled every other mode to "other", which left us with a total of 5 different classes for our model. In terms of configuration, we used the Rectified Linear Unit (ReLU) as activation function for the input and hidden layers and the softmax activation in the output layer. We compiled the model using the adam optimizer [10] and the loss

Table 1. Model configuration and accuracy multiclass

Feature Selection Method	Features	Hidden Layers	Epochs	Batch Size	Training Data	Test Data
CART	21	2	150	32	0.815	0.812
				64	0.815	0.811
			1000	32	0.821	0.817
				64	0.800	0.804
Random Forest	39	5	150	32	0.872	0.863
				64	0.872	0.863
			1000	32	0.892	0.879
				64	0.892	0.880
XGBoost	27	3	150	32	0.829	0.824
				64	0.800	0.798
			1000	32	0.839	0.835
				64	0.850	0.844
ANOVA f-test	34	4	150	32	0.813	0.810
				64	0.808	0.804
			1000	32	0.825	0.819
				64	0.838	0.831
Mutual Information	47	6	150	32	0.888	0.877
				64	0.890	0.880
			1000	32	0.902	0.885
				64	0.909	0.891
Intersection	56	8	150	32	0.901	0.892
				64	0.902	0.890
			1000	32	0.920	0.901
				64	0.935	0.906

function sparse categorical crossentropy. We set up the multilayer perceptron for multiclass classification and trained 24 models with different configurations. For each feature selection technique we tested out two different amounts of training epochs and for each of these, two different batch sizes. More training epochs are usually better, however, it was interesting to see whether we could achieve a similar accuracy using less training epochs. Less epochs, require less processing and, in turn, leads to faster training of the model and less resources consumed. There is a relation between batch size and the speed and stability of the learning process. Therefore, we tested out two different batch sizes in order to investigate whether a high or low batch size yielded the better result. Surprisingly, for many of the models, a high batch size yielded a higher accuracy as seen in Table 1.

Table 1 shows the different accuracies we achieved for the different configurations based on the different features identified through each of the feature importance techniques. The table shows the accuracy achieved based on both the data used for training the model, in addition to a holdout set which is data not used during the training. The holdout set consisted of 33% of the total data, while we trained the model on the remaining 66%. We highlighted the accuracies, based on the holdout set, that were over 90% (green). We can see that the best accuracy was achieved using the features derived from the intersection of the other feature selection methods and this model is henceforth referred to as the best model.

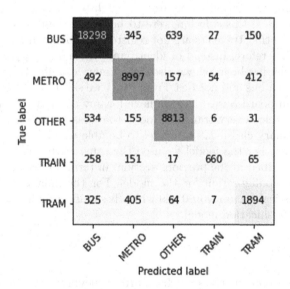

Fig. 7. Confusion matrix

Figure 7 shows the confusion matrix for the best model. The matrix demonstrates the number of correct predictions for each class, in this case, mode of transportation. We see the number of correctly predicted modes are highest for

Table 2. Classification report best model

	Precision	Recall	F1-Score	Support
BUS	0.91	0.96	0.93	19331
METRO	0.90	0.89	0.90	10271
OTHER	0.93	0.92	0.92	9428
TRAIN	0.83	0.65	0.73	1174
TRAM	0.79	0.67	0.73	2752
Accuracy			0.91	42956
Micro Avg	0.87	0.82	0.84	42956
Weighted Avg	0.90	0.91	0.90	42956

bus with 18298 correct predictions and lowest for train with only 660 correct predictions. Table 2 presents the precision, recall and F1-Score of the best model. Support refers to the number of occurrences of the given class in the training dataset.

5.2   Binary Classification

An accuracy above 90% is quite significant, however, for a large-scale implementation for public transport operators, a slightly better accuracy would be preferred. After all, if this solution were to be used for automated fare collection, it is essential that travelers are not registered as boarded for a vehicle they did not board. Therefore, instead of identifying which type of public transport vehicle the traveler has boarded, we also did a binary classification where we distinguished between bus and not bus. From Fig. 1 we saw that we have a lot more data collected on board buses than we have for any other transport mode and, as such, we re-labeled every transport mode that was not a bus into "not bus" and created a binary classification model to be able to infer whether a traveler is on a bus or not. For the model we used the same approach as for multiclass classification described in the previous section, in terms of feature selection and finding the best configuration for the model. For the binary classification we achieved a statistical accuracy of 0.949 which is significantly higher than that of the multiclass classification model.

6   Discussion

In this work, we proposed an approach towards achieving Be-In/Be-Out in public transportation using a pre-trained machine learning model for transport mode inference on-device. This approach is completely void of any on-board sensors or devices. The results presented in the previous sections indicated a fairly high accuracy and attests to the viability of the approach.

Our approach differentiate from similar approaches on two key points. Firstly, our approach does not require any on-board equipment, as opposed to previous research such as [2,17]. Reducing the amount of vehicle-mounted sensors and devices can contribute to ensure scalability for the public transport operators, in addition to reduce cost related to both installation and maintenance. In dialog with public transport operators in Norway, it became apparent that this would be an important factor for them if they were to utilize such a solution. We assume that this is ideal for any public transport operator anywhere due to the aforementioned benefits. As such, by employing a solution which does not require any physical equipment, the solution will be easy and effortless to test out and deploy for any public transport operator anywhere in the world, regardless of location and affluence. Secondly, our model can run the inference on the traveler's personal smartphone. This is also to the contrary of previous research that send the necessary data from the traveler's device to an on-board system, which in turn communicates with a remote server or cloud [15,17]. The researches who has employed machine learning in order to solve this issue, have placed the model in the cloud [13,17,19] which may cause an increased cost both for the public transport operators in terms of maintenance and computation cost, as well as, an increased cost for the travelers, in terms of network cost. Furthermore, by running inference on-device, no data needs to leave the traveler's device in order to establish a presence within the given mode of transport. This contributes to the security and privacy of the solution since eliminating data transmission prohibits any potential man-in-the-middle attacks. Moreover, sensitive data is not available in any cloud solution which also mitigates the risk of malicious insiders working at the public transport companies. A fully integrated solution would, of course, need some sort of data transmission in order to deduct the required amount for the journey and so forth, however, the presence detection itself does not require this.

Even though there are many advantages of the proposed solution, there are also some potential disadvantages. A potential disadvantage to our approach could be elevated energy consumption on-device. Experimental testing does not indicate significant energy usage, however, this particular issue needs further investigation. Another apparent drawback is the accuracy of our solution. We achieved a statistical accuracy for the multiclass classification of 0.906, compared to that of [17] which reached a statistical accuracy of 0.978, although using an on-board device and with the machine learning model residing in the cloud. As stated earlier, we enlisted 101 participants to gather data on-board public transportation vehicles and it resulted in a fairly skewed data collection. We assume the lack of data collection in public transport vehicles other than bus may be the reason for the suboptimal accuracy of our model. If we look at the confusion matrix in Fig. 3 we see that bus was correctly classified 18298 times of a total of 19459 times. This corresponds to a theoretical accuracy of roughly 94% which is what we achieved with the binary classification. From there, metro has the second highest amount of correct classifications, then tram and lastly train. This correlates with the amount of sensor data collected within each mode of transport shown in Fig. 1. It is thus reasonable to assume that more data collected within each mode of transport will result in a higher classification accuracy for each of the classes, which is also supported by [13]. Another potential way to build on this solution and to improve the overall accuracy for public transport mode inference is to take advantage of ad hoc collaboration. In our previous work we investigated the energy consumption of distributing sensor data collection amongst travellers on-board the same public transport vehicle [20]. By employing the same technology, we could use ad hoc collaboration between collocated passengers in order to reach a consensus if the probability of a given class is below a certain threshold.

7   Conclusion and Future Work

We suggest the use of a pre-trained, on-device machine learning model for public transport mode inference. Our approach differentiate itself from previous research mainly in two aspects. Firstly, our approach does not require any form of on-board device or sensors, and secondly, the transport mode inference is being done on-device. This comes with the potential benefits of reduced cost related to installation, maintenance network and cloud calculations, in addition to, potentially reducing the network cost for the traveler. Our solution achieved a statistical accuracy of 0.906, however, due to the skewed data foundation, it is reasonable to assume that a larger data foundation will lead to an increased accuracy of the model.

Future work entails amassing a larger, more diverse dataset, which could lead to a significant increase in the model accuracy. Further, we would like to investigate the performance of this solution in terms of network load and energy consumption compared to cloud-based machine learning models. It would also be interesting to address and evaluate security aspects related to this kind of solution.

References

1. Bieler, M., Mukkamala, R.R., Grønli, T.M.: A context- and trajectory-based destination prediction of public transportation users. IEEE Intell. Transp. Syst. Mag., 2–19 (2022). https://doi.org/10.1109/MITS.2021.3132772
2. Bitew, M.A., Muhammad, A., Fandiantoro, D.H., Boedinoegroho, H., Kurniawan, A.: E-payment for public transportation using BIBO method based on Bluetooth low energy beacon. In: 2020 International Conference on Computer Engineering, Network, and Intelligent Multimedia (CENIM), pp. 199–204 (2020). https://doi.org/10.1109/CENIM51130.2020.9297901
3. Chen, C., et al.: Improving protein-protein interactions prediction accuracy using XGBoost feature selection and stacked ensemble classifier **123**, 103899 (2020). https://doi.org/10.1016/j.compbiomed.2020.103899
4. Chui, K.T., Tsang, K.F., Chi, H.R., Ling, B.W.K., Wu, C.K.: An accurate ECG-based transportation safety drowsiness detection scheme. IEEE Trans. Ind. Inf. **12**(4), 1438–1452 (2016). https://doi.org/10.1109/TII.2016.2573259
5. Dong, N., Zhai, M., Zhao, L., Wu, C.H.: Cervical cell classification based on the CART feature selection algorithm. J. Ambient. Intell. Humaniz. Comput. **12**(2), 1837–1849 (2020). https://doi.org/10.1007/s12652-020-02256-9

6. Estevez, P.A., Tesmer, M., Perez, C.A., Zurada, J.M.: Normalized mutual information feature selection **20**(2), 189–201 (2009). https://doi.org/10.1109/TNN.2008. 2005601
7. Han, H., Siebert, J.: TinyML: a systematic review and synthesis of existing research. In: 2022 International Conference on Artificial Intelligence in Information and Communication (ICAIIC), pp. 269–274 (2022). https://doi.org/10.1109/ ICAIIC54071.2022.9722636
8. Handte, M., Foell, S., Wagner, S., Kortuem, G., Marrón, P.J.: An internet-of-things enabled connected navigation system for urban bus riders. IEEE Internet Things J. **3**(5), 735–744 (2016). https://doi.org/10.1109/JIOT.2016.2554146
9. Jankowski, S., Szymański, Z., Dziomin, U., Mazurek, P., Wagner, J.: Deep learning classifier for fall detection based on IR distance sensor data. In: 2015 IEEE 8th International Conference on Intelligent Data Acquisition and Advanced Computing Systems: Technology and Applications (IDAACS), vol. 2, pp. 723–727 (2015). https://doi.org/10.1109/IDAACS.2015.7341398
10. Kingma, D.P., Ba, J.: Adam: a method for stochastic optimization (2014)
11. Kostakos, V., Camacho, T., Mantero, C.: Wireless detection of end-to-end passenger trips on public transport buses. In: 13th International IEEE Conference on Intelligent Transportation Systems, pp. 1795–1800 (2010). https://doi.org/10. 1109/ITSC.2010.5625062
12. Li, X., Chen, W., Zhang, Q., Wu, L.: Building auto-encoder intrusion detection system based on random forest feature selection **95**, 101851 (2020). https://doi. org/10.1016/j.cose.2020.101851
13. Mastalerz, M.W., Malinowski, A., Kwiatkowski, S., Śniegula, A., Wieczorek, B.: Passenger BIBO detection with IoT support and machine learning techniques for intelligent transport systems **176**, 3780–3793 (2020). https://doi.org/10.1016/j. procs.2020.09.009
14. Mishra, K.M., Huhtala, K.J.: Fault detection of elevator systems using multilayer perceptron neural network. In: 2019 24th IEEE International Conference on Emerging Technologies and Factory Automation (ETFA), pp. 904–909 (2019). https:// doi.org/10.1109/ETFA.2019.8869230. ISSN: 1946-0759
15. Narzt, W., Mayerhofer, S., Weichselbaum, O., Haselböck, S., Höfler, N.: Be-In/Be-Out with Bluetooth low energy: implicit ticketing for public transportation systems. In: 2015 IEEE 18th International Conference on Intelligent Transportation Systems, pp. 1551–1556 (2015). https://doi.org/10.1109/ITSC.2015.253
16. Narzt, W., Mayerhofer, S., Weichselbaum, O., Haselböck, S., Höfler, N.: Bluetooth low energy as enabling technology for Be-In/Be-Out systems. In: 2016 13th IEEE Annual Consumer Communications Networking Conference (CCNC), pp. 423–428 (2016). https://doi.org/10.1109/CCNC.2016.7444817
17. Oplenskedal, M., Taherkordi, A., Herrmann, P.: DeepMatch: deep matching for in-vehicle presence detection in transportation. In: Proceedings of the 14th ACM International Conference on Distributed and Event-Based Systems, DEBS 2020, pp. 97–108. Association for Computing Machinery (2020). https://doi.org/10. 1145/3401025.3401741
18. Patlins, A., Kunicina, N.: The new approach for passenger counting in public transport system. In: 2015 IEEE 8th International Conference on Intelligent Data Acquisition and Advanced Computing Systems: Technology and Applications (IDAACS), vol. 1, pp. 53–57 (2015). https://doi.org/10.1109/IDAACS.2015.7340700
19. Servizi, V., et al.: Context-aware sensing and implicit ground truth collection: building a foundation for event triggered surveys on autonomous shuttles **28**(1) (2021). https://doi.org/10.5278/ojs.td.v28i1.6862

20. Skretting, A., Grønli, T.M.: Distributed sensor data collection using mobile clouds for public transportation. In: 2021 IEEE 17th International Conference on Intelligent Computer Communication and Processing (ICCP), pp. 61–68 (2021). https://doi.org/10.1109/ICCP53602.2021.9733560

21. Wieczorek, B., Poniszewska-Marańda, A.: Be in/Be out model for intelligent transport in SmartCity approach. In: Proceedings of the 17th International Conference on Advances in Mobile Computing & Multimedia, pp. 226–230. ACM (2019). https://doi.org/10.1145/3365921.3365945

22. Zhuang, H., et al.: Diagnosis of early stage Parkinson's disease on quantitative susceptibility mapping using complex network with one-way ANOVA F-test feature selection **21**(05), 2140026 (2021). https://doi.org/10.1142/S0219519421400261

Data-Driven Federated Autonomous Driving

Ahmad Hammoud[1] , Azzam Mourad[2,3]([✉]) , Hadi Otrok[4] ,
and Zbigniew Dziong[1]

[1] Department of Electrical Engineering, Ecole de Technologie Superieure (ETS),
Montreal, Canada
`ahmad.hammoud.1@ens.etsmtl.ca, zbigniew.dziong@etsmtl.ca`
[2] Department of Computer Science and Mathematics, Lebanese American University,
Beirut, Lebanon
`azzam.mourad@lau.edu.lb`
[3] Science Division, New York University, Abu Dhabi, UAE
[4] Department of EECS, Khalifa University, Abu Dhabi, United Arab Emirates
`hadi.otrok@ku.ac.ae`

Abstract. Intelligent vehicles optimize road traveling through their
reliance on autonomous driving applications to navigate. These applications integrate machine learning to extract statistical patterns and
sets of rules for the vehicles to follow when facing decision-making scenarios. The immaturity of such systems, caused by the lack of a diverse
dataset, can lead to inaccurate on-road decisions that could affect road
safety. In this paper, we devise a decentralized scheme based on federating autonomous driving companies in order to expand their access to data
and resources during the learning phase. Our scheme federates companies
in an optimal manner by studying the compatibility of the federations'
dataset in the federations formation process, without exposing private
data to rivalries. We implement our scheme for evaluation against other
formation mechanisms. Experiments show that our approach can achieve
higher model accuracy, reduce model loss, and increase the utility of the
individuals on average when compared to other techniques.

Keywords: Autonomous driving · Federations · Machine learning ·
Intelligent vehicles · IoV

1 Introduction

The current era has introduced many advancements in a variety of sectors, among
which the Internet of Vehicles (IoV) and Autonomous Driving rise as part of the
Intelligent Transportation Systems (ITS) [1,2]. IoV integrates sensors into the
intelligent vehicles, such as Cameras and LIDARs (Light Detection and Ranging), to allow scanning of their surrounding. The vehicles, afterward, intercept
the scanned data and pass them through their OBUs (On-Board Units) trigger-
ing an autonomous driving application that decides whether or not to take a specific driving action, e.g. changing speed, rotating wheels [3]. In order to develop

© The Author(s), under exclusive license to Springer Nature Switzerland AG 2022
I. Awan et al. (Eds.): MobiWIS 2022, LNCS 13475, pp. 79–90, 2022.
https://doi.org/10.1007/978-3-031-14391-5_6

autonomous driving applications, autonomous driving companies rely on analyzing data, collected from the vehicles through Vehicle-to-Infrastructure (V2I) communications [4], by discovering statistically significant patterns out of the available data using machine learning techniques [5]. For instance, Autonomous Driving systems, such as Alphabet's Waymo[1] and Tesla's FSD[2], are examples of the widely studied IoV applications that are critical for improving road safety in the future.

1.1 Problem Statement and Objectives

Mainly, generating an autonomous driving model strongly depends on the quality of the dataset and the availability of computing resources for training such data. One of the main problems that a company might face during the development of its model is the lack of sufficient data and computing resources. To begin with, the lack of significant data can be interpreted in two ways: 1) the data is too small in terms of size, thus, generalizing a certain pattern out of it can be a difficult/impossible task to do. 2) The dataset is biased and does not cover all possible cases. Hence, extracting the knowledge out of that sample data might not be safe for production. Therefore, a problem arises as these inaccurate models may endanger road safety.

One of the considered methods in the literature to compensate on the missing resources is to federate entities by merging their available resources. For instance, the authors in [6] have addressed the problem of online team formations in social networks. They devised algorithms to form teams that are able to complete their assigned tasks while reducing the communication overhead. From a different aspect, the authors in [7] advanced evolutionary models using genetic algorithms and evolutionary game theory to reach a cloud federations formation that is highly profitable, while reinforcing the stability among cloud providers. The authors of [8] addressed the cloud formation problem by using trust as a measurement among providers. They claimed to reach stability, profit maximization, and fairness through their formation mechanism. The formation techniques were further extended to cover fog federations formation as well; For instance, [9] studied forming the federations by embedding a machine learning technique within a genetic model in order to estimate the impact of the federations on the QoS. The authors in [10] addressed forming coalitions of fog providers according to their available computing resources in order to ensure a smooth execution of the federated learning processes. Their objective was to migrate services on the fogs within the same federations in a way that maximizes the delivered QoS. The authors in [11] emphasized the collaboration among all entities by forming a grand federation and exchanging knowledge in a federated learning architecture. Nevertheless, a structureless formation of the federation or forming the grand federation may result in instabilities of the federation in a

---

[1] Alphabet, the parent company of Google. https://waymo.com/waymo-driver/.
[2] Tesla's Full Self-Driving system. https://www.tesla.com/en_CA/support/full-self-driving-computer.

competitive environment where all of the companies are looking for supremacy in full vehicle autonomy.

To the best of our knowledge, no work has addressed team formations while acknowledging the requirements of autonomous driving. Hence, the objective of this paper is to find a suitable solution that overcomes the resource shortage while reducing the number of members within a single federation to avoid unnecessary interactions.

1.2 Contributions

To overcome the aforementioned problems, we devise a decentralized scheme based on cooperative game theory [12,13] to form the federations while respecting the condition of maximizing their efficiency. Our game consists of having the set of players cooperating to construct a federation that can overcome the accuracy limitation while respecting the privacy of the data between rivalries. We implement our scheme using python as a proof of concept. Our experiments reveal that the approach used in this paper can lead to better accuracy and less model loss while maximizing the efficiency of the resources than other federating schemes. Our contribution, in this paper, can be summarized as the follows:

- Devising a decentralized solution for coalition formation to overcome the resources shortage for the federations while maximizing the efficiency of the federations and minimizing its members.
- Providing a numerical example using MNIST dataset to explain the steps of our federation formation approach.
- Implementing our scheme and comparing its results with other federation techniques in terms of the machine learning model's accuracy and loss, in addition to the theoretical utility of the entities.

Outline of the paper The rest of the paper is organized as follows. In Sect. 2, we detail our problem and demonstrate our scheme. In Sect. 3, we provide a numerical example for forming the set of federations. Afterward, in Sect. 4, we discuss the results obtained using our scheme and compare them with other methods. In Sect. 5, we conclude this work.

2 Federation Formation Mechanism

2.1 System Model and Problem Formulation

Let us consider a set of autonomous driving companies $C = c_1, c_2, ..., c_n$. All companies possess a set of data $D(c_i)$ that needs to be processed. We assume that the set C are all developing similar models that utilize similar datasets in terms of features, e.g., traffic signs recognition model or lane following model. When c_i performs the learning operation on its dataset, it obtains a certain autonomous driving model with accuracy $Acc(c_i)$ and loss $Loss(c_i)$. For a prototype product (i.e. autonomous driving model) to be ready for production, it should be certified to do so based on testing its accuracy. We introduce a variable min_acc which determines the minimum required accuracy for the model. Nevertheless, some of the problems that a company might face during the development process are the lack of a representative dataset or not having enough resources to process the available dataset. These problems could prevent the companies from reaching an acceptable model accuracy. When this accuracy is reached, the company can charge $R(Acc(c_i)) = \rho \times Acc(c_i)$ per each product it sells as a reward, where ρ is the selling price of a fully mature model. This can be interpreted as the following:

$$R_{c_i} = \begin{cases} R(Acc(c_i)), & \text{if } Acc(c_i) \geq min\_acc \\ 0, & \text{otherwise} \end{cases} \tag{1}$$

Thus, the rationality of the entities pushes them to collaborate with others, rather than not being able to achieve their targets. Therefore, to avoid wasting the data and resources of the companies that are unable to reach the targeted accuracy, we introduce $f_i = c_1, c_2, ..., c_m$ which represents a federation of m members collaborating. A federation of autonomous driving companies is intended to enhance the efficiency and increase the accuracy of their product by merging their resources strategically, where all members can benefit from the federation. In a cooperative and competitive environment, multiple federations can be formed, represented by the set $F = f_1, f_2, ..., f_n$, with unique members each. In other words, federations f_i and f_j can exist while having no members in common. Thus, the members of a federation f_i collaborate to generate a model with accuracy $Acc(f_i)$ and loss $Loss(f_i)$. Accordingly, the reward obtained for this federation can be interpreted as $R(Acc(f_i)) = \rho \times Acc(f_i)$, which will be distributed among the federation members. The utility of a member is considered as its revenue per one sold model, represented by the below equation:

$$U_{c_i, f_j} = \frac{\rho \times Acc(f_j)}{|f_j|} \tag{2}$$

where f_j is the federation joined by c_i, and $|f_j|$ is the number of participants in that federation.

As a rational decision-maker, a company c_i might break from its federation due to the lack of incentives to maintain its commitment. This act can lead to instabilities and deteriorates the effectiveness of the abandoned federation. Hence, there should be a designated policy for forming the set of federations that increases the efficiency and assures the stability of these federations. In addition, due to the profit distribution according to the members in the same federation, it gets more beneficial for the companies to consider minimizing the number of the members.

Game theory is the science of the optimal decision-making of independent and competing players in a strategic environment [12]. In game theory, *cooperative games* are games with competition between groups of players due to the possibility of external enforcement of cooperative behavior [14]. Players can cooperate with others through contract law. These types of games are also known as *coalitional games*. In contrast to non-cooperative games that focus on predicting the individual payoffs, cooperative games focus on predicting the coalitions that will form and the collective actions that the players will take. Game theory has been adopted in many fields and has proven its efficiency in reaching satisfactory solutions [14,15].

2.2 Decentralized Federation Formation Scheme

In this context, we refer to an autonomous driving company as a player who seeks to achieve its objective, that is reaching its desired model accuracy, by contracting with a suitable coalition, i.e. federation. Our proposed scheme evolves in rounds where, at each round, a player makes its decision to join a coalition based on certain criteria. We assume that a player is expected to always be welcomed by a federation of its choice if the latter still has not reached its desired outcome yet. Below, we briefly overview the scheme.

Algorithm 1: Federation Formation Mechanism

Input: C
Output: F
```
// federations initialization
```
1 $F \leftarrow \emptyset$;
2 $F' \leftarrow \emptyset$;
3 **foreach** $c_i \in C$ **do**
4      $tmp\_fed \leftarrow initialize\_fed(c_i)$;
5      $F' \leftarrow tmp\_fed \cup F'$;

```
// evaluate initial federations
```
6 **foreach** $f_i \in F'$ **do**
```
   // train model
```
7      $f_i.model \leftarrow train(f_i, d_i)$;
```
   // evaluate model
```
8      $f_i.acc, f_i.loss \leftarrow Acc(f_i), Loss(f_i)$;
```
   // check federation qualification
```
9   **if** $f_i.acc \geq min\_acc$ **then**
10        $F.add(f_i)$;
11        $F'.remove(f_i)$;

```
// federations restructuring
```
12 **while** $|F'| > 1$ **do**
13   **foreach** $f_i \in F'$ **do**
14        $f_j \leftarrow Get\_Merge\_Decision(f_i, F'[i+1:])$;
15        $f_i \leftarrow f_i \cup f_j$;
16        $F'.remove(f_j)$;
```
      // evaluate changes
```
17        $f_i.model \leftarrow train(f_i, d_i)$;
18        $f_i.acc, f_i.loss \leftarrow Acc(f_i), Loss(f_i)$;
19   **if** $f_i.acc \geq min\_acc$ **then**
20          $F.add(f_i)$;
21          $F'.remove(f_i)$;

22   **return** F;

The scheme begins by initializing every company as an independent federation. Afterward, each company initiates its training process to measure the quality of its output by interpreting its accuracy. Then, a round of reinforcing the coalitions takes place in a decentralized manner, where players who were not able to reach their desired accuracy seek to federate with others. The process for joining a certain federation in our scheme is based upon the compatibility of the player with the federation. That is to say, a player studies its harmony with the set of all available federations and chooses the best federation accordingly. The compatibility study is based on testing the resulted model of the federation on a representative chunk of the player's dataset. In order to protect the data of the player, it downloads the model from the federation and test it locally on its own dataset. The player then chooses to merge with the federation that showed the most opposed features by selecting the least accurate model (as can be shown in Algorithm 2). Our scheme is organized as the following (Algorithm 1):

1. Identifying the set of companies developing a similar autonomous driving model.
2. Creating n federations where n is the number of companies and assigning each company to be the leader of a unique federation.
3. Training the data and evaluating the results obtained.
4. Merging unsatisfactory federations with others based on Algorithm 2. Then reevaluate the performance of the changed federations.
5. Repeat Steps 3 and 4 until no further merge is needed.

Algorithm 2: Get Merge Decision

Input: f_i, F'
Output: f_j

1 $f_j \leftarrow NULL$;
2 $min\_accuracy \leftarrow 1$;
   // search for the least accurate model according to the player's dataset
3 **foreach** $f_k \in F'$ **do**
4 $\quad$ $f_k\_accuracy \leftarrow Acc(f_k, f_i.data)$;
5 $\quad$ **if** $min\_accuracy < f_k\_accuracy$ **then**
6 $\quad\quad$ $min\_accuracy \leftarrow f_k\_accuracy$;
7 $\quad\quad$ $f_j \leftarrow f_k$;

8 return f_j;

---

3 Numerical Example

In this section, we illustrate our federation formation process using an example based on MNIST dataset for its simplicity. We assume the existence of 10 companies, $C_1...C_{10}$. We consider $20,000$ records randomly selected from this data. Then, we distribute the dataset among the companies in a random non-independent and identical distributed manner. The distribution is shown in Table 1. We assume that the threshold for a model to be publicly accepted is 0.6.

Table 1. MNIST dataset - initial step

		\multicolumn{10}{c	}{Labels}		
		0	1	2	3	4	5	6	7	8	9	Accuracy
Companies	C_1	400	0	400	400	0	400	0	0	0	400	0.45
	C_2	0	0	0	0	0	0	2000	0	0	0	0.19
	C_3	0	500	0	0	500	0	0	500	500	0	0.41
	C_4	0	0	1000	0	0	1000	0	0	0	0	0.20
	C_5	500	0	0	500	0	0	500	0	0	500	0.43
	C_6	0	0	0	0	0	0	0	0	2000	0	0.14
	C_7	0	500	500	0	500	0	0	500	0	0	0.42
	C_8	400	0	0	400	0	400	400	0	0	400	0.45
	C_9	0	500	0	0	500	0	0	500	500	0	0.42
	C_{10}	0	0	1000	0	0	1000	0	0	0	0	0.23

The first step is to initiate 10 federations where each company belongs to a separate one. Then, it generates a model and makes it accessible to other companies if the accuracy is below the threshold. The game starts and federation i starts looking for another to join. In our example, we assume that federation $f_1 = [C_1]$ initiates the game by downloading all of the available models generated by the other federations. It then evaluates the accuracy of the model according to its own data to assess whether or not the data used for training is similar or not to its own. The accuracy rate of the 9 models according to f_1's data are the following:

$$Acc(f_2, f_1.data) = 0.09$$
$$Acc(f_3, f_1.data) = 0.04$$
$$Acc(f_4, f_1.data) = 0.39$$
$$Acc(f_5, f_1.data) = 0.58$$
$$Acc(f_6, f_1.data) = 0.06$$
$$Acc(f_7, f_1.data) = 0.24$$
$$Acc(f_8, f_1.data) = 0.73$$
$$Acc(f_9, f_1.data) = 0.05$$
$$Acc(f_{10}, f_1.data) = 0.42$$

The model that was trained with the least similar dataset belongs to f_3. f_1 then decides to merge with f_3 in order to benefit from their resources combined. The game proceeds afterward and the turn comes to f_2 to select a federation to join in during the second round. The process repeats for all the unsatisfied federations where each one takes a turn to decide its best strategy to follow. After convergence, the final set of federations is shown in Table 2 where there exist 4 federations, f_3, f_5, f_7, f_9, and 3 of these federations were able to surpass the accuracy threshold.

Table 2. MNIST dataset - formed federations

		Labels										Accuracy
		0	1	2	3	4	5	6	7	8	9	
Federations	C_3, C_1	400	500	400	400	500	400	0	500	500	400	0.76
	C_5, C_4	500	0	1000	500	0	1000	500	0	0	500	0.52
	C_7, C_8, C_6	400	500	500	400	500	400	400	500	2000	400	0.79
	C_9, C_{10}, C_2	0	500	1000	0	500	1000	2000	500	500	0	0.61

4   Experimental Evaluation

To assess the efficiency of our devised scheme, we implement the algorithms using python. The simulation took place on a computer equipped with 16 GB of RAMs and NVIDIA GeForce GTX 1060 Mobile. To set up a realistic working environment, we developed a non-identical distribution algorithm to split the MNIST dataset into biased subsets, similar to what was proposed in [16]. This way, each company can possess a distinguished subset that differs from others in terms of labels and features. The number of companies is set to 10 and the threshold min_acc is set to 0.7. Each federation can execute its training process for up to 50 epochs to show how it evolves. Similar to Tesla's FSD price, the selling price ρ of a fully aware model is set to 12,000\$[3]. The evaluation of our technique is assessed by measuring its results in terms of Average Federation Accuracy, Average Federation Loss, and Average Federation Utility against other techniques, i.e., a Fair Allocation technique, and a Random Formation technique. In these two techniques, Algorithm 1 executes as usual, whereas we replace Algorithm 2, i.e. the federation merge selection process, with Algorithm 3 for the Fair Allocation scheme, and by a random federation selection for the Random Formation technique. Algorithm 3 presents the heuristic that attempts to form the federations by reducing the variance of the number of companies in the federations. In other words, at each round, a federation merges with another that has the least number of members. The utility considered is the revenue obtained per company on average, if the product meets the minimum accuracy required (Eq. 2). The loss is calculated through the below equation:

$$D(S, L) = - \sum_i L_i \times log(S_i) \qquad (3)$$

where the set S is the set of probabilities of the classes the prediction belongs to, and L is the one hot encoded labels set that indicates the correct prediction.

---

[3] https://electrek.co/2022/01/18/tesla-increases-full-self-driving-package-price-but-not-monthly-subscription-service/.

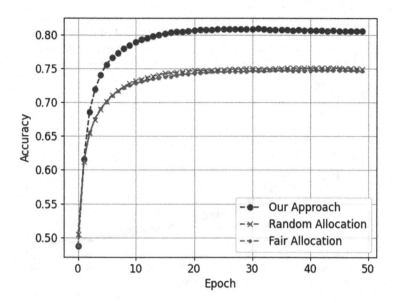

Fig. 1. Accuracy

In Fig. 1, we illustrate the results obtained in terms of accuracy (y-axis) and how it evolves according to the training process. The values represent the average accuracy of all of the formed federations. We notice that the Random allocation and the Fair allocation approaches achieved very similar results to one another and converged to 0.75 at $epoch = 20$, whereas our approach was able to achieve higher accuracy and to converge up to 0.81. In terms of loss, in Fig. 2, our approach achieved a loss of 1.82 and both of the other approaches reached 1.83 on average. The average utility measured in Fig. 3 shows that our approach achieves a faster way to reach the desired accuracy threshold (i.e., min_acc), which allows the federations to make a profit faster. The other two approaches struggle at the beginning but were able to reach a value of $utility = 1900$ at the end of the training process, compared to our $utility = 2400$.

We deduce from this simulation that our approach, with its mechanism of fitting players together according to their missing data, is able to achieve higher results than other random and heuristics, thus achieving higher profitability for the entities.

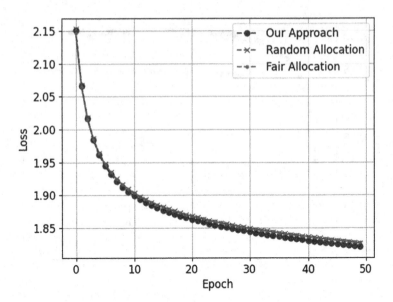

Fig. 2. Loss

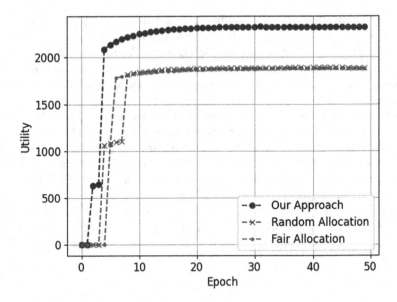

Fig. 3. Utility

Algorithm 3: Get Federation With Least Members

Input: F'
Output: f_j
1   $f_j \leftarrow NULL$;
2   $min\_members \leftarrow +inf$;
    // search for the federation with the least members
3   **foreach** $f_k \in F'$ **do**
4   **if** $min\_members < members(f_k)$ **then**
5       $min\_members \leftarrow members(f_k)$;
6       $f_j \leftarrow f_k$;

7   **return** f_j;

---

5   Conclusion and Future Work

In this work, we emphasized the importance of autonomous driving and the role of devising federations of autonomous driving companies for achieving greater road safety. The approach that was proposed in this paper is based on federating companies according to their lack of representative data to produce their autonomous driving applications. The approach preserves the privacy of the individuals that are not in the same federation. Results showed that our scheme is able to increase the average model accuracy and the average profit of the companies by up to 8% compared to other federation methods. For future work, we will extend this paper by reinforcing the privacy measurements within the same federation as well, by utilizing federated learning to unify the knowledge without the need to share raw data. Federated learning assures the privacy of the participants by training their data locally and sharing only the extracted knowledge patterns [17]. In addition, we will consider the resources of these companies in terms of processing power when training the models. Also, we will devise a recovery mechanism in case a member dropped from a federation by adopting evolutionary techniques such as evolutionary game theoretical model [18]. Finally, the study will cover a diverse set of autonomous driving datasets when evaluating the proposed model to assure being efficient in its intended environment.

References

1. Aloqaily, M., Hussain, R., Khalaf, D., Hani, D., Oracevic, A.: On the role of futuristic technologies in securing UAV-supported autonomous vehicles. IEEE Consum. Electron. Mag. (2022)
2. Rahman, S.A., Mourad, A., El Barachi, M., Al Orabi, W.: A novel on-demand vehicular sensing framework for traffic condition monitoring. Veh. Commun. **12**, 165–178 (2018)
3. Hammoud, A., Sami, H., Mourad, A., Otrok, H., Mizouni, R., Bentahar, J.: AI, blockchain, and vehicular edge computing for smart and secure IoV: challenges and directions. IEEE Internet Things Mag. **3**(2), 68–73 (2020)

4. Salahuddin, M.A., Al-Fuqaha, A., Guizani, M.: Software-defined networking for RSU clouds in support of the internet of vehicles. IEEE Internet Things J. **2**(2), 133–144 (2014)

5. Wahab, O.A., Kara, N., Edstrom, C., Lemieux, Y.: MAPLE: a machine learning approach for efficient placement and adjustment of virtual network functions. J. Netw. Comput. Appl. **142**, 37–50 (2019)

6. Anagnostopoulos, A., Becchetti, L., Castillo, C., Gionis, A., Leonardi, S.: Online team formation in social networks. In: Proceedings of the 21st International Conference on World Wide Web, pp. 839–848, April 2012

7. Hammoud, A., Mourad, A., Otrok, H., Wahab, O.A., Harmanani, H.: Cloud federation formation using genetic and evolutionary game theoretical models. Futur. Gener. Comput. Syst. **104**, 92–104 (2020)

8. Dhole, A., Thomas, M.V., Chandrasekaran, K.: An efficient trust-based Game-Theoretic approach for cloud federation formation. In: 2016 3rd International Conference on Advanced Computing and Communication Systems (ICACCS), vol. 1, pp. 1–6. IEEE, January 2016

9. Shamseddine, H., et al.: A novel federated fog architecture embedding intelligent formation. IEEE Netw. **35**(3), 198–204 (2020)

10. Hammoud, A., Otrok, H., Mourad, A., Dziong, Z.: On demand fog federations for horizontal federated learning in IoV. IEEE Trans. Netw. Serv. Manage. (2022)

11. Rjoub, G., Wahab, O.A., Bentahar, J., Bataineh, A.S.: Improving autonomous vehicles safety in snow weather using federated YOLO CNN learning. In: Bentahar, J., Awan, I., Younas, M., Grønli, T.-M. (eds.) MobiWIS 2021. LNCS, vol. 12814, pp. 121–134. Springer, Cham (2021). https://doi.org/10.1007/978-3-030-83164-6_10

12. Curiel, I.: Cooperative Game Theory and Applications: Cooperative Games Arising from Combinatorial Optimization Problems, vol. 16. Springer, New York (1997). https://doi.org/10.1007/978-1-4757-4871-0

13. Bataineh, A.S., Bentahar, J., Wahab, O.A., Mizouni, R., Rjoub, G.: Cloud as platform for monetizing complementary data for AI-driven services: a two-sided cooperative game. In: 2021 IEEE International Conference on Services Computing (SCC), pp. 443–449. IEEE, September 2021

14. Bataineh, A.S., Bentahar, J., Mizouni, R., Wahab, O.A., Rjoub, G., El Barachi, M.: Cloud computing as a platform for monetizing data services: a two-sided game business model. IEEE Trans. Netw. Serv. Manage. **19**, 1336–1350 (2021)

15. Bataineh, A.S., Bentahar, J., Abdel Wahab, O., Mizouni, R., Rjoub, G.: A game-based secure trading of big data and IoT services: blockchain as a two-sided market. In: Kafeza, E., Benatallah, B., Martinelli, F., Hacid, H., Bouguettaya, A., Motahari, H. (eds.) ICSOC 2020. LNCS, vol. 12571, pp. 85–100. Springer, Cham (2020). https://doi.org/10.1007/978-3-030-65310-1_7

16. McMahan, B., Moore, E., Ramage, D., Hampson, S., Arcas, B.A.: Communication-efficient learning of deep networks from decentralized data. In: Artificial Intelligence and Statistics, pp. 1273–1282. PMLR, April 2017

17. AbdulRahman, S., Tout, H., Ould-Slimane, H., Mourad, A., Talhi, C., Guizani, M.: A survey on federated learning: the journey from centralized to distributed on-site learning and beyond. IEEE Internet Things J. **8**(7), 5476–5497 (2020)

18. Weibull, J.W.: Evolutionary Game Theory. MIT Press (1997)

Security in Healthcare and Smart Cities Environment

Case Study on a Session Hijacking Attack: The 2021 CVS Health Data Breach

Aversa Prentosito$^{(\boxtimes)}$, McKenna Skoczen, Lauren Kahrs, and Suman Bhunia

Miami University, Oxford, OH 45056, USA
{prentoam,skoczemm,kahrslg,bhunias}@miamioh.edu

Abstract. The CVS medical data breach in March of 2021 was a source of anxiety, fear, and anger in many users, leading to lower customer loyalty. Our study found that their websites used misconfigured databases, allowing an adversary to steal healthcare data through session hijacking attacks. Customers' search metadata containing email addresses, prescriptions, and other medical search queries, were stored in cloud-hosted log files. Although no concrete evidence of data misuse was uncovered, the research found that over a billion confidential search queries were potentially exposed to adversaries. This paper analyzes the data breach methodology and impact in detail and provides possible defense strategies against such attacks. It violates the security and protection regulations mandating proper confidentiality of users' private medical and healthcare information. This paper also outlines possible defense measures against healthcare data session hijacking attacks, including having policies in place, such as an incident response plan, preserving evidence of the breach, and isolating the data breach.

Keywords: CVS · Session Hijacking · IoMT · Data breach

1 Introduction

The medical data breach we are analyzing is from a CVS website hack. In late March of 2021, a data breach occurred with over a billion search records from CVS Health discovered to have been posted online [1]. CVS' site allows customers to perform tasks such as search and purchase products, schedule vaccines, and find resources for health related items. For most of these records, data could not be traced back to a single user. Most of the records included search data for COVID-19 and medication, but for some, if Session ID was matched with what a user searched for or something was added to their shopping cart as part of that session, that user could possibly be identified along with their exposed email [1]. Subsequently, the news was widely covered in the major media outlets as can be see in Fig. 1. Additionally, it has been stated that it could be possible to match the Session ID to a specific user and specific user information. A security researcher who worked with an IT Research Team for Website Planet, issued a report stating that it was likely misconfiguration that resulted in CVS Health

I. Awan et al. (Eds.): MobiWIS 2022, LNCS 13475, pp. 93–105, 2022.
https://doi.org/10.1007/978-3-031-14391-5_7

Fig. 1. News Articles addressing the data breach

website's database not being secure [2]. The whole database was not downloaded so Fowler couldn't determine the number of email addresses that were in the database [3]. CVS stated that a vendor was responsible for hosting the databases and they were taken down in a timely manner. Additionally, CVS states that they had made sure to communicate with the vendor to prevent a recurrence in the future.

There are multiple strict governmental regulations for healthcare data such as Health Insurance Portability and Accountability Act (HIPAA) and Protected Health Information (PHI), to ensure that users' medical information is secured by the companies who hold it. Data breaches in the medical field are especially important because these unforeseen gaps in security can be a criminal offense in certain circumstances [4]. A data breach can be defined as "a confirmed incident of unlawful access/disclosure of sensitive, confidential or otherwise protected data, including personal health or personally identifiable information, trade secrets, or intellectual property" [5]. Some of the risks of data breaches in the medical field specifically can include the customers becoming targets for phishing attacks, giving competitors an advantage, vulnerability to attacks of more sensitive data, increased knowledge of public to entire system structure, losing stock value, and losing customers that might not feel safe after a data breach has occurred. Phishing can occur when data is compared to what people have ordered to give hackers a better look into what things a certain customer could be interested in and fall prey to [6]. Competitors could also use leaked information to target their customers based on the data obtained through the leak, information that would have taken years to procure on their own in some cases [7].

Studies have noted both fear and anger from affected customers from past CVS data breaches, that could lead to lower customer loyalty and less customers in total coming back and going to a competitor medical service provider [5].

Unlike other non-medical companies, CVS has an enforced responsibility to keep customer data private, and that is the importance of looking into the CVS data breach in its entirety to better understand how breaches like this could be better prevented in the future.

The goal of this paper is to describe the CVS health data breach, from how the breach occurred to its implications for CVS and its customers, including remedies for such breaches and how to guard against future breaches of this nature. Background on the CVS company and their privacy policy is presented in Sect. 2. An overview of the timeline and description of the CVS health data breach is in Sect. 3. Section 3 also includes more detail into the CVS health data breach, going into specifics of how the breach occurred. A discussion on how CVS's customers were impacted as a result of their data being breached, as well as the impact on CVS as a company and others involved (such as the third-party vendor), is in Sect. 4. In Sect. 5, the steps CVS took to mitigate the attack are listed. Also discussed in Sect. 5 are deliberations on how to work towards preventing these kinds of breaches and maintaining a defense against possible attackers in both the case of CVS and the healthcare industry in general. In Sect. 6, it's all brought together into a summary of findings and conclusion.

2 Background

In this section, we talk about what CVS is as a whole, the standard they hold themselves to, their online presence, the architecture of their search system, and an in depth view of the data breach itself to help give light to the attack and methodologies used in the data breach itself.

2.1 CVS Health

CVS Health is a chain store for everyday goods and health related items. It was ranked number 5 in the fortune 500 list in 2020 and has more than 9,000 locations around the world, serving more than 4.5 million customers daily [8]. Because of the scope that CVS reaches, the database of information that it has about healthcare in the U.S. is vast. CVS has been able to run a Healthcare Insights report for the past 4 years, because of its reach, to get information about healthcare in the U.S. and individuals [9]. Overall, CVS Health has the power to effect great change based on the security and the decisions it makes.

CVS Health's privacy policy is updated each year and stresses on the importance of protecting people's medical information for legal and ethical reasons. Consent is required to store medical information when creating a CVS account. CVS will use personal information given to contact and identify and communicate with the account holder. CVS has the right to view and disclose personal information to business and the government, as long as it does not personally identify the account holder. CVS collects personal information for analytical, monetary, communication, marketing, optimization, and security purposes. CVS does not have the right to sell or disclose patient information that has not been unidentified. Overall, CVS Health spells out very clearly what they are allowed to do with the data given to them [4].

Table 1. Different websites CVS has. In this study, CVS Health was the targeted site in this data breach.

Website address	Description	Requirements
cvs.com	Search and purchase products, have virtual clinics, refill prescriptions, schedule vaccines, and find resources for different health related items	CVS account that requires your name, email, password, address, phone number, date of birth and gender and to agree to a privacy policy
cvshealth.com	An informational site about the company itself	None
caremark.com	Mail pharmacy system	A sign in with name and birth date

2.2 CVS Websites

CVS Health has a number of online websites that they use to connect with their consumer base, including cvs.com, cvshealth.com, and caremark.com. Table 1 shows these websites and their purpose. The main site, cvs, allows customers to search and purchase products, have virtual clinics, refill prescriptions, schedule vaccines, and find resources for different health related items. Most of these services require a CVS account that stores personal information such as name, email, password, address, phone number, date of birth and gender. The user is required to agree to a terms of use agreement [4]. The associated website, cvshealth, is an informational site about the company itself that includes information like services offered, an overview of who CVS is, current health and company news, career and investment opportunities, contact information, as well as other CVS related documentation. Cvshealth also has a search feature to more easily find specific information on the site [9]. The offshoot website, caremark, was created to act as the main website for their mail pharmacy system that also requires a sign in with name and birth date. Caremark provides a way for CVS customers to order prescriptions online and have their order delivered to their door or available for pickup at a local pharmacy location to save money and avoid contact [10]. All three of these websites have a large amount of data they are processing and storing on a daily basis whether its orders, prescription, or documentation.

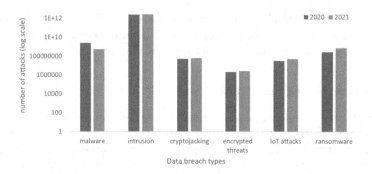

Fig. 2. Malware attacks have decreased 22%; intrusion attempts have increased by 9%. Cryptojacking attacks have increased by 23% while encrypted threats are up 26%. IoT attacks have increased 59% and ransomware attacks have increased 151%.

2.3   Recent Trend in Cybersecurity Attacks

As stated in SonicWall's Cyber Threat Report, there have been a total of about 304.7 million ransomware attacks, 51.1 million cryptojacking attacks, and 2.5 trillion intrusion attempts globally. Figure 2 details the current trends in cybersecurity attacks. The most increasingly common type of malicious cyberattack is a ransomware attack. During these attacks, a form of malware encrypts the victim's files. The attacker demands a monetary fee from the victims in order for them to receive a decryption key. One of the most common deliveries of ransomware is phishing emails. These scams have attachments that seem like a trustworthy file; once a user downloads and opens the file, the attacker can take control of the user's computer. These are very similar to phishing attacks, using targeted messages to entice users into clicking a link. These links can then download viruses, steal private data, and obtain permission on hosts and the connected systems.

Another increasingly common attack is an IoT attack [11]. These attacks target Internet of Things devices such as smart doorbells and other smart home equipment. These devices are frequently gathering passive data on users, getting highly detailed data from their environments. Many of these devices are also connecting their virtual environments to their physical environments, making it possible for cyberthreats to escalate to physical attacks. IoT attacks typically target these devices, taking advantage of insecure default settings and outdated software. Network intrusions are similarly popular cyber threats [11]. Network intrusions are any type of unauthorized activity on a network. These can include port scans and network mapping. These activities can also target network resources and compromise the security of the network and its data.

3   Attack Methodology

It all started with over 1 billion search records for CVS Health discovered online, not password protected, in March 2021 [7]. The CVS data breach was the result of the cloud storage database being misconfigured, as there were no passwords or multi-factor authentication, thus an overall lack of security. In this section, we describe how the attack happened using session hijacking.

3.1 Session Hijacking Attack

This attack was a session hijacking attack, an attack consisting of the exploitation of web session control mechanisms. These attacks compromise session tokens by stealing or predicting a valid session token to gain access to the server. The timeline of the health breach from the time the cloud storage was configured to the time of the attack is:

1. CVS metadata cloud storage configured without password or multi-factor authentication.
2. CVS health log file created. Session ID and Shopper ID encrypted.
3. CVS health log file stored.
4. cloud storage of log file accessed.

The database tracked search functions such as medical conditions, as well as some accidentally entered emails. A cyber-criminal could match Session IDs and search queries and compare these searches with medications a customer is looking for, using it to make more successful targeted phishing attempts [12]. CVS' database that wasn't secure, was posted online, later discovered by a group of researchers [13].

Luckily a research team discovered the unprotected database, however if a hacker looking to exploit vulnerabilities had access to the database, CVS and its customers could be very negatively impacted. The database not making users authenticate is violating an essential requirement of cyber security. With access to the information in the database, a hacker could possibly use consumers' search queries to uncover a consumer's identity. Search queries revealed that many users accidentally entered their emails as searches, potentially allowing hackers access to this information [14]. The emails could be used to identify a customer and then a hacker could perform an attack like spear phishing emails.

Jeremiah Fowler, a researcher involved in discovering the breach, recognized that with regards to medical data, cyber criminals are great at phishing and social engineering. He said that the search entries including email addresses should encourage companies to make sure their data is safe [15]. Email addresses in the search bar correlated with a visitor ID and user ID, as well as what was searched, connecting consumers to their searches.

The data breach attack on CVS was not malicious. As stated previously, this attack was the result of improper configuration of a database. Although this breach was accidental, there could have been horrible consequences. Most of the data exposed was client log files containing search data, but there were some users who entered their emails as search queries. Regardless of whether the CVS data breach was accidental, if user email accounts were exposed, these emails could be targets of phishing attacks and similar scams.

3.2   Storing Data on Third Party Vendor

CVS Health stores a large amount of their data using a private third party vendor. The breach that this study looked into was related to how data was stored in the search bar. CVS's search bar stores all the information typed and entered into a log file. They do this to improve their website performance and get insights into their online consumer base. The log file used can contain metadata and error logs as well. The shopper ID is encrypted in the log file to help ensure anonymity of the shopper. This is the same with the Session ID as well [7]. Overall, CVS Health uses a third party cloud vendor to store their log information about search queries which contain what was searched as well as an encrypted Session and Shopper ID.

The attack came from the log storage mentioned earlier. On March 21st 2021, a data breach occurred resulting in 1 billion records being leaked from the log files because they were not password protected [7].

– 204 gigabytes of data leaked
– database leaked and removed the same day
– 1,148,327,940 records leaked

The information that was obtained included things like medications, COVID vaccination queries, and other personal health items as well as products the customer searched [6]. Some other things that the data contained was configuration settings of how the logging system of CVS operated on the server side [16]. The data on its own was not a big breach, but sensitive information about customers could be obtained if the correct cross referencing methods on the database were performed [6]. The size of the data breach was 204 Gigabytes which comprised a little over a billion records, a very large data breach.

3.3   Database Logs

This attack would not have been as concerning if it wasn't for the fact that many online customers typed in their emails to the search bar, through user error, when they were trying to log into their account. These emails provided a way for hackers to possibly connect their Session ID to their account and see their searches. They did this by using key email words such as gmail or outlook to find customers' email in the log files. CVS re-secured their site in a number of days through the third party vendor by removing the database [7]. There was no evidence that this data breach was harmful to CVS or the individual consumer because of how quickly CVS responded after finding the data breach, but the repercussions of how this data could have been used as well as how big the data breach was and how big CVS as a company and online presence is makes this case study worth exploring and analyzing to ensure that large data breaches that affect so many people's private data does not happen again. Figure 3 illustrates how the leak was discovered.

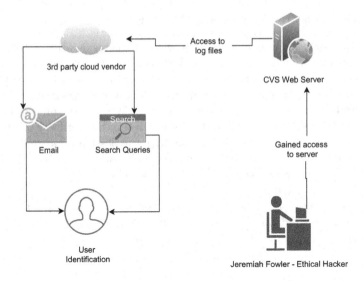

Fig. 3. Jeremiah Fowler discovered the leak in the CVS website to access logs contained in a 3rd party vendor that, if matched with users emails, could identify the user and the searches that they made during that session

4   Impact

Healthcare data has become more digitized over time, involving the Internet of Medical Things (IOMT). "Sensitive data are collected by healthcare organizations from their customers and stored on network servers to make them accessible all the time" [17]. While this increased accessibility is beneficial in many ways to healthcare companies and their customers, unfortunately, it can lead to many privacy breaches. Databases have the possibility of being accessed by unauthorized users because of failures in security, vulnerabilities in software, as well as human error [17]. Sensitive healthcare data could be stolen, lost, or disclosed by attackers. Hacking and unauthorized internal disclosure have increased within the healthcare industry, and the CVS data breach of March 21, 2021, is just one example of this.

4.1   Effects in Healthcare

The healthcare industry tends to be affected more than other industries in terms of data because the cost of records can be a lot more in the healthcare industry. Over a couple hundred million people have been affected by healthcare data breaches from 2005–2019. Healthcare data is some of the most sensitive data, so as attackers target healthcare data more, it makes the data more vulnerable and confidentiality and privacy become more important. Over time, healthcare data breach costs have increased more quickly than the average data breach costs [17].

As previously mentioned, the March 2021 session hijacking attack and data breach was huge in terms of scope, with 204 gigabytes of data - over a billion records - being breached. The large amount of healthcare data stored digitally makes it even more vital that safeguards are in place to protect against such breaches, especially given the sensitivity of such data and the cost involved. PHI being breached could negatively impact both the customers and the business. Attackers gaining access to private medical records has many impacts. Healthcare data breaches can result in customers' medical identity theft, which out of all identity theft types, can be the worst in terms of time and expenses [18]. Victims of medical identity theft can end up losing their health care coverage and end up having to pay their own money to restore their coverage, and this is a big consequence on the part of the customer. Victims don't often realize the theft has occurred until once they get expenses they did not charge, making this sort of theft expensive to fix.

While the CVS breach was unlikely to result in medical identity theft since it involved records from log files of customer searches, more information could be obtained about the customer if the customer had accidentally typed in their email address when trying to log into their account. With an email address to go by, a hacker could potentially connect a specific customer to his or her searches, thus revealing more personal information.

A PHI breach also affects the business in that it comes at a financial cost as well as loss of customers. A healthcare provider breaking the trust of its customers by not keeping their personal health information protected will result in a large amount of damage and fines [16]. "The average expense incurred for a company to address a medical data breach is $211 per record" [18], so this comes at a great cost. There is also a HITECH Act (Health Information Technology for Economic and Clinical Health) which has requirements for privacy and security that healthcare companies should follow, otherwise more expenses could be incurred. In addition, many customers lose trust in the healthcare company, as well as many who switch to a different healthcare organization. A company should be closely following the standards in the HITECH Act and HIPAA (Health Insurance Portability and Accountability Act) [18].

4.2   Reactions from Customers

There are many reactions that a data breach can cause in customers. Fear and anger both play a role in customers' reactions to a data breach. This can relate to the scope of the breach (how many customers are affected). With a larger scope, customers become more fearful about purchasing from the company. As a reaction to a data breach, angry customers are more concerned about how it affects them personally rather than being concerned about the scope of the breach, and are less likely to intend to repurchase [5]. Figure 4 details reactions of previous data breaches. It was considered one of the worst data breaches of 2021, as 204 GB of data, with over 1 billion records, were leaked, including queries for medications and vaccines. Widespread publicity about the breach undoubtedly shook customer confidence in CVS.

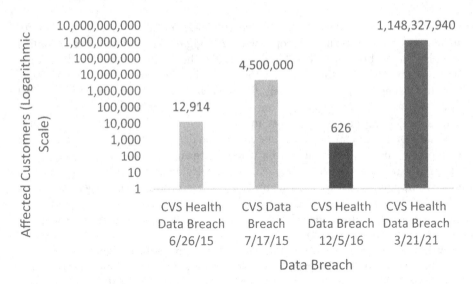

Fig. 4. Past CVS data breaches comparing their scope as well as emotional reactions of customers to each. Orange = Fear, Red = Anger, Green = Neutral, Blue = Reaction is not known (Color figure online)

There are negative implications on the market value of a company after it experiences a data breach. In addition to this financial impact, there could also be damage to the company's reputation. This impact on reputation is significant [19]. Data breaches, in general, can also affect stock volatility, the rate that stock increases or decreases over a certain amount of time. Technology has a big impact on the business of public institutions. Privacy and security concerns are gradually increasing in this digital environment. "Data breach disclosure destabilizes the volatility of the stock market, which might also influence investors' confidence and reactions" [20].

5   Defense Solution

Something that's needed to prevent data breaches are laws and policies. There should be standards in place that companies are required to follow to prevent attacks. Cyberspace needs to be safe for economic development to be sustainable, including in the healthcare sector [21].

5.1   Steps to Manage Healthcare Data Breach

In terms of managing a healthcare data breach after it has already occurred, some courses of action would help protect the customers and the company, listed in Fig. 5. These could be used after a healthcare data breach to prevent more damage and get operations back to normal, as well as to prevent a data breach in the first place. One thing to do is start an incident response plan (IRP). "A well-executed incident response plan can minimize breach impact, reduce fines, decrease negative press, and help you get back to business more quickly" [22]. Mistakes are more likely to be made when there is no plan for how to deal with a potential breach.

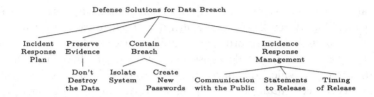

Fig. 5. Strategies to counter healthcare and medical data breach

Another thing to do is preserve evidence. You don't want to destroy any of the data in the process of fixing the breach, because that data could be used to learn more about the breach itself and determine how to protect from it in the future [22].

It is important to contain the breach. The system that's affected should be isolated as much as possible, to avoid any more damage. Some steps can be taken to prevent stealing of information and lessen the effect of damage and get operations back in order efficiently if a breach does occur [22]. It's also good to create new passwords while keeping track of old passwords. In addition, HHS (The United States Department of Health and Human Services) should be contacted so they are aware of what happened [22].

Another remedy is to start incidence response management, in which you have a team where each person helps manage an aspect of the breach. You should think about how you will communicate with the public and determine statements that will be released, as well as the timing of the release, so it does not appear that you are stalling or keeping information from the public [22].

5.2   CVS' Response

CVS took steps to remedy the breach itself, as well as to appease their angry customers and reassure them it wouldn't happen again. CVS worked to quickly get the database down and investigated to make sure identifiable information was not included [23]. Overall, it appears that CVS responded quickly and effectively once the data breach was discovered, by removing the database in a matter of days. However, if the log files had originally been password protected, likely, the breach would not have occurred in the first place. CVS could improve its security by password-protecting its log files of customer searches, implementing a plan to respond in a matter of hours rather than days once a breach is detected, and tightening up its monitoring of its third-party vendors.

When a data breach occurs, it is vital to fully investigate and fix all aspects of the system. You want to get the system back to normal, prevent it from happening again, and become prepared for if it did happen again [22].

6 Conclusion

Health data breaches are some of the most expensive and damaging cyber security incidents. The March 2021 CVS health data breach was one such example, with over a billion health records being publicly exposed. This massive data breach was the result of the database of customer search records not being password-protected, which demonstrated a serious lack of security measures. With the records containing emails along with searched terms, hackers could more easily perform phishing attacks on those emails. A data breach like this can have negative impacts on the company, such as the costs to fix the breach, the loss of customers' trust, and a negative effect on the market valuation of the corporation. CVS reacted quickly, taking down the database soon after being notified of the breach, but there are ways that CVS could better protect its data and prevent a similar data breach in the future. This could include multi-factor authentication, password protection, and formulating an incident response plan in advance to mitigate any breaches that occur. Improving the security of sensitive information like CVS' health records will be vital in preventing or limiting potential breaches in the future.

References

1. McKeon, J.: CVS health faces data breach, 1B search records exposed, June 2021. https://healthitsecurity.com/news/cvs-health-faces-data-breach1b-search-records-exposed
2. McGee, M.K., Ross, R.: Researcher: 1 billion CVS health website records exposed, June 2021. https://www.govinfosecurity.com/researcher-1-billion-cvs-health-website-records-exposed-a-16890
3. Alder, S.: 1 billion-record database of searches of CVS website exposed online, June 2021. https://www.hipaajournal.com/1-billion-record-database-of-searches-of-cvs-website-exposed-online/
4. CVS: CVS health notice of privacy practices. https://www.cvs.com/content/patient-privacy
5. Chatterjee, S., Gao, X., Sarkar, S., Uzmanoglu, C.: Reacting to the scope of a data breach: the differential role of fear and anger. J. Bus. Res. **101**, 183–193 (2019)
6. CyberTalk: CVS accidentally leaks more than 1 billion records. https://www.cybertalk.org/2021/06/16/cvs-accidentally-leaks-more-than-1-billion-records
7. Fowler, J.: Report: CVS health exposed search records online. https://www.websiteplanet.com/blog/cvs-health-leak-report/
8. Leggate, J.: What is CVS health? https://www.foxbusiness.com/markets/what-is-cvs-health
9. CVS: About CVS health. https://www.foxbusiness.com/markets/what-is-cvs-health

10. Caremark. https://www.caremark.com/
11. Conner, B.: Mid-year update: 2021 SonicWall cyber threat report (2021)
12. 1 billion CVS health records breached, June 2021. https://rocketit.com/cvs-health-data-breach/
13. Brewster, T.: CVS accidentally leaks 1 billion website records-including Covid-19 vaccine searches. https://www.forbes.com/sites/thomasbrewster/2021/06/16/cvs-accidentally-leaks-1-billion-website-records-including-covid-19-vaccine-searches/?sh=1986e4d92c4f
14. Paganini, P.: Over a billion records belonging to CVS Health exposed online, June 2021
15. More than 1 billion CVS data records accidentally exposed, researcher says, June 2021. https://abc30.com/cvs-data-breach-medical-records-health-cyber-attack/10798172/
16. Turea, M.: CVS health suffers database breach leaving 1b records exposed online, July 2021. https://healthcareweekly.com/cvs-health-database-breach
17. Hussain Seh, A., et al.: Healthcare data breaches: insights and implications. Healthcare 8(2), 133 (2020)
18. The potential damages and consequences of medical identity theft and healthcare data breaches, April 2010. https://www.experian.com/assets/data-breach/white-papers/consequences-medical-id-theft-healthcare.pdf
19. Sinanaj, G., Zafar, H.: Who wins in a data breach?-A comparative study on the intangible costs of data breach incidents. In: PACIS, p. 60 (2016)
20. Tweneboah-Koduah, S., Atsu, F., Prasad, R.: Reaction of stock volatility to data breach: an event study. J. Cyber Secur. Mob. 9(3), 355–384 (2020)
21. Azubuike, S.: Cybersecurity attacks: regulatory and practical approach towards preventing data breach and cyber-attacks in USA (2021)
22. Stone, J.: How to manage a healthcare data breach. https://www.securitymetrics.com/blog/how-manage-healthcare-data-breach
23. Landi, H.: CVS health database leak left 1B user records exposed online, June 2021. https://www.fiercehealthcare.com/tech/cvs-health-database-leak-leaves-1-billion-user-records-exposed-online

Blockchain for Cybersecure Healthcare

Avnish Singh Jat and Tor-Morten Grønli[(✉)]

Mobile Technology Lab, Department of Information Technology, Kristiania University College,
Oslo, Norway
Tor-Morten.Gronli@kristiania.no

Abstract. The medical care industry is especially at risk and focused on cyber-attacks on the grounds that they have a huge amount of data of high financial and knowledge worth to hackers. Thus, there is an urgent need for the implementation of countermeasures to the consequences of such crimes in priority areas like law, technology, and education. This article discusses the recent cyber threats and the utilization of blockchain to secure electronic healthcare technologies. Further, this article talks about various blockchain-empowered digital secure answers for medical care zeroing in on added regard, including immutability, auditability, and accountability in processes, for example, user-device binding, registration, maintenance, and alerting. We have likewise proposed a blockchain design that executes a smart contract (SC) to convey safer administrations in the medical service industry.

Keywords: eHealth · mHealth · Cyber security · Cyber threats in Healthcare · Blockchain

1 Introduction

1.1 Background

In recent years utilization of healthcare practice supported by electronic processes and communication has significantly increased and is termed Digital Health. WHO defines "Electronic health (eHealth) or digital health (digital health) as the cost-effective and secure use of information and communications technologies in support of health and health-related fields, including health-care services, health surveillance, health literature, and health education, knowledge and research" [1].

In recent documents, WHO operates with the concept of "digital health." The content of this concept includes e-health, including the use of mobile wireless communications (mHealth), as well as other actively developing new areas, such as the collection and processing of "Big Data" (Big Data), computer technologies in genomics and the implementation of artificial intelligence. The Global Strategy for Digital Health (2020–2025) defines digital health as "a field of knowledge and practice related to the development and use of modern digital technologies to improve health" [2], thus covering the entire range of applications of high-tech devices in solving the problems of protecting the health of citizens. More precisely, the Internet of Things (IoT) (more precisely, the Internet of

I. Awan et al. (Eds.): MobiWIS 2022, LNCS 13475, pp. 106–117, 2022.
https://doi.org/10.1007/978-3-031-14391-5_8

Medical Things or IoMT), promising computer technologies, and robotics have been added to the previously named areas.

WHO attaches particular importance to the development of digital health and defines its objectives and principles. Thus, on May 26, 2018, the highest body of the WHO (World Health Assembly) approved the Resolution on Digital Health, calling on the Member States "to consider, if necessary, how digital technologies can be integrated into existing health system infrastructures and regulatory systems in order to strengthen national and global health priorities by optimizing existing platforms and services to strengthen the social orientation of health care and disease prevention measures, as well as to reduce the burden on health systems" [3].

As emphasized in the Global Strategy, digital health must become "an integral part of health priorities and benefit people from the point of view of ethics and safety." The use of information and communication technologies must be "safe, reliable, fair, and sustainable." Digital healthcare innovation should be developed based on such principles as transparency, accessibility, interoperability, confidentiality, and security, among others. The goals of digital health, in addition to improving the quality and accessibility of medical services, are "giving the individual a central role in caring for their health and well-being" "using the huge potential of data in the interests of health care," and facilitating the transition "towards predictive and preventive models of medical care delivery." A wide range of subjects are involved in digital health relations, including a) patients and their legal representatives; b) doctors and other medical workers; c) organizations providing medical care, regardless of the economic and legal form and departmental affiliation; d) authorized bodies carrying out regulation in the field of healthcare (federal and regional); e) scientific community (this segment is presented as a research educational and educational institutions medical profile, as well as individual scientists and scientific teams; e) pharmacy organizations; g) insurance organizations.

1.2 Digital Security in Healthcare

In practice, digital innovation is already serving the personal health needs of citizens and include, among other things, the organization of electronic services for contacting medical organizations, maintaining electronic medical records, providing targeted communication with specific patients, and remote monitoring of their health, development of a clinical decision support system and organization with the help of telemedicine consultations of highly qualified specialists for patients and doctors, control of production and supply of products for medical purposes and medicinal funds, creation of medical databases for co- improving diagnostic and treatment protocols, conducting clinical trials and research follow. A list of main ways to use digital technologies in the industry is contained in the document by WHO Classification of digital health care v 1.0 [4]. In 2019, the size of the global digital health market defense was estimated at more than $106 billion. Forecasts up to 2026, this market's cumulative average growth rate will be 28.5%, and the total sales cost will reach 639.4 billion dollars. Growth in sales of mobile applications is predicted for health (by 28.9%), medical equipment (by 31%), and telemedicine services (26.2%) [5]. Much lower growth is expected in the market segment of the copper Qing analytics (9.7%).

The volume of products sold on the global market and digital health services requires government state regulation of the industry to provide quality, efficacy, and safety implemented digital technologies. One of the ways the basis of such regulation is the development of darts, which such technologies must comply with. In national documents, often recommendatory in nature but which blow in practice, special attention is paid to control of reliability, efficiency, and safety devices used for medical purposes, their protection from cyber-attacks, rules of good medical practice, and the protected medical information. The exceptional importance of confidentiality of medical information motion requiring "high standards [providing] security" of such personal data is celebrated at the international level. A study of applications of digital technologies in health care and requirements for them, already subject to regulation in various countries (USA, UK, Spain, France, Germany, Canada) showed that the number of users for the evaluation of technologies and devices of the criteria of variable ranges from two to ten. Most verifiable are such qualities as safety, including data security, clinical effectiveness, usability, and functional compatibility. The authors' attention to the guidelines also deals with economic issues, particularly the cost of implementing the technology. Still, none of the sources studied provided the full proof application for the development of a feasibility study or quantitative analysis of the potential actual losses and profits. As a result, the study's authors found that more than half of the criteria recommended for evaluating key digital innovations in their implementation in practice health care relate to the organization's rational consequences of the decision, safety data, and specifications.

1.3 Objectives

In this article, we intend to focus on the vulnerabilities of cyber security in eHealth and discuss recent cyber-attacks in healthcare. We have reviewed different research works on utilizing blockchain for securing healthcare. Additionally, we have implemented a use case to highlight the blockchain utilization in eHealth.

2 Cyber Security Breaches in Healthcare

According to medical care network safety statistics for 2022, the medical services industry alone lost $25 billion in the last two years. The report, delivered by Singapore-based Cyber Risk Management (CyRiM), accepts medical care and will be one of the businesses generally impacted by cyber-attacks. Cyber-attacks in healthcare hit an unequaled high in 2021, uncovering a record number of patients' protected health information (PHI), as per a report from online protection organization Critical Insights [6]. In 2021, 45 million people were impacted by medical services assaults, up from 34 million in 2020. That number has significantly increased in only three years, developing from 14 million out in 2018, as indicated by the report, which breaks down break information answered to the U.S. Branch of Health and Human Services (HHS) by medical care associations [7].

The absolute number of people impacted expanded 32% north of 2020, implying that more records are uncovered per break every year. The absolute number of breaks just rose 2.4% from 663 in 2020 to 679 in 2021 yet at the same time hit memorable highs. In the following subsections, we will look in detail at different types of cyber vulnerabilities and recent cyber-attacks in the Health care industry [8].

2.1 Ransomware

It is difficult to disregard the new expansion in revealing clinics targeted by ransomware. In the first place, cyber thieves try to make medical services activities inoperable. The Healthcare industry isn't similar to different industries that can wait for some time if their system is compromised. In the event that a clinic can't get to its records or its capacity to serve patients is compromised, that is a big problem. Ransomware is a sort of malware that contaminates frameworks and records, making them inoperable until demanded payment is paid. Whenever this happens in the medical services industry, digital tasks associated with healthcare are slowed or become totally inoperable. Recently, the "Maryland Department of Health was designated with a ransomware assault which left emergency clinics battling in the midst of COVID-19 cases" [10]. It's not yet known what group of cyber thieves were behind the assault. Additionally, East Tennessee Children's Hospital revealed that they had been a casualty of an "IT security issue" on the evening of Sunday, March thirteenth. In an articulation, they said, "keeping up with the wellbeing and security of our patients and their consideration is our first concern. We are as yet ready to really focus on our patients. Our cyber forensics department and other experts are doing all that could be within reach to limit any interruption. We apologize for this and request your understanding as we address this issue." No further details were accessible [11].

2.2 Data Breaches

Data breaches are observed on a large scale in the healthcare industry. It is an occurrence wherein data is taken or hacked from a framework without the information or approval of the framework's proprietor. In the year between 2009 and 2021, 4,419 medical care data breaches of at least 500 records have been accounted for by the HHS' Office for Civil Rights [23]. These breaches have brought about the misfortune, burglary, and exposure of 314,063,186 medical care records. Recently, Adaptive Health Integrations confronted a hacking occurrence that affected 510,574 people, as per the Office for Civil Rights (OCR) data breach portal [12]. The occurrence was the third-biggest detailed healthcare information break in 2022 up to this point. An aggregate of 78.8 million patient records was taken. Albeit this sounds adequately terrible, the sort of information taken was profoundly delicate and included records like social security numbers, birthdate, and address. Notwithstanding most casualties being Anthem plan individuals, some were not. This is on the grounds that Anthem additionally worked with the various insurance agency, dealing with their administrative work too [13].

2.3 Phishing Attacks, Email Spoofing

Phishing is when assailants send pernicious messages intended to fool individuals into succumbing to a trick. The expectation is frequently to get clients to uncover monetary data, organization email access, or other vital information. Email spoofing to fool clients into thinking a message came from their organization or someone they know. Generally, the attacker develops email headers in such a way that client programming shows the deceitful source address, which most clients fully trust. A phishing attack against

Charleston Area Medical Center (CAMC) affected 54,000 people. On January tenth and eleventh, an unapproved attacker accessed some CAMC representative email accounts by means of a phishing trick. In a notification on its site, CAMC said it did whatever it may take to end access and secure the records as quickly as time permits [14].

3 Blockchain for Cyber Secure Healthcare

3.1 Why Blockchain

Blockchain technology offers the medical industry an approach to storing and processing clinical records over an organization without compromising patients' data security or being targeted by cyberattacks. Besides, it guarantees information integrity and clinical record auditability. Blockchain gives a few other likely advantages to healthcare frameworks, like decentralization, data possession, and robustness [9]. Nonetheless, in blockchain-based healthcare, the board framework would be created. For example, creating blockchain-based electronic clinical records implies that health or personal records would be shared over an organization. Smart contracts have been found to be reasonable for saving and processing clinical records as they guarantee security and protection highlights [25]. The basic infrastructure model of blockchain is displayed in Fig. 1. These applications are dissected to investigate the key prerequisites in blockchain-based healthcare frameworks like information interoperability, security, integrity, cost/assets adequacy, untrusted and transparent, and the intricacy of the proposed work. Despite the fact that Blockchain has been broadly used in the development of digital currency, most uses of blockchain in healthcare are still in the conceptualization stage or carried out in testbed [24]. In conventional cyber security, the organization writes the majority of the code and weaknesses can emerge from code that the organization controls. On the other hand, the development on the blockchain is highly encrypted and decentralized. It can also eliminate the requirement for certain passwords, which are much of the time depicted as the most vulnerable connection in online protection.

3.2 Blockchain in Healthcare

In total, the authors of the study substantively analyzed a few research works containing recommendations for the utilization of blockchain in Healthcare. Publications for analysis, published between September 2016 and December 2021, were selected in international information Pub-med, Scopus, and Science Direct databases for keywords "digital health," "mHealth," "mobile health," "telemedicine," "health app," and "wearables" in combination with the terms "blockchain," "Ethereum " and "cybersecurity." The authors themselves note its specific limitation value. The results obtained allow us to outline ways of developing and improving cybersecurity in digital health through blockchain.

1. Teleconsultation and mHealth: In today's world, mobile phones are commonly used in every house and utilized in day-to-day tasks by every individual. The innovation of mobile applications is additionally on the ascent. More friendly applications are being

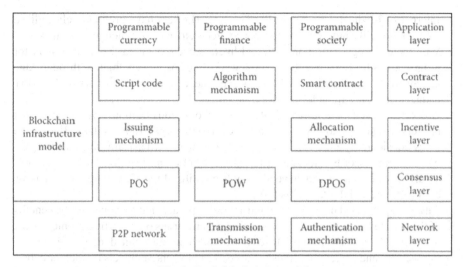

Blockchain infrastructure model	Programmable currency	Programmable finance	Programmable society	Application layer
	Script code	Algorithm mechanism	Smart contract	Contract layer
	Issuing mechanism		Allocation mechanism	Incentive layer
	POS	POW	DPOS	Consensus layer
	P2P network	Transmission mechanism	Authentication mechanism	Network layer

Fig. 1. Basic blockchain model

developed in every industry, including healthcare. Colossal measures of metadata are gathered during this development. Mobile-based application clients safeguard the administrations and their information with feeble, temperamental passwords. Thus, many organizations are looking for ways to utilize the blockchain to safeguard mobile applications from cyber-attacks. Blockchain can be utilized to make a standard security convention. It has features like traceability, transparency, and decentralization, which can be extremely helpful in creating tamper-proof mobile health infrastructure [22, 27]. Figure 2 presents a sequence diagram of data stored on the blockchain through the mobile application and the transaction hash stored in an intra planetary file management system.

In research proposed by Daisuke Ichikawa, authors found that "Blockchain serves as a tamperproof system for mHealth. Combining mHealth with blockchain technology may provide a novel solution that enables both accessibility and data transparency without a third party such as a contract research organization" [15]. In recent research, researchers presented methods to take advantage of Blockchain to implement cybersecure messaging. To start with, they developed a message confirmation model based on SM2 to stay away from counterfeit attacks and replay attacks. Second, they develop a cryptographic hash mode on SM3 to confirm the integrity of the message. and then they develop a message encryption model on SM4 to safeguard the security of clients [16].

In the new past, various attacks have been executed on social stages like Twitter and Facebook, which are used by physicians to build interactive patient strategies, such as direct patient engagement. These attacks brought about information breaks with a great many records being penetrated and client information arriving into some unacceptable hands. Blockchain innovations, if all around carried out in these informing frameworks, may forestall such future cyberattacks.

2. Internet of Medical Things (IoMT) Security: Hackers have progressively utilized edge gadgets, like indoor regulators and switches, to get close enough to frameworks. With the ongoing fixation on Artificial Intelligence (AI), it has become simpler for programmers to get by with large frameworks like hospital automation through edge gadgets like 'smart' switches. Much of the time, an enormous number of these IoT gadgets have questionable security highlights [21].

   Utilizing blockchain to store IoT information would add one more layer of safety that hackers would have to bypass to gain access to the organization's data. Blockchain gives considerably high-level encryption that makes it basically difficult to over-write existing records. Blockchain-based frameworks can be utilized to reinforce IoT security. Such frameworks have already been utilized to safely store data, identity, certifications, and digital rights [26].

   An article published in 2018 presented a novel approach that consolidates the benefits of the private key, public key, blockchain, and numerous other cryptographic natives to foster a patient-driven admittance control for electronic clinical records, fit for giv-ing security and protection. It also discusses implemented models to counter cyber-attacks, for example, DoS, modification attacks, and so on [17]. Recently, researchers proposed a "decentralized, interoperable trust model that suffuses Blockchains in healthcare IoHT. DIT Blockchain IoHT framework is a resilient ecosystem that sup-ports semantic annotations for health edge layers in IoHT." They also presented how their model outperforms all other blockchain models [18].

3. Distributed Denial of Service (DDoS) Attack: It happens when clients of an objective asset, like an organization asset, server, or site, are denied admittance or admin-istration to the objective asset. These assaults shut down or dial back the asset frameworks.

   Then again, an unblemished Domain Name System (DNS) is extremely brought together, causing it an ideal objective for programmers who invade the association between the IP address and the name of a site. This assault delivers a site that is difficult to reach, cashable, and, surprisingly, redirectable to other trick sites. By applying decentralized arrangements, blockchain would have eliminated the weak single focus taken advantage of by programmers. Article by Anthony Ugochukwu Nwosu discusses in detail the utilization of blockchain for countering Distributed Denial-of-Service (DDoS) attacks [9].

4. Decentralizing Medium Storage: Healthcare information hacks and ransomware are turning into vital reasons for the Healthcare industry to invest in cyber security. Such an attack leaks delicate and classified information, like healthcare monetary records and confidential patient data.

   By utilizing blockchain, "data might be safeguarded by guaranteeing a decentralized type of information stockpiling. This moderation strategy would make it harder and surprisingly inconceivable for programmers to infiltrate information capacity frameworks. Numerous Healthcare organizations are evaluating ways blockchain can shield information from hackers" [19].

   Article by discusses how Blockchain and decentralization are utilized in monitoring patient data to blockchain-based supply chain management of drugs, Blockchain in medical care could tackle a portion of the medical care industry's greatest impediments [20].

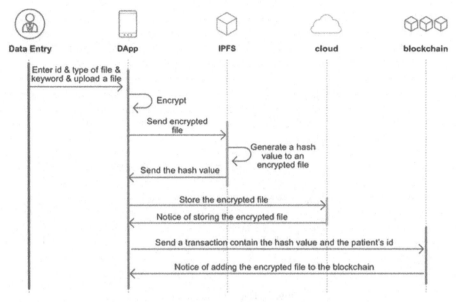

Fig. 2. Decentralized application sequence diagram

4 Case Study

4.1 Blockchain for Transparency in Organ Transplant

To understand in-depth the utilization of blockchain in healthcare, we developed a decentralized application for streamlining the organ donation and transplant matching process with the help of Blockchain technology. The application will connect donors to patients with hospitals acting as a mediator and automates the process using smart contracts. We have used Ethereum to add traceability security along with immutability of data and functionality with proper authentication to the organ donation process between donors and recipients. It acts as a needed fast decentralized, and secure platform to regularize organ donation by connecting hospitals, donors, and recipients. Figure 3 explains the data flow diagram of the system where the donor registers in the system over blockchain, and the hospital administration process the recipient and donor details.

4.2 Architectural Diagram

The system was developed by using the Ethereum network to provide security and maintain a distributed tracking system. React and NodeJS are used for the frontend and backend of the application, respectively, and Ganache Developer tools to recreate the blockchain environment and test smart contracts. To access the application on a browser, Metamask is required that enable browsers with web 3.0 functionalities to explore the decentralized application. Figure 4 presents the architecture diagram of the application.

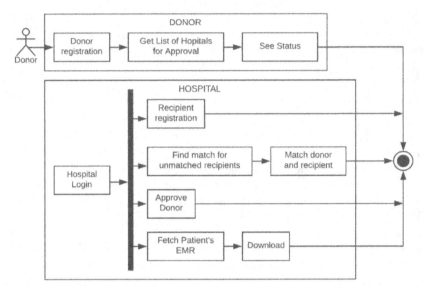

Fig. 3. Data flow diagram

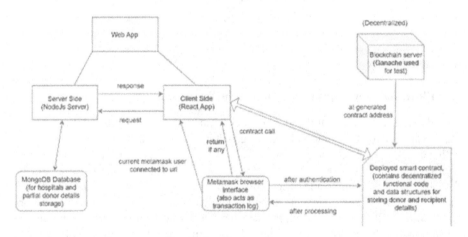

Fig. 4. Architecture diagram

4.3 Deployment and Security Advantages

The application is deployed on localhost, and the smart contract is deployed on the Remix platform. The Metamask plugin is utilized to connect the smart contract with the Ethereum test network. Figure 5 shows the snapshot of the smart contract implementation on the Remix platform. Organized and more available to the end-users: This Will help the donors, recipients, and healthcare organizations come together in a single holistic platform, making the process more available to the users, and reducing middlemen, fraud, and trafficking. Robust, Secure, and Traceable system: Blockchain adds traceability and security along with immutability of data and functionality with proper inbuilt authentication to the organ donation process between donors and recipients. Timely access to transplant: Instead of manually looking up for or finding suitable transplant matches, it will automate the process. Due to this, instant and automated matching of organ transplants are more efficient and faster. Automation: To an extent where IOT and healthcare devices could be integrated using smart contracts and made to work as a whole workforce. Creating a universal secure patient profile: Could be used for faster and proper healthcare availability and improving diagnostics and could be used to improve patient experience and for research.

Fig. 5. Smart contract snapshot

5 Conclusion

Really advancing and distant serious consequences of cyber-attacks on healthcare organizations, increasingly using digital technologies, make counteraction such a criminal encroachment, priority and vital. Not excluding other areas of development and implementation of countermeasures to the consequences of such crimes, we believe that the priority areas are law, technology, and education. Legal measures should include, first of all, the regulation of the legal regime of digital health care, as well as improving the legislation both nationally and internationally international level, including the conclusion of relevant agreements. Technical measures play a very crucial role in ensuring cybersecurity healthcare systems. Such measures should include software, hardware, and software-hardware countermeasures. We have discussed the utilization of blockchain for providing security to healthcare in different domains. Technical measures also include standardization procedures and control before obtaining permission to use digital medical devices and using blockchain technology to protect medical information. We have also implemented the use case to show the potential of blockchain in healthcare transparency. Educational Measures should include regular awareness-raising of an educational nature with medical personnel and other employees of medical organizations that use in their activities digital technologies. Need to develop relevant cybersecurity guides for healthcare organizations.

References

1. WHO EMRO | eHealth | Health topics. www.emro.who.int. http://www.emro.who.int/health-topics/ehealth/. Accessed 12 Mar 2022
2. Global strategy on digital health 2020–2025. Geneva: World Health Organization; 2021. License: CC BY-NC-SA 3.0 IGO
3. Seventy-first World Health Assembly update, 25 May. www.who.int. https://www.who.int/news/item/25-05-2018-seventy-first-world-health-assembly-update-25-may. Accessed 15 Mar 2022
4. World Health Organization. Classification of digital health interventions v1. 0: a shared language to describe the uses of digital technology for health. No. WHO/RHR/18.06. World Health Organization (2018)
5. Rachh, A.: A study of future opportunities and challenges in digital healthcare sector: cyber security vs. crimes in digital healthcare sector. Asia Pac. J. Health Manage. 16(3), 7–15 (2021)
6. Seh, A.H. et al.: Healthcare data breaches: insights and implications. Healthcare. vol. 8. no. 2. Multidisciplinary Digital Publishing Institute (2020)
7. Zarour, M., et al.: Ensuring data integrity of healthcare information in the era of digital health. Healthcare Technol. Lett. 8(3), 66 (2021)
8. Walden, A., Cortelyou-Ward, K., Gabriel, M.H., Noblin, A.: To report or not to report health care data breaches. Am. J. Manage Care 26(12), e395–e402 (2020)
9. Nwosu, A.U., Goyal, S.B., Bedi, P.: Blockchain transforming cyber-attacks: healthcare industry. In: Abraham, A., Sasaki, H., Rios, R., Gandhi, N., Singh, U., Ma, K. (eds.) IBICA 2020. AISC, vol. 1372, pp. 258–266. Springer, Cham (2021). https://doi.org/10.1007/978-3-030-73603-3_24
10. Maryland Department of Health Network Security Incident. health.maryland.gov. https://health.maryland.gov/incidentupdate/Pages/default.aspx. Accessed 28 Mar 2022
11. McKeon, J.: East Tennessee Children's Hospital Experiencing Security Issue" healthitsecurity.com. Xtelligent Healthcare Media, 17 Apr 2022. Accessed 28 Mar 2022
12. McKeon, J.: Adaptive Health Integrations Data Breach Impacts 510K" healthitsecurity.com. Xtelligent Healthcare Media, 17 Apr 2022. Accessed 28 Mar 2022
13. Kadam, S., Motwani, D.: Protected admittance E-health record system using blockchain technology. In: Smys, S., Bestak, R., Palanisamy, R., Kotuliak, I. (eds.) Computer Networks and Inventive Communication Technologies. LNDECT, vol. 75, pp. 723–739. Springer, Singapore (2022). https://doi.org/10.1007/978-981-16-3728-5_54
14. "USA: Charleston Area Medical Center notifies OCR of data security incident." www.dataguidance.com. https://www.dataguidance.com/news/usa-charleston-area-medical-center-notifies-ocr-data (Last accessed April 28, 2022)
15. Ichikawa, D., Kashiyama, M., Ueno, T.: Tamper-resistant mobile health using blockchain technology. JMIR mHealth uHealth 5(7), e111 (2017)
16. Yi, H.: Securing instant messaging based on blockchain with machine learning. Saf. Sci. 120, 6–13 (2019)
17. Dwivedi, A.D., Srivastava, G., Dhar, S., Singh, R.: A decentralized privacy-preserving healthcare blockchain for IoT. Sensors 19(2), 326 (2019). https://doi.org/10.3390/s19020326
18. Abou-Nassar, E.M., et al.: DITrust chain: towards blockchain-based trust models for sustainable healthcare IoT systems. IEEE Access 8, 111223–111238 (2020)
19. Omar, I.A., Jayaraman, R., Salah, K., Simsekler, M.C.E., Yaqoob, I., Ellahham, S.: Ensuring protocol compliance and data transparency in clinical trials using blockchain smart contracts. BMC Med. Res. Methodol. 20(1), 1–17 (2020)
20. Jamil, F., Hang, L., Kim, K.H., Kim, D.H.: A novel medical blockchain model for drug supply chain integrity management in a smart hospital. Electronics 8(5), 505 (2019)

21. Alam, T.: mHealth communication framework using blockchain and IoT technologies. Int. J. Sci. Technol. Res. **9**(6) (2020)
22. Taralunga, D.D., Florea, B.C.: A blockchain-enabled framework for mhealth systems. Sensors **21**, 2828 (2021). https://doi.org/10.3390/s21082828
23. Sengupta, A., Subramanian, H.: User control of personal mHealth data using a mobile blockchain app: design science perspective. JMIR mHealth and uHealth **10**(1), e32104 (2022)
24. Clim, A., Zota, R.D., Constantinescu, R.: Data exchanges based on blockchain in m-Health applications. Procedia Comput. Sci. **160**, 281–288 (2019)
25. Peña, C.A.N., Díaz, A.E.G., Aguirre, J.A.A., Molina, J.M.M.: Security model to protect patient data in mHealth systems through a blockchain network. In: Proceedings of the LACCEI international Multiconference for Engineering, Education and Technology (2019)
26. Zhang, G., Yang, Z., Liu, W.: Blockchain-based privacy preserving e-health system for healthcare data in cloud. Comput. Netw. **203**, 108586 (2022)
27. Liu, Y., Shan, G., Liu, Y., Alghamdi, A., Alam, I., Biswas, S.: Blockchain bridges critical national infrastructures: E-healthcare data migration perspective. IEEE Access **10**, 28509–28519 (2022)

Design of a Method for Setting IoT Security Standards in Smart Cities

Hana Svecova[✉] [iD]

Faculty of Management and Informatics, University of Hradec Kralove,
Rokitanskeho 62, 50003 Hradec Kralove, Czech Republic
hana.svecova@uhk.cz

Abstract. Legal norms of international standards have so far been developed inconsistently and non-comprehensively. Cities, municipalities, regional self-governments or state security forces have no support in legislation or international standards in the form of security standards that they could implement in connection with the integration of the Smart Cities concept. Cyber security leaders involved in drafting legislation have not yet addressed this issue. From the point of view of IoT development, it is necessary to analyse and propose, using a suitable method, security standards for IoT, which could integrate the Smart Cities concept. No method or software is used to design suitable security standards that speed up and streamline preparing legislative documents. Standard MS Office software applications are used to prepare legislative documents, and the overall preparation and processing are not efficient and comprehensive.

The article's primary goal is to analyse existing security standards and design a suitable method for comprehensively processing security standards in IoT in Smart Cities. Furthermore, this method could be used to prepare and process other documents in cyber security.

Keywords: Content analysis · Smart Cities · IoT · Cyber security · Safety

1 Introduction

Today is a time of massive digitisation and the deployment of conceptually new technologies. Closely related to this is the need to store enormous data. It follows that the stored data is duplicated and all the more vulnerable. Moreover, we rely on a public data network when transmitting them, where endpoints are exposed to possible cyber attacks. As developments in recent years have shown, due to basic transmission technology and inadequate global, in terms of international legislation, impunity for attacks on any commercial and infrastructural targets is possible. Attacks often escalate precisely in crises, when people are expected to be more prone to error under work pressure. A clear example was the attacks on healthcare facilities at the height of the corona crisis when patient care was exacerbated by the failure of the NIS, to which devices used to examine or support patients' vital functions are tied.

The data generated during the emergency may include the content of all affected system components. For example, during an arson attack, where they are wounded, the

I. Awan et al. (Eds.): MobiWIS 2022, LNCS 13475, pp. 118–128, 2022.
https://doi.org/10.1007/978-3-031-14391-5_9

fire brigade will deal with the liquidation of the fire, the fire brigade will take care of the wounded, and the Police will search for the attackers. The centres cannot be located on the same as all the units involved in the intervention, only minimally due to travel times. Various IoT sensors flow information to the appropriate stations to attend the event.

The current system of registration and transmission of patient data is decentralised. For example, suppose the patient is transported to the emergency room first. In that case, his data is entered into the IS emergency room system without the possibility of obtaining information on his health condition or current medication based on the identification of the person. If an event involving the same person occurs in the future, this data can already be retrieved, checked and updated. This is where this information ends.

Hospital Information Systems (NIS) are not involved in this global system. They do not have immediate information about patients at risk of medical treatment. Instead, paramedics report patient status information to the target hospital through the reception centre. The implementation of NIS is a matter of the founder; therefore, even within one region, individual hospitals may operate different systems. Some regions (e.g. Pardubický) are already trying to eliminate this inefficiency and centralise data management.

If the trend of using Smart, and thus IoT technologies, is to be applied, the systems must be significantly better secured. Single-purpose miniature devices with low energy consumption and memory capacity cannot defend against massive and sophisticated attacks. Scenarios for their deployment do not always allow for recommended wiring that relies on ideal conditions. If there is no international law on cyber security and the probability of catching offenders is minimal, redress does not seem realistic, and appropriate technical measures should be taken, supported by legislation. The critical infrastructure information systems of the state, and therefore of the EU states, should be operated in a mode that does not allow immediate attacks from the commercial space of the internet network. At the same time, it must be specified how the data will be entered into the systems and, if necessary, exported without infecting the system by introducing malicious code. The security standards for IoT that will be designed and implemented should include a repressive section so that operators' responsibilities for compliance are clearly defined. For the design and elaboration of IoT safety standards, it is necessary to choose a suitable method that will apply to other processes associated with analysing and preparing other legislative documents. This method combines qualitative and quantitative content analysis using software that implements a statistical survey module. The research of the content parts of the existing legislative documents (National and International) and standards with the subsequent verification of the outputs using statistical research will thus objectively verify the integrity of the processed outputs.

The article aims to analyse existing safety standards and design a suitable method for comprehensively processing safety standards in IoT. This method could prepare and elaborate IoT security standards for Smart Cities and prepare other legislative documents, standards, or recommendations.

The article is divided into sections:

1. **Safety standards and legislation in IoT** – This section contains an analysis of existing standards and legislative documents in IoT.

2. **Content analysis for processing IoT security** standards - This part characterises the content analysis, including the definition of sub-parts including the preparation and examination of existing legislative documents and standards.

3. **Examination of documents – alternative method** – This section compares the content analysis with another existing method for examining texts. Content analysis was used in research to write technical proposals for construction contractors [1].

Content analysis was used only to analyse court findings [2] and the analysis of regional legislation in Russia [3].

Furthermore, content analysis is used to process political texts [4] or for the empirical study of the effects of film music [5].

From the above, it can be stated that qualitative and quantitative content analysis methods for preparing and processing legislative documents, standards and safety standards have not yet been used. Content analysis is used in various scientific disciplines for word processing, frequencies and relationships between words. However, it is not used in legal and information sciences nor in connection with preparing documents for implementing Smart Cities. Using content analysis for the processing and designing safety standards for IoT in Smart Cities or other industries could bring innovation and work efficiency elements to the preparation and processing of output documents.

2   Safety Standards and Legislation in IoT

Security standards and legislation in cyber security must be viewed from several perspectives. The first aspect is legislation in the European Union, the other is international legislation, which is contained in the sources of international law [3], and the third is national legislation.

A few years ago, leading Member States' experts also drew attention to fragmented cyber security legislation. As a result, the Member States of the European Union have sought to establish a uniform cyber certification of products, processes and services. These efforts adopted the EU Cyber Security Regulation, which came into force in 2019 [6]. The regulation aims to unify cyber security at the European Union level and eliminate potentially dangerous supplier companies. The regulation establishes the institute of European certification of products, processes and services according to uniform certification schemes. Hardware certification is preferred.

If all hardware is certified when many new products enter the market daily, the certification process will be lengthy, costly and inefficient. Unfortunately, IoT certification schemes are unknown, nor are there IoT security standards that define sub-criteria for security.

IoT is a large group of devices that use various subsystems, software and hardware base. Therefore, it is necessary to approach IoT in a different individual way.

IoT hardware certification comes into play with the certificate of services or processes.

Finland has defined safety standards for IoT certification used in the consumer chain according to ETSI TS 103 645 Cyber Security for Consumer Internet of Things [7].

The issue of defining safety standards for IoT has been addressed in the US by the National Institute of Standards and Technology (NIST). A study group and program called the NIST Cybersecurity for IoT Program was established to study this issue [8]. The IoT-Enabled Smart City Framework standards are recognised worldwide [9]. The above standards are based on a general framework that applies to multiple industries. Recent research has focused on sub-sections that have examined cyber security in the context of IoT. Li and Liao researched IoT vulnerabilities and proposed a vulnerability identification process [10].

Other specialised working groups have been set up worldwide to deal with security and IoT issues, but security issues with IoT in Smart Cities have not yet been addressed. First, IoT safety standards can be developed generally, and IoT safety standards for sub-sectors (sectors) will be developed in the coming years. However, the design and elaboration of suitable IoT security standards applicable in Smart Cities in cooperation with public administration, self-government or state security forces will not be elaborated at all or will be elaborated in the perspective of 5–10 years. The process set up in this way will be lengthy. In contrast to the dynamic technological development, the IoT technologies implemented in Smart Cities will not be secured against cyber threats.

From a historical point of view, security standards for information technology are contained in ČSN, ISO, and IEC standards, which are general in content and are only recommended. The most used standards include ISO/IEC 27001 Information Security Management [11], ISO/IEC 27002 Information Technology [12], ISO/IEC 27005 Information technology – Security techniques – Information security risk management [13].

Cyber Security is supervised by the National Office for Cyber and Information Security (NUKIB) in the Czech Republic, established in 2017 and is the primary authority in this area. The Office was established by separation from the National Security Office. Through its activities, the Office has demonstrated well-developed legislation in the field of cyber security, including implementing regulations [14].

NUKIB operates in several sectors and cooperates significantly with public administration entities. However, the main goal of NUKIB is mainly a legislative and control initiative of obligated entities falling under national legislation.

The Action Plan for the National Cyber Security Strategy of the Czech Republic for the period 2021 to 2025 (NÚKIB) [18] envisages the involvement of the professional public in cooperation with legislative changes in the field of cyber security. Furthermore, the aim is to identify practical problems with the requirements for the professional public and obliged entities by law and help eliminate them using practical experience [19]. For these reasons, the processing of legislative comments will be effective using appropriate methods and software.

The most suitable method for analysing and designing suitable security standards is combining qualitative and quantitative content analysis using appropriate software.

3   Content Analysis for Processing IoT Security Standards

Qualitative and quantitative content analysis was chosen to analyse and design suitable security standards.

Content analysis is called a synonym for the more precise name quantitative content analysis or formal content analysis. Content analysis is an objective, systematic, valid, and reliable method. The content analysis subject is communication, transmitted as an image, text or sound recording. Content analysis is further divided into conceptual and relational analyses.

The content analysis examines the text about the occurrence of selected characters (letters, words, phrases). Conceptual analysis is used for a narrower selection of the examined features, using which "concepts" are examined – words, phrases, and their occurrence frequency. Conceptual analysis can be characterised as a research method that quantifies the presence of a particular feature and compares the occurrence of words in the examined group. We, therefore, classify conceptual analysis into quantitative research. The results of quantitative content analysis can be further investigated using statistical methods and appropriate software.

Content analysis is often associated with relational analysis (semantic analysis) qualitative research. The relational analysis is focused on the occurrence of concepts (characters) in the researched document, but at the same time, it is also focused on the research of the relationships between the researched concepts (characters, phrases). The relational analysis results from the so-called mental models, characters, and groups (decision map). Content analysis is an observational research method to evaluate the content of recorded communications based on a set of procedures [15].

Authors Burton, Jirák and Hendl characterise content analysis as a method in which the authors first choose the types of categories in which the frequency of occurrence of words is subsequently determined using appropriate statistical methods [16].

Content analysis can generally be defined as an analysis of the content of a record of a particular communication. This method was defined for analysing texts or a set of texts. The main goal of this method, based on the traditions of positivist methodology, is to search for specific words and concepts in the analysed communication and determine the frequency of their occurrence, meaning, and mutual relationship [17].

Content analysis is an observational research method to evaluate content recorded communications based on a set of procedures [15].

3.1 Methodological Procedure of Content Analysis

The processing of content analysis must always be preceded by a formal analysis (identification analysis) and the selection of suitable software for processing content analysis and statistical surveys. Formal analysis (identification analysis) focuses on the formal characteristics, which allow the document to be unambiguously identified, identified and distinguished from other, formally similar documents [18].

The qualitative and quantitative content analysis process, including statistical data verification, would include importing existing legislative documents, security standards, and methodological recommendations in cyber security (national legislation, international legislation, ISO/IEC standards). All documents would be imported into the appropriate software to process content analysis. After import and processing, research questions focusing on IoT cyber security will be identified. After processing the content analysis, security standards for IoT would be proposed, including the possibility of statistical examination of the analysed data.

IoT security can be viewed from three levels: hardware, network communication, and application interface security.

The methodological procedure of content analysis would include partial parts listed in Table 1.

Table 1. Partial parts of content analysis

Partial parts for content analysis processing	Description of partial parts of content analysis
Characteristics of IoT	Identification and analysis of the overall technical and safety concept for IoT
Select files to import	Search, and import existing legislative sources, international standards and safety standards in IoT
Determination of unit/depth for document processing	Performing word frequency analysis using lemmatisation, determining research questions related to the performed word frequency analysis
Determination of primary and additional sources of description and identification data	Identify primary and additional description sources, including detailed data on the examined documents
Statistical verification of the examined questions using the module included in the software	Statistical verification of research questions using the module included in the MAXQDA Analytics Pro software
Processing of the final report	Draft safety rules/standards for IoT

The process of examining qualitative content analysis can also be viewed from the three approaches he characterised in his article by Hsiu-Fang, Sarah E. Shannon [19]. First, inductive Content Analysis is used without previous studies dealing with the phenomenon [20].

Self-analysis and methodological research using content analysis is time-consuming, and it is necessary to know in detail the whole content analysis process, including basic concepts and statistics methods.

Methodological research in performing content analysis using Atlas Ti software is shown in Fig. 1.

3.2 Content Analysis using MAXQDA software

The MAXQDA software from VERBI was chosen from the exact point of view for elaborating the sampling procedure because it also has an integrated statistical module with which the results can be statistically verified [21].

MAXQDA is a software program for computer, qualitative and mixed data, text and multimedia analysis in academic, scientific and business institutions. It is developed and distributed by VERBI Software, based in Berlin, Germany.

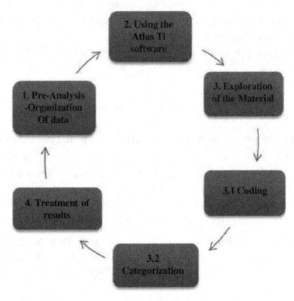

Fig. 1. Using software Atlas Ti for content analyses

The software is used to process professional content analyses, especially in marketing and journalism. The software includes three modules that can be used separately or together. The licensing policy is based on individual modules:

- MAXQDA Standard,
- MAXQDA Analytics Pro,
- MAXQDA Reader.

The software is supported for MS Windows and MAC OS platforms. The software is not supported on the Linux platform. The software allows importing various formats (PDF, DOC, SPPSS, video recordings, audio recordings) into the Document System.

The software also has an integrated lemmatisation function and a word cloud.

Other software that is used for content analysis includes Provalis Research, Text Analytics Software, Atlas Ti software,

The methodological process for processing the content analysis included the partial parts listed in Table 1.

First, two primary legal sources in the field of cyber security of Act No. 181/2014 on Cyber Security (ZoKB) [22] and Decree No. 82/2014 on Cyber Security [23], were selected. Then, these two legislative documents were imported automatically into MAXQDA software. After import, research questions were set:

Are the imported documents focused on IoT security standards?

Is the issue of using a secure password when using IoT technologies included in the documents?

Do the research documents include solutions for IoT and the use of secure password login?

At the same time, the process of examining content analysis also included determining the list of words for which the frequency was examined, including the search for relationships. Furthermore, Lemmatization (a procedure that converts words into a basic grammatical form, i.e. stem or root) was performed [24].

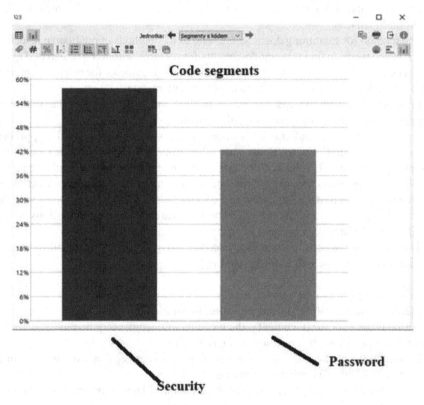

Fig. 2. Code segments

Another functionality used in the content analysis was graphically displaying the word frequency or generating a word cloud. Furthermore, questions were identified, including a possible examination of the interrelationships with the subsequent verification of outputs using a statistical module. However, the content analysis process also includes risks, particularly incorrect interpretation of the information obtained based on preliminary and unfounded conclusions. Therefore, when processing content analysis, it is necessary to focus on all the details of the occurrence of word frequency, including the determination of all research questions divided into categories (Fig. 2).

The content analysis process is extensive, and it is impossible to characterise all parts in detail in this article.

4 Document Examination – Alternative Method

To evaluate the choice of the chosen method of qualitative and quantitative content analysis it was necessary to compare with other methods used for examining texts to justify the choice of the chosen method. Another method for analysing the content of documents is Textual Examination. This method is one of the alternative methods that is used minimally.

The method for examining documents is one of the methods of qualitative research. First, it is necessary to find relevant documents for research within the researched questions. Then, after finding and determining appropriate documents for research, internal and external documents are assessed to interpret content data.

In the case of applying this alternative method for the design and elaboration of safety standards for IoT, the process would be as follows:

Legal acts, international standards or feasibility studies would first be appropriately identified (found), written down and ranked from a historical point of view to the present. Furthermore, the types of documents and research questions would be specified. Research questions should be formulated according to the historical context of the researched documents at the same time as the formulation of research questions with the documents that are currently up to date. The formulation of research questions would be followed by source criticism and interpretation of the documents.

The value of the legal documents, international guidelines or feasibility studies examined would be assessed according to the following criteria:

- Document type – legal norms, international directives and standards.
- External characters of the document – font, illustration.
- Internal features of the document – the meaning of documents, guidelines.
- The intentionality of the document – scientific value.
- The proximity of the document – connections between legal norms, international directives and other examined documents.
- Origin of the document – the origin of the creation of legal norms and international directives.

This alternative method for examining documents cannot be considered suitable given the absence of suitable software for statistical verification of results or other missing modules. However, this method can examine historical documents in the context of attitudes, values, or customs.

5 Conclusion

The Cyber security solution of IoT components is driven by needs in the environment of corporations using networks of miniature computers and, at the same time, is based on knowledge of the increased vulnerability. Therefore, legislation for IoT, Smart Technologies and other state-level strategic projects should be based on documented knowledge based mainly on recognised international and security standards developed by cybersecurity managers (NIST, ENISA).

The proposed methodological procedure for analysing and creating safety rules and recommendations could be used in other activities, such as other analytical activities, to create normative documents. In addition, with the help of content analysis, it would be possible to streamline and speed up the lengthy process of examining existing documents.

The mentioned methodology for text examination and the resulting goal of creating draft security standards could streamline the use of modern software tools and sub-modules (e.g. statistical module), which are based on proven methodological procedures used worldwide.

Last but not least, the proposed solution could also have positive benefits for the environment by reducing the burden on staff capacity in organisations or reducing air emissions through the use of a comprehensive, effective software tool and appropriately selected methodology.

The result of the content analysis can be used to create a legislative document or internal guidelines for the use of IoT in the security forces of the state, regional governments, or cities in implementing the Smart Cities strategy.

Acknowledgement. The Faculty of Informatics and management UHK specific research project 2107 Computer Networks for Cloud, Distributed Computing, and internet of Things III has partially supported the research.

References

1. Lines, B., Miao, F.: Writing more competitive proposals: content analysis of selected (and Unselected) construction contractor technical proposals, pp. 457–466, May 2016. https://doi.org/10.1061/9780784479827.047
2. Hall, M.A., Wright, R.F.: Systematic content analysis of judicial opinions. Calif. L. Rev. **96**, 63 (2008)
3. Koptseva, N.P., Luzan, V.S., Razumovskaya, V.A., Kirko, V.I.: The content analysis of the Russian federal and regional basic legislation on the cultural policy. Int. J. Semiot. Law **30**(1), 23–50 (2016). https://doi.org/10.1007/s11196-016-9479-4
4. Text as data: the promise and pitfalls of automatic content analysis methods for political texts, Political Analysis, Cambridge Core. https://www.cambridge.org/core/journals/political-analysis/article/text-as-data-the-promise-and-pitfalls-of-automatic-content-analysis-methods-for-political-texts/F7AAC8B2909441603FEB25C156448F20. 29 December 2021
5. Bullerjahn, C., Güldenring, M.: An empirical investigation of effects of film music using qualitative content analysis. Psychomusicology J. Res. Music Cogn. **13**(1–2), 99–118 (1994). https://doi.org/10.1037/h0094100
6. Regulation (EU) 2019/881 of the European Parliament and of the Council of April 17, 2019, on ENISA (the European Union Agency for Cybersecurity) and information and communications technology cybersecurity certification and repealing Regulation (EU) No 526/2013 (Cybersecurity Act) (Text with EEA relevance), roč. 151. 2019. Seen 27 May 2021. http://data.europa.eu/eli/reg/2019/881/oj/eng
7. Dahmen-Lhuissier, S.: ETSI – Consumer IoT security, ETSI. https://www.etsi.org/technologies/consumer-iot-security (viděno bře. 27, 2021)
8. paul.hernandez@nist.gov, NIST Cybersecurity for IoT Program, NIST, zář. 25, 2019. https://www.nist.gov/itl/applied-cybersecurity/nist-cybersecurity-iot-program. 27 March 2021
9. Burns, M.J.: IES-City Framework, s. 150 (2018)

10. Li, Z., Liao, Q.: Economic solutions to improve cybersecurity of governments and smart cities via vulnerability markets. Gov. Inf. Quart. **35**(1), 151–160 (2018). https://doi.org/10.1016/j.giq.2017.10.006
11. ISO 27001. https://itgovernance.co.uk/iso27001 (viděno říj. 06, 2021)
12. ČSN EN ISO/IEC 27002 (369798) - Technical standards ČSN. http://www.technicke-normy-csn.cz/369798-csn-en-iso-iec-27002_4_95679.html. 6 November 2021
13. ČSN ISO/IEC 27005 (369790) - Technical standards ČSN. http://www.technicke-normy-csn.cz/369790-csn-iso-iec-27005_4_83193.html. 06 November 2021
14. National cyber and information security agency – legislation. https://nukib.cz/en/cyber-security/regulation-and-audit/legislation/. 27 March 2021
15. (PDF) Practical resources for assessing and reporting intercoder reliability in content analysis research projects. https://www.researchgate.net/publication/242785900_Practical_Resources_for_Assessing_and_Reporting_Intercoder_Reliability_in_Content_Analysis_Research_Projects. 24 January 2021
16. Hendl, J.: Qualitative research: fundamental theories, methods and applications (2016)
17. Content analyses, department of anthropology. http://www.antropologie.org/cs/metodologie/obsahova-analyza. 27 March 2021
18. 04_formalni_a_obsahova_analyza_textu_05.pdf. 27 March 2021. https://www.mzk.cz/sites/mzk.cz/files/04_formalni_a_obsahova_analyza_textu_05.pdf
19. Three Approaches to Qualitative Content Analysis – Hsiu-Fang Hsieh, Sarah E. Shannon 2005. https://journals.sagepub.com/doi/abs/10.1177/1049732305276687. 29 December 2021
20. The qualitative content analysis process – Elo - 2008 - Journal of Advanced Nursing – Wiley Online Library. https://onlinelibrary.wiley.com/doi/abs/10.1111/j.1365-2648.2007.04569.x. 29 December 2021
21. Top 14 Qualitative Data Analysis Software in 2021 - Reviews, Features, Pricing, Comparison, PAT RESEARCH: B2B Reviews, Buying Guides & Best Practices, 29 Juni 2020. https://www.predictiveanalyticstoday.com/top-qualitative-data-analysis-software/. 27 December 2021
22. A. C.- info@aion.cz, 181/2014 Sb. Cyber Security Act, Laws for People. https://www.zakonyprolidi.cz/cs/2014-181. 01 January 2022
23. A. C.- info@aion.cz, „The Decree No 82/2018 Coll. on Security Measures, Cybersecurity Incidents, Reactive Measures, Cybersecurity Reporting Requirements, and Data Disposal (the Cybersecurity Decree)., Laws for people. https://www.zakonyprolidi.cz/cs/2018-82. 01 January 2022
24. Lemmatizace, cestinaveslovniku.cz, January 2017. https://www.cestinaveslovniku.cz/lemmatizace/. 24 January 2021

Software-Defined Networks

Mathematical Models for Minimizing Latency in Software-Defined Networks

Pablo Adasme[1]([✉])[iD], Andres Viveros[2][iD], Ali Dehghan Firoozabadi[3][iD], and Ismael Soto[1][iD]

[1] Department of Electrical Engineering, Universidad de Santiago de Chile,
Av. Victor Jara 3519, Santiago, Chile
{pablo.adasme,ismael.soto}@usach.cl
[2] Department of Industrial Engineering, Universidad de Santiago de Chile,
Av. Victor Jara 3769, Santiago, Chile
andres.viveros11@usach.cl
[3] Department of Electricity, Universidad Tecnológica Metropolitana,
Av. Jose Pedro Alessandri 1242, 7800002 Santiago, Chile
adehghanfirouzabadi@utem.cl

Abstract. In this paper, we propose mixed-integer quadratic and linear programming models to minimize the worst latency in software-defined wireless networks (SDNs). Our models are adapted from classical combinatorial optimization problems referred to as the p-median and stable set problems in the literature. For each of the two adapted models, we further derive two additional formulations. The latter is achieved by applying simple convex and linearization techniques. In summary, we obtain six mathematical formulations for minimizing latency in SDNs. We conduct substantial numerical experiments to compare the behavior of all the proposed models in terms of CPU times, the number of branch and bound nodes, and the optimal solutions obtained with the CPLEX solver. Our numerical results indicate that the first linear model allows one to obtain the optimal solution of each instance in significantly less CPU time than the other ones. Finally, we test all our models for different numbers of controllers and switches in the network while varying the degree of importance between the worst shortest path distances of switch-controller and inter-controller pairs.

Keywords: Mixed-integer quadratic and linear programming models · Software-defined networking · Wireless networks · p-Median and stable set problems

1 Introduction

Software-defined networks are programmable network architectures that separate the control or logic plane from the data forwarding plane in order to provide flexible operation to the networks. Mainly, two types of nodes are identified in a software-defined network, switches, and controllers. Switches are nodes in the

I. Awan et al. (Eds.): MobiWIS 2022, LNCS 13475, pp. 131–142, 2022.
https://doi.org/10.1007/978-3-031-14391-5_10

network that captures information data to be sent to other nodes in the network. Whilst controllers are the nodes composing the backbone of the network. Commonly a message is received by a switch node and then passed to a controller. In turn, the controller decides how to manage the traffic it receives in order to resent the messages to other switches and/or controllers. Notice that latency is a major issue in software-defined networking since it reflects the quality of service offered by the network. The larger the distance between a switch and a controller to which the switch is assigned, the higher the latency experienced by the network. Consequently, it is a major challenge to minimize latency in an SDN as it is equivalent to minimizing the existing distances between pairs of switch controllers or between controllers themselves [6].

To simultaneously minimize the worst latencies for all switch-controller and inter-controller pairs in an SDN, in this paper, we propose mathematical programming models in the form of mixed-integer quadratic and linear programming models. Our proposed models are derived from classical combinatorial optimization problems referred to as the p-median and stable set problems in the literature [7,8,10]. We further derive two additional formulations for each of the two proposed optimization models. The latter is achieved by applying traditional convex and standard linearization techniques [9]. In summary, six mathematical formulations are obtained for minimizing latency in SDNs. Finally, we test all our models for different numbers of controllers and switches using several networks while varying the importance of the worst existing distance between switches and controllers and between controllers themselves.

A few related works closer to our work in this paper can be described as follows. In [3], the authors argue that the controller placement problem (CPP) is a relevant problem to handle large-size networks. They argue that dealing with this problem in an efficient manner allows one to improve the scalability and influences the latency and performance of the whole network. Consequently, the authors define an accumulated latency metric to solve the CPP while taking into account the latency between the controller and their switches and the inter-controller latencies simultaneously. In particular, the authors formulate a mathematical programming model subject to latency constraints while minimizing the total number of controllers in the network. Finally, they evaluate the performance of their approach using network topologies from the literature. Similarly in [4], the authors intend to find the optimum location and the minimum number of controllers to be deployed in order to improve the scalability of the network using several controllers. The authors propose an algorithm that is based on the K-means and K-center algorithms. In reference [5], the authors propose the use of capacitated controllers for the global latency control placement problem. They define the latter concept as the combination of the switch-controller and inter-controller latencies as well. Thus, the optimization objective in their approach is to minimize the global latency using randomly generated network topologies.

In [6], the authors present a recent survey highlighting the importance of software-defined networking as a fundamental topic not only for data-centers and wide-area networks but also to be considered for next-generation architectures including vehicular Ad-hoc networks and networks using 5G technologies. The authors refer to the importance of controller placements since their location in a network impacts a wide range of issues such as latency, resiliency, energy efficiency, and load balancing, to name a few. The authors also present a classical CPP formulation and discuss a wide range of CPP modeling approaches while using several associated metrics and solution approaches. They further examine recent applications including mobile/cellular networks, 5G, data networks, wireless mesh networks, and vehicle Ad-hoc networks. Finally, they conclude and discuss open issues and future research directions for these topics. Further reading, for instance, can also be consulted in the recently published works [1,2].

In this paper, our main contribution is to propose new controller placement formulations based on classical combinatorial optimization problems from the literature to minimize the worst latency of switch-controller and inter-controllers simultaneously using the shortest path distances between the nodes of the network. Our first formulation is obtained from a classical p-median formulation [7]. Whereas the second one is obtained using a formulation from [10]. In the latter work, the authors show that the p-median problem can be represented as an integral slice of the stable set polytope [8,10]. The latter allows imposing a set of constraints that avoid forming cliques with the arcs of the solution obtained. Since the proposed models contain quadratic terms in the objective function, we further consider traditional convexification and linearization techniques leading to six mathematical programming models at the end. In contrast to the problem considered in [3], we impose a pre-defined number of controllers to be located in the network. On the other hand, similarly as in [5], so far we consider randomly generated graph instances with up to 80 nodes as they could also represent sensor network deployments. Finally, our proposed models allow us to solve all the generated graph instances optimally.

The paper is organized as follows. In Sect. 2, we present the proposed mathematical formulations and show through an example an input graph representing the network and the optimal solution obtained for this input graph. Then, in Sect. 3, we conduct numerical results to compare the behavior of all our proposed models in terms of CPU time, the number of branch and bound nodes, and best or optimal solutions obtained. Finally, in Sect. 4 we present our conclusions and provide some insight for future research.

2   Mathematical Formulations

In order to illustrate a feasible and optimal solution to the problem, in Fig. 1 we present an input connected graph instance representing a wireless network. Hereafter, we denote this graph as $G = (V, E)$ where $V = \{1, \ldots, n\}$ represents the set of nodes of the graph and $E = \{1, \ldots, m\}$ the set of edges connecting nodes in the network. In particular, the network in Fig. 1 is composed of $n = 60$ nodes where $k = 20$ controllers are to be located. Notice that the input network need not be fully connected. We randomly generated the network of Fig. 1 while

a) Input graph

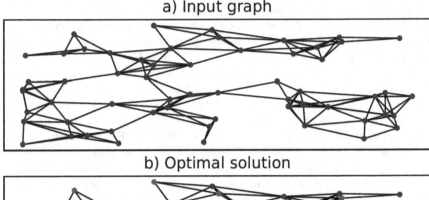

b) Optimal solution

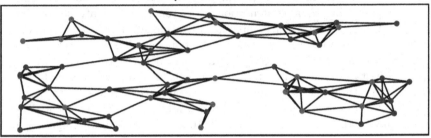

Fig. 1. An input graph instance together with its optimal solution for an SDN composed of $n = 60$ nodes where $k = 20$ controllers are to be located while using a node transmission radius of 200 m, and a value of parameter $\alpha = 0.75$ (Color figure online)

using a transmission radius of each node of 200 m. For this purpose, we generated different graphs until a connected one was obtained. Finally, for this example, we use a weighting parameter $\alpha = 0.75$ where $\alpha = [0; 1]$ is used to give a higher degree of importance to the first objective of the optimization problem which in this case corresponds to the worst switch-controller distance. In Fig. 1.a), all nodes of the network appear as blue nodes and each one of them represents a potential candidate for locating a controller. Whilst in Fig. 1.b), the red nodes represent the $k = 20$ controllers already located in the network according to the optimal solution obtained.

In order to obtain optimal solutions for the problem, first, we define the following binary variables

$$y_j = \begin{cases} 1, & \text{if controller } j \in V \text{ is located in the index position } j. \\ 0, & \text{otherwise.} \end{cases}$$

Similarly, we define the binary variables

$$x_{ij} = \begin{cases} 1, & \text{if switch } i \in V \text{ is assigned to controller } j \in V. \\ 0, & \text{otherwise.} \end{cases}$$

Thus, a first formulation can be written as

$$\min_{\{x,y\}} \left\{ \alpha \max_{\substack{\{i,j\} \in V}} \{D_{ij}x_{ij}\} + (1-\alpha) \max_{\substack{\{i,j\} \in V \\ (i<j)}} \{D_{ij}y_iy_j\} \right\} \tag{1}$$

$$\text{st.} \sum_{j \in V} y_j = k \tag{2}$$

$$\sum_{j \in V} x_{ij} = 1, \quad \forall i \in V \tag{3}$$

$$x_{ij} \leq y_j, \quad \forall i,j \in V \tag{4}$$

$$x \in \{0,1\}^{n^2}, y \in \{0,1\}^n \tag{5}$$

Notice that in the objective function (1), each entry in matrix $D = D(i,j)$ for all $\{i,j\} \in V$ denotes the shortest path distance between nodes i and j. Also, notice that in our solution to the problem, both nodes i and j can act as a switch or a controller or vice-versa. Consequently, matrix D is symmetric and all the elements of its diagonal must be equal to zero. In order to obtain a more tractable version of problem (1)–(5). We introduce the non-negative variables t_1 and t_2. This allows writing the problem in the following equivalent form

$$M_1 : \min_{\{x,y,t_1,t_2\}} \{\alpha t_1 + (1-\alpha)t_2\} \tag{6}$$

$$\text{st.} \ D_{ij}x_{ij} \leq t_1, \quad \forall i,j \in V \tag{7}$$

$$D_{ij}y_iy_j \leq t_2, \quad \forall i,j \in V, (i<j) \tag{8}$$

$$(2)-(5)$$

$$t_1 \geq 0, t_2 \geq 0$$

From the quadratic model M_1, we further notice that the constraints (8) can be equivalently written as

$$D_{ij}y_iy_j + y_i^2 - y_i + y_j^2 - y_j \leq t_2, \quad \forall i,j \in V, (i<j) \tag{9}$$

This is clear since for each $i \in V$ we have that $y_i^2 - y_i = 0$ since the y variable vector is binary. The latter allows obtaining the convex constraints (9) in contrast to the ones in (8) which are not. Thus, we can formulate another equivalent model as

$$M_2 : \min_{\{x,y,t_1,t_2\}} \{\alpha t_1 + (1-\alpha)t_2\}$$

$$\text{st.} \ (2)-(5), (7), (9)$$

$$t_1 \geq 0, t_2 \geq 0$$

Finally, it is also possible to obtain a mixed-integer linear model by introducing linearization variables $z_{ij} = y_i y_j$ for all $i, j \in V, (i < j)$ [9]. This allows obtaining the following model

$$M_3: \min_{\{x,y,t_1,t_2,z\}} \{\alpha t_1 + (1-\alpha)t_2\}$$

$$\text{st. } D_{ij}z_{ij} \leq t_2, \quad \forall i, j \in V, (i < j) \tag{10}$$

$$(2) - (5), (7)$$

$$z_{ij} \leq y_i \quad \forall i, j \in V, (i < j) \tag{11}$$

$$z_{ij} \leq y_j \quad \forall i, j \in V, (i < j) \tag{12}$$

$$z_{ij} \geq y_i + y_j - 1 \quad \forall i, j \in V, (i < j) \tag{13}$$

$$t_1 \geq 0, t_2 \geq 0$$

Notice that the same steps required to obtain models M_1, M_2, and M_3 can be applied to derive three additional formulations while adapting the p-median formulation proposed in [10]. In this reference [10], the authors assume that the p-median problem consists of a directed graph in which a feasible solution can be obtained if and only if the set of arcs in the solution form an independent set [8,10]. A particular set of arcs in an obtained solution form an independent set if and only if each tail of each arc starts from a particular median node. Since there are p nodes acting as medians in the classical p-median problem, then we can have exactly $n - p$ arcs in a feasible solution to the problem. This allows obtaining an equivalent formulation for the software-defined networking problem as follows

$$\min_{\{x,y\}} \left\{ \alpha \max_{\{i,j\} \in V} \{D_{ij}x_{ij}\} + (1-\alpha) \max_{\substack{\{i,j\} \in V \\ (i<j)}} \{D_{ij}y_iy_j\} \right\} \tag{14}$$

$$\text{st. } \sum_{j \in V} y_j = k \tag{15}$$

$$\sum_{i,j \in V} x_{ij} = n \tag{16}$$

$$x_{ij} \leq y_i, \quad \forall i, j \in V \tag{17}$$

$$\sum_{i \in V \setminus \{j\}} x_{ij} + x_{js} \leq 1, \quad \forall j, s \in V \tag{18}$$

$$x \in \{0,1\}^{n^2}, y \in \{0,1\}^n \tag{19}$$

Similarly as we did for the model (1)–(5), for short we omit writing explicitly all the equivalent formulations that can be derived from model (14)–(19). However, hereafter we denote these new models by M_4, M_5 and M_6. Recall that these models can be easily obtained by first introducing the non-negative variables t_1 and t_2, then by applying the convex approach, and finally by using the linearization method [9], respectively.

As it can be observed the main differences of model (14)–(19) w.r.t. the model (1)–(5) are constraints (16) which ensure that all nodes have to be assigned to a particular controller. Next, the constraints (17) ensure the independent set property which states that any directed arc starts from i to j if and only if node i acts as a controller. The constraints (18) avoid forming cliques with the arcs obtained in the output solution of the problem. Finally, constraints (19) are domain constraints for the decision variables.

3   Computational Numerical Experiments

In this section, we conduct computational numerical experiments in order to compare all the proposed models. For this purpose, we implement Python codes using CPLEX 20.1.0 solver [11] to solve the linear and quadratic models. The numerical experiments have been performed on an Intel(R) 64 bits core (TM) with 3 GHz and 8 G of RAM under Windows 10. CPLEX solver is used with default options. In our preliminary numerical experiments we consider graph instances with dimensions of $n = \{50, 70, 80\}$ using values of $k = \{5, 10\}$ for connected sparse networks with densities smaller than 10%. Notice that independently of the density of the input SDN, we can always obtain the shortest path distance for all pairs of nodes since the network is connected. More precisely, we generate connected graph networks using a transmission radius of 150 m and test the performance of each model while varying the parameter values of α ranging from zero to one. In Tables 1 and 2, we report numerical results for models M_1, M_2, M_3, and for models M_4, M_5, M_6, respectively. More precisely, we report the best or optimal objective function value obtained for each model, its number of branch and bound nodes, and the CPU time in seconds CPLEX requires to solve each particular model. Each network in these tables is generated with plane coordinate values which are randomly drawn from the interval $[0; 1]$. Consequently, the objective function values can be scaled up to 1km by multiplying each value by 1000. Finally, notice that the instances reported for a particular number of nodes in both tables are exactly the same. This is intentionally done for better comparison purposes. It is also relevant to mention that all the numerical results reported in Tables 1 and 2 allow deciding which of the proposed models would be preferred to use when applied to practical applications as it could be the case of a sensor network deployment for example.

From Table 1, we observe that all the instances are solved to optimality using CPLEX and for all the parameter values of α. However, when incrementing the value of k, in particular, we see that for small values of α, the objective function values are higher. Whereas for the larger values the opposite occurs. Next, we also see that the number of branch and bound nodes are higher for the quadratic models than for the linear model. Finally, we see that the linear model solves most of the tested instances in significantly less CPU time.

From Table 2, we observe similar trends as in Table 1 for the models M_4, M_5, and M_6. Again, we see that the linear models require less computational effort than the quadratic ones. We further notice that the models M_4, M_5, and

Table 1. Numerical results obtained with models M_1, M_2 and M_3

Den.	n	k	M_1			M_2			M_3		
			Best	$B\&B$	CPU(s)	Best	$B\&B$	CPU(s)	Best	$B\&B$	CPU(s)
Using a transmission radius of 150 m and $\alpha = 0$											
7.67	50	5	0.09	365	3.67	0.09	116	5.53	0.09	0	0.98
	50	10	0.2	628	4.78	0.2	405	3.7	0.2	0	1.23
7.28	70	5	0.1	596	25.96	0.1	403	8.17	0.1	0	2.6
	70	10	0.22	1123	20.2	0.22	1152	28.54	0.22	0	4.31
6.55	80	5	0.09	135	29.57	0.09	400	47.59	0.09	0	2.82
	80	10	0.22	923	55.43	0.22	5681	56.46	0.22	0	7.17
Using a transmission radius of 150 m and $\alpha = 0.25$											
7.67	50	5	0.36	5969	19.17	0.36	8691	36.39	0.36	872	8.35
	50	10	0.41	3872	25.09	0.41	9273	35.65	0.41	2779	12.31
7.28	70	5	0.39	5199	79.39	0.39	10752	104.93	0.39	1925	36.28
	70	10	0.47	182258	1190.59	0.47	108353	538.78	0.47	4527	114.26
6.55	80	5	0.32	19430	238.09	0.32	7057	146.34	0.32	2362	144.01
	80	10	0.43	320110	2784.26	0.43	169938	1838.73	0.43	6500	220.89
Using a transmission radius of 150 m and $\alpha = 0.5$											
7.67	50	5	0.53	7027	45.9	0.53	4928	23.48	0.53	1822	21.35
	50	10	0.58	93442	266.28	0.58	25014	92.32	0.58	4584	25.65
7.28	70	5	0.64	12854	687.57	0.64	5703	122.56	0.64	4281	229.79
	70	10	0.66	167192	2711.7	0.66	22335	1050.28	0.66	6552	151.53
6.55	80	5	0.46	13787	219.71	0.46	6836	163.79	0.46	3273	194.31
	80	10	0.5	121902	2171.98	0.5	328247	3448.71	0.5	6537	247.42
Using a transmission radius of 150 m and $\alpha = 0.75$											
7.67	50	5	0.54	2297	28.56	0.54	1775	27.45	0.54	2242	25.0
	50	10	0.5	2691	22.89	0.5	6286	32.85	0.5	2055	18.06
7.28	70	5	0.68	6646	233.93	0.68	8912	231.92	0.68	5390	245.45
	70	10	0.65	9200	470.29	0.65	13213	626.79	0.65	7242	208.7
6.55	80	5	0.49	10764	509.17	0.49	10299	608.1	0.49	2059	167.32
	80	10	0.48	11928	398.71	0.48	13262	462.09	0.48	2868	228.43
Using a transmission radius of 150 m and $\alpha = 1$											
7.67	50	5	0.37	85	5.46	0.37	172	6.67	0.37	0	3.87
	50	10	0.22	118	6.59	0.22	91	6.79	0.22	0	5.0
7.28	70	5	0.4	429	50.35	0.4	316	32.7	0.4	80	20.59
	70	10	0.23	828	40.87	0.23	727	41.5	0.23	11	17.89
6.55	80	5	0.35	1092	166.23	0.35	1029	143.56	0.35	131	27.73
	80	10	0.22	139	31.06	0.22	271	31.4	0.22	73	30.03

Table 2. Numerical results obtained with models M_4, M_5 and M_6

n	k	M_4			M_5			M_6		
		Best	B&B	CPU(s)	Best	B&B	CPU(s)	Best	B&B	CPU(s)
Using a transmission radius of 150 m and $\alpha = 0$										
50	5	0.09	330	9.59	0.09	148	13.76	0.09	0	4.92
50	10	0.2	140	28.85	0.2	188	22.34	0.2	51	7.0
70	5	0.1	122	39.31	0.1	226	38.75	0.1	87	16.62
70	10	0.22	756	112.76	0.22	2029	119.14	0.22	250	53.25
80	5	0.09	150	235.26	0.09	411	212.96	0.09	26	42.73
80	10	0.22	2787	164.28	0.22	294	190.14	0.22	87	58.48
Using a transmission radius of 150 m and $\alpha = 0.25$										
50	5	0.36	8109	62.53	0.36	4018	45.26	0.36	2529	52.14
50	10	0.41	12934	92.39	0.41	8740	76.09	0.41	2630	66.26
70	5	0.39	9664	221.12	0.39	35236	512.56	0.39	4011	544.76
70	10	0.47	17478	594.35	0.47	77853	3600.67*	0.47	4224	504.9
80	5	0.32	6265	518.17	0.32	9647	562.92	0.32	2711	586.51
80	10	0.43	44347	1957.45	0.43	28748	1811.89	0.43	4677	856.51
Using a transmission radius of 150 m and $\alpha = 0.5$										
50	5	0.53	2697	41.12	0.53	3601	72.46	0.53	2758	172.31
50	10	0.58	18356	171.62	0.58	10975	142.93	0.58	2876	110.42
70	5	0.64	7341	456.84	0.64	9544	868.34	0.64	2825	796.67
70	10	0.66	51827	2435.51	0.66	100906	2554.06	0.66	3077	871.67
80	5	0.46	5892	665.82	0.46	7176	709.03	0.46	3780	1843.15
80	10	0.5	37617	2366.95	0.5	10052	910.37	0.5	3268	823.17
Using a transmission radius of 150 m and $\alpha = 0.75$										
50	5	0.54	4118	148.07	0.54	3460	120.09	0.54	3230	124.03
50	10	0.5	9231	101.78	0.5	5999	74.51	0.5	2929	81.56
70	5	0.68	9925	915.5	0.68	7920	1194.45	0.68	2632	665.01
70	10	0.65	20049	1193.98	0.65	62281	2748.15	0.65	2170	653.9
80	5	0.49	10653	1696.7	0.49	7539	931.87	0.49	3636	1543.43
80	10	0.48	28902	2295.68	0.48	17792	1262.76	0.48	4886	1356.95
Using a transmission radius of 150 m and $\alpha = 1$										
50	5	0.37	58	11.35	0.37	46	10.21	0.37	127	11.84
50	10	0.22	294	14.35	0.22	213	11.68	0.22	181	15.09
70	5	0.4	457	105.84	0.4	2581	212.93	0.4	947	382.96
70	10	0.23	3717	162.59	0.23	3634	169.78	0.23	646	120.43
80	5	0.35	2977	546.51	0.35	2911	399.06	0.35	906	364.6
80	10	0.22	3443	237.53	0.22	3626	242.89	0.22	421	160.82

*: Instance not solved to optimality in one hour of CPU time

M_6 are harder to solve optimally when compared to models M_1, M_2, and M_3, respectively. Only a few instances can be solved faster in Table 2 when compared to Table 1. From the numerical results of both tables, we can conclude that the models presented in Table 1 are preferable to the ones reported in Table 2. Finally, we observe that one instance in Table 2 could not be solved optimally in one hour of CPU time which was the limit imposed for all the models.

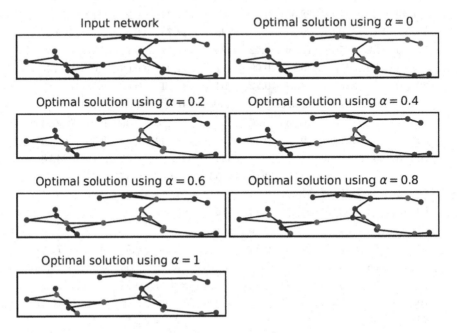

Fig. 2. An input graph instance of $n = 20$ using $k = 8$ together with the optimal solutions obtained for different values of parameter α using a node transmission radius of 200 m

In order to give more insights with respect to the optimal positions the controller should take depending on the value of parameter α, we plot in Fig. 2 a SDN example for an input graph composed of $n = 20$ and $k = 8$ while varying the parameter α for values ranging from zero to one as $\alpha = \{0, 0.2, 0.4, 0.6, 0.8, 1\}$. In Fig. 2, the blue nodes represent the nodes of the network before it is decided if a controller is going to be located at that particular location. Whilst the red nodes represent the controllers already in their optimal positions for each particular value of α.

From Fig. 2, we clearly observe that for small values of α, the controllers are closer to each other. On the opposite, we see that for larger values of α, the controller positions seem to be more dispersed. These observations are correct since the lower the values of α, the larger the degree of importance for the inter-controller distance. On the opposite, the larger the values of α, the larger the degree of importance for the inter-switch node distances.

4 Conclusions

In this paper, we have proposed mixed-integer quadratic and linear programming formulations that allow for minimizing the worst latency in terms of distance for software-defined networks. The proposed models are obtained as adapted versions from classical combinatorial optimization problems referred to as the p-median and stable set problems in the literature. We further derive two additional formulations for each of the two optimization models. This is achieved by applying well-known convex and linearization techniques. In summary, we have proposed six mathematical formulations for minimizing latency in SDNs. We conduct substantial numerical experiments in order to compare the behavior of all the proposed models in terms of CPU times, the number of branch and bound nodes, and the optimal or best solutions obtained with the CPLEX solver. So far, our preliminary numerical results indicated that the first linear model allows one to obtain the optimal solution of each instance in significantly less CPU time than the other ones. Finally, we test all our models for different numbers of controllers and switches and for different network sizes while varying the degree of importance between the worst shortest path distance between pairs of switches and controllers and between controllers themselves.

In future research, we plan to formulate new additional models, use more realistic networks from the literature, and develop low complexity algorithms in order to obtain optimal or good feasible solutions for large-size networks.

Acknowledgements. The authors acknowledge the financial support from Competition for Research Regular Projects, year 2021, code LPR21-02, Universidad Tecnológica Metropolitana, and from projects Dicyt 062117S, and FONDEF No. ID21110191.

References

1. Mohanty, S., Shekhawat, A. S., Sahoo, B., Apat, H.K., Khare, P.: Minimizing latency for controller placement problem in SDN. In: 2021 19th OITS International Conference on Information Technology (OCIT), pp. 393–398 (2021). https://doi.org/10.1109/OCIT53463.2021.00083
2. Chen, Y.H., Wang, P.C.: Concise retrieval of flow statistics for software-defined networks. IEEE Syst. J. **16**(1), 554–565 (2022). https://doi.org/10.1109/JSYST.2021.3065306
3. Rasol, K.A., Domingo-Pascual, J.: Joint placement latency optimization of the control plane. In: International Symposium on Networks, Computers and Communications (ISNCC), pp. 1–6 (2020). https://doi.org/10.1109/ISNCC49221.2020.9297271
4. Heller, B., Sherwood, R., McKeown, N.: The controller placement problem. In: Proceedings of the First Workshop on Hot Topics in Software Defined Networks. Helsinki, Finland. ACM, pp. 7–12 (2012)
5. Gao, C., Wang, H., Zhu, F., Zhai, L., Yi, S.: A particle swarm optimization algorithm for controller placement problem in software defined network. In: Proceedings of the International Conference on Algorithms and Architectures for Parallel Processing (ICA3PP 2015). Zhangjiajie, China (2015)

6. Das, T., Sridharan, V., Gurusamy, M.: A survey on controller placement in SDN. IEEE Commun. Surv. Tutor. **22**(1), 472–503 (2020). https://doi.org/10.1109/COMST.2019.2935453
7. Sandoval, C., Adasme, P., Firoozabadi, A.D.: Quadratic p-median formulations with connectivity costs between facilities. In: Bentahar, J., Awan, I., Younas, M., Grønli, T.-M. (eds.) MobiWIS 2021. LNCS, vol. 12814, pp. 99–107. Springer, Cham (2021). https://doi.org/10.1007/978-3-030-83164-6_8
8. Korshunov, A.D.: Coefficient of internal stability. Kibernetika **10**(1), 17–28 (1974). https://doi.org/10.1007/BF01069014
9. Fortet, R.: Applications de lálgebre de boole en recherche operationelle. Rev. Fr. Rech. Oper. **4**, 17–26 (1960)
10. Avella, P., Sassano, A.: On the p-median polytope. Math. Program. **89**(3), 395–411 (2001)
11. IBM ILOG CPLEX high-performance mathematical programming engine (2022). https://www.ibm.com/docs/en/icos/22.1.0

Analyzing the Impact of DNN Hardware Accelerators-Oriented Compression Techniques on General-Purpose Low-End Boards

Giuliano Canzonieri[1], Salvatore Monteleone[2]([✉])[iD], Maurizio Palesi[1][iD], Enrico Russo[1][iD], and Davide Patti[1][iD]

[1] Department of Electrical, Electronic and Computer Engineering (DIEEI), University of Catania, Catania, Italy
{giuliano.canzonieri,enrico.russo7}@studium.unict.it
{maurizio.palesi,davide.patti}@dieei.unict.it
[2] Department of Engineering, Niccolò Cusano University, Rome, Italy
salvatore.monteleone@unicusano.it

Abstract. Deep Neural Networks emerged in the last years as the most promising approach to the smart processing of data. However, their effectiveness is still a challenge when they are implemented in resource-constrained architectures, such as those of edge devices often requiring at least the inference phase. This work investigates the impact of two different weight compression techniques initially designed and tested for DNN hardware accelerators in a scenario involving general-purpose low-end hardware. After applying several levels of weight compression on the MobileNet DNN model, we show how accelerator-oriented weight compression techniques can positively impact both memory traffic pressure and inference/latency figures, resulting in some cases in a good trade-off in terms of accuracy loss.

Keywords: DNN · Compression techniques · Experimental implementation

1 Introduction and Background

Over the last decade, Deep Neural Networks (DNNs) have been successfully exploited in a huge number of different applications, ranging from offline tasks such as handwriting, image classification/recognition to real-time video flows processing for autonomous driving or detection of threat situations in security systems. While the initial training phase of such networks can be usually performed by means of high-performance machines, some application scenarios require their actual usage (*i.e.*, the inference) to be deployed on resource-constrained devices, such as mobile systems [10,11,13].

Current DNN models rely on millions or even billions of parameters, thus exacerbating the role played by the processing, communication, and memory

I. Awan et al. (Eds.): MobiWIS 2022, LNCS 13475, pp. 143–155, 2022.
https://doi.org/10.1007/978-3-031-14391-5_11

sub-systems for moving such high data volume during the inference phase. In particular, three main types of traffic determine the above latency and energy figures, as follows: 1) the traffic for fetching the input feature map and model parameters (*i.e.*, weights) from memory; 2) the on-chip traffic for dispatching the weights and the input feature maps 3) the traffic for storing back the output feature maps to the main memory in case of the local memory does not suffice. In particular, the fraction of traffic due to transfer weights accounts for a significant fraction of the overall traffic, as shown in Fig. 1 for the most commonly used DNN models. Further, in contrast to the traffic induced by the output feature maps that decreases as the local memory size increases, the weights induced traffic is not affected by the amount of local memory. Thus, as the local memory size increases, the memory traffic becomes more and more dominated by the weights-induced traffic.

Based on the above observations, it is clear that reducing the memory footprint to store the model parameters would have a relevant positive impact on both the performance and energy metrics.

In this regard, different compression methods that have been proposed in the literature focus on minimizing the model size. Some methods rely on parameters' pruning and sharing to remove parameters that are not crucial to the model performance, as in [7]. Other methods modify the network structure to compress weights [1]. A method to compress intermediate feature maps to decrease memory storage and bandwidth requirements during inference is presented in [6]. Another interesting approach is the one shown in EBPC [3], a hardware-friendly and lossless compression scheme for the feature maps present within Convolutional Neural Networks (CNNs). However, it is limited on the compression of the feature maps, while the model parameters are responsible for a major fraction of the overall memory/communication traffic (as already shown in Fig. 1). A further class of approaches is based on the reduction in the number of bits required to represent weights, with a consequent reduction of the memory footprint for storing the network parameters [5]. To summarize, compression methods in the field of DNN is a growing research topic involving different hardware/software complexity trade-offs. With this regard, the interested reader can also refer to [4] for a survey of model compression and acceleration for DNNs.

In our previous work [9], we introduced a weight footprint reduction technique (*DNNZip*), whose major point is that of being orthogonal to the compression strategies, *i.e.*, it is suitable for application on top of all the above-discussed approaches for further increasing their compression effectiveness. Another technique (*LineCompress*), has been introduced in subsequent work, aimed at further increasing the compression ratio, but also allowing a simplified hardware accelerator implementation and thus especially targeted for the IoT accelerators [12]. An extensive comparison of both approaches, in terms of accuracy, compression, energy, and power metrics has been presented in recent works [2,9,12]. While the above techniques have been designed assuming DNN accelerators as target architecture, which remains the most promising solution for future DNN applications, in this paper, we aim to extend our analysis to investigate their impact on commonly available small-sized architecture for mobile IoT prototypes and low-end applications, such as the Raspberry Pi board series.

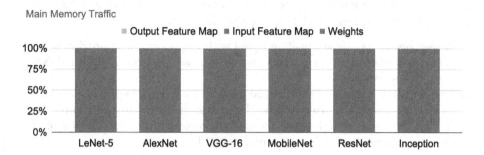

Fig. 1. Breakdown of inference memory traffic for some reference DNN models.

In particular, we describe the setup through which we experimentally tested and compared both techniques, taking into account the inference of a MobileNet model deployed on a Raspberry Pi 3 board performing a video frame processing task. The results we achieved in the test experiment are reported in Sect. 3.

2 Experimental Setup

In the following, we illustrate the instruments and the methodology adopted in our experiment. The main goal is to perform video processing and image classification using a low-end resource-constrained device, thus testing the impact of the above-discussed compression techniques in a different target architecture from the DNN hardware accelerators scenario.

2.1 Compression Data Flow Overview

The *DNNZip* [9] and *LineCompress* [12] compression techniques perform a lossy compression of the model's parameters, in order to decrease the energy consumption and the latency in the inference process of the deep neural network.

As already discussed, the idea behind such approaches originates from the necessity to reduce the traffic caused by delivering parameters from the main memory to the processing units. We remind that, during the inference process, the input feature maps and parameters are firstly fetched from the main memory and then dispatched in order to be processed. Lastly, they can be stored in local memory, but in most cases, the local memory is not capable of containing the huge amount of parameters of the deep neural network, so they are moved to the main memory. While the delay introduced by such movement could be reduced by increasing local memory caches, we can assume that, for a given memory size, more parameters imply more used bandwidth between local and main memory. It also should be noticed that when using the compressed model for the weights, there is no need to retrain the model, because it does not modify the structure of the deep neural network.

The algorithm underlying DNNZip requires as input the DNN model and a user-defined *maximum tolerated error* (MTE), while the output is the compressed model. The steps performed by the algorithm are:

1. It searches for the most sensitive layers with respect to the approximation to their parameters. For this purpose, parameters are perturbed, and the DNN's top-1 accuracy is tested.
2. The sensitivity level and the size are used to compute the score of each layer. It is more convenient to compress layers less sensitive to the compression of their parameters and whose parameters consist of a large fraction of the overall parameters of the deep neural network.
3. Layers are sorted based on their score
4. The generic layer is analyzed to extract monotonic sub-sequences of parameters, and for each sub-sequence, a linear regression is used to compute two coefficients that approximate the sub-sequence. Then δ is used to relax the strict monotonic sub-sequence into a weak monotonic one. The value of δ is the maximum value that can be used to compress layers without exceeding the maximum tolerated error provided in input. This error is expressed as the *normalized mean square error* with respect to the amplitude of parameters of the generic layer.

The LineCompress technique improves DNNZip in terms of hardware overhead and removes the requirement for the δ since monotonic sequences of parameters are automatically created by sorting them in fixed-size clusters (see [12] for details). Of course, since in this work we will be using those techniques in a different architecture from hardware accelerators, the required weights decompression operations performed on-the-fly right before the inference are not required.

2.2 Hardware and Software Setup

In our experiment, we used the MobileNet model provided by the Keras deep learning API, whose documentation is available online[1], to execute frame by frame image classification on videos assuming that the model is pre-trained on an ImageNET data set [8]. The device in which we embedded the model is a Raspberry Pi 3 B+, with 1 GB of SDRAM, a 32 GB micro SD card, and a Broadcom BCM2837B0 quad-core A53 (ARMv8) 64-bit processor at 1.4 GHz. We firstly performed the model's inference using 80 MP4 videos of 10 different objects, recorded from a Raspberry Pi Camera V2, each of them with a resolution of 640 × 480, a frame rate of 25 fps, and a length of 5 s (Fig. 2).

The objects, each of them of different shapes, were recorded while they were moving through a drill powered conveyor belt, in two different light conditions (one scenario with natural indoor light and one scenario where a 405 lm light bulb was placed near the object), to test the network behavior in several scenarios.

---
[1] https://keras.io/api/applications/mobilenet/.

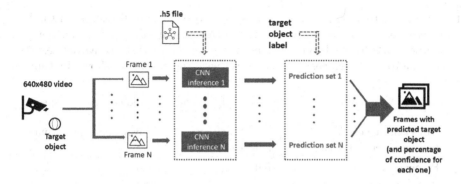

Fig. 2. This is the workflow followed in the experiment. Firstly, a video dataset was created, then each video was split into its frames, and each frame was given in input to the model with the chosen H5 file. Once the model's predictions are produced, we search for the frames in which the correct prediction appears.

The convey belt consists in a PVC frame 80 cm long, at whose ends there are a pulley and an aluminum bar. The bar is attached to the drill to let the cloth belt slide trough the pulley (Figs. 3 and 4).

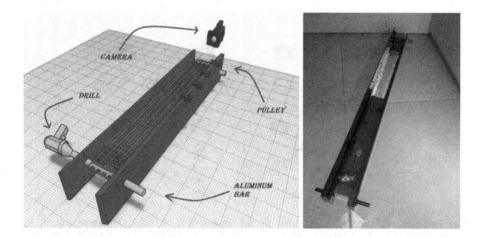

Fig. 3. Model of the convey belt, and all its parts (left). Prototype of the convey belt used in the experiments (right).

In the first 40 videos, the conveyor belt was placed perpendicular to the Pi camera and 18 cm away from it, and the drill rounds per minute were set to 400 in the first 20 videos, and 1500 in the other 20. The aluminum bar's diameter is 1 cm, so we can approximately calculate the objects speed, ignoring the friction and their weight. The diameter is 1 cm, so the circumference is about 3.14 cm. Then, if the drill is set to 400 rpm, the objects will move at about 0.21 m/s, if the drill is set to 1500 rpm the objects will move at about 0.70 m/s. In the last 40 videos, the conveyor belt was placed in the camera's direction, in such a way that objects approached to the camera when we actuated the conveyor belt. We recorded a total of 8 videos for each object with the parameter shown in Table 1.

Table 1. Values of movement directions, light condition, and convey belt speed.

Object movement direction (with respect to the camera)	Light conditions (Low/High)	Convey belt speed (rpm)
Perpendicular	High	400
Perpendicular	High	1500
Perpendicular	Low	400
Perpendicular	Low	1500
Towards	High	400
Towards	High	1500
Towards	Low	400
Towards	Low	1500

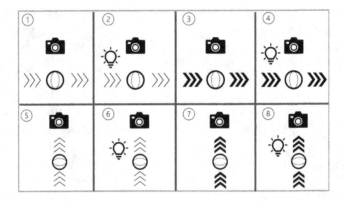

Fig. 4. These are the eight scenarios we set up for each object in the experiment. In the upper part of the figure, we can see the four scenarios where the object is moving perpendicular to the camera. In the lower part, there are the four scenarios where the object is approaching towards the camera. The bold arrows refer to the highest value in velocity.

We firstly performed inference using the original model's H5[2] file provided by Keras, we then used compressed model versions to process the same dataset, so we could compare the several accuracy values.

---

[2] Fifth version of the Hierarchical Data Format (HDF) a file format designed to store and organize large amounts of data.

All inferences were done through python scripts. As aforementioned, model's compression was executed by using the above discussed weight compression algorithms.

3   Results

In this section, we show the results of the experiments when processing the MobileNet model weights with the above discussed techniques, employing different levels of compression.

In the case of DNNZip, three different values of the maximum tolerated error MTE have been considered: a maximum tolerated error value of 0, then 10, and lastly 20. For LineCompress, having a fixed compression ratio that cannot be tuned, we tried different compression levels by changing the number of layers for which the compression has been applied, indicated with xN, where N is the number of layers, sorted according their impact on the accuracy, according to the sensivity metric defined in [12]. As the flow of frames are being processed by the inference, the object can be not recognized or recognized with different class probabilities.

The tables in the following report, for each model instance, the maximum class probability at which the object in the video was recognized, thus representing the value obtained for the frame in which the confidence of detecting the correct one was at the top level.

Ten target objects have been considered, numbered as: (1) coffee mug, (2) cellular phone, (3) mouse, (4) candle, (5) ruler, (6) remote controller, (7) screwdriver, (8) lighter, (9) sunglasses, and (10) ping-pong ball. These objects have been selected because they are representative of different physical characteristics (shape, color, and opacity), thus allowing to test the model's behavior in a wide range of scenarios. There are two videos for each object, the first in low light conditions and the second in better (high) light conditions.

Tables 2 *(top)* and *(bottom)* show the probabilities computed by models when the convey belt were powered by a drill working at 400 rpm (V1), in the third and fourth tables the drill worked at 1500 rpm (V2). We see how, in some cases, the compressed model computes higher probabilities than the ones of the original model, such as the predictions of objects #1, #4, #7 and #9, due to input noise carrying not useful information that maybe get discarded by compressed model. While this should not intended as an accuracy improvement of the compressed model, which is lossy by definition, still confirms an acceptable degradation of the weights quality occurring when manipulating the network parameters to perform the compression.

Tables 3 *(top)* and *(bottom)* show the results produced when the objects approached to the camera. In each cell we annotate the maximum distance from which the object was recognized (from less than 10 cm, and from 10 cm to 50 cm with steps of 10 cm), and the relative class probability. We notice better performance in videos of objects #6 and #10 as the recognition distance increased.

In Tables 4 and 5, there can be found the predictions related to the H5 files compressed by using the LineCompress algorithm.

Table 2. Maximum rates at with which the object was correctly recognized by the model when the drill rpm were set to the V1 *(top)* and V2 *(bottom)*. For each compression level of the H5 file, we performed the inference once per video. "Low" and "High" refer to the light condition.

Object predictions (V1 = 400 rpm)

Compression level	OBJECTS																			
	#1		#2		#3		#4		#5		#6		#7		#8		#9		#10	
	Low	High	Low	High	Low	High	Low	High	Low	High	Low	High	Low	High	Low	High	Low	High	Low	High
Not compressed	18.0%	86.0%	16.0%	95.0%	36.0%	40.0%	12.0%	70.0%	52.0%	37.0%	—	66.0%	13.0%	30.0%	6.0%	73.0%	—	12.0%	79.0%	79.0%
0 MTE	—	12.2%	—	—	—	—	—	6.6%	—	—	—	—	—	—	—	—	—	12.5%	—	18.1%
10 MTE	12.0%	97.0%	—	72.0%	—	—	9.3%	53.0%	—	7.6%	—	34.4%	—	—	—	—	23.5%	47.1%	22.3%	38.0%
20 MTE	14.2%	92.7%	6.2%	87.3%	—	3.7%	18.0%	83.9%	26.2%	18.6%	—	45.2%	11.7%	31.5%	—	34.7%	10.2%	27.4%	38.4%	64.0%

Object predictions (V2 = 1500 rpm)

Compression level	OBJECTS																			
	#1		#2		#3		#4		#5		#6		#7		#8		#9		#10	
	Low	High	Low	High	Low	High	Low	High	Low	High	Low	High	Low	High	Low	High	Low	High	Low	High
Not compressed	—	72.0%	—	89.0%	17.0%	95.0%	—	43.0%	—	34.0%	—	—	—	3.0%	—	—	—	3.0%	—	38.0%
0 MTE	—	5.5%	—	—	—	—	—	—	—	—	—	—	—	—	—	—	—	—	—	—
10 MTE	—	88.0%	—	48.8%	5.0%	41.7%	—	—	—	5.6%	—	—	—	—	—	—	—	9.2%	—	9.0%
20 MTE	—	81.4%	—	65.7%	—	66.4%	—	4.7%	—	12.5%	—	—	—	6.4%	—	—	—	6.3%	—	19.2%

Fig. 5. For each H5 file is shown the percentage difference of *(a)* accuracy *(b)* average inference time *(c)* average CPU usage *(d)* average memory usage, all with respect to the nominal values (*i.e.*, those related to the non compressed H5 files).

The comparison of the accuracy values related to the recognition of object #1, in high light condition and with velocity V1, is shown in Fig. 5a. In order to keep a measure of the performance improvement among the compression levels, we took note of the average latency regarding the inference, taking into account just 10 frames from the videos related to the coffee mug (object #1).

Table 3. Maximum recognition distances when the objects move towards the camera and respective class probabilities. The drill rpm were set to V1 *(top)* and V2 *(bottom)*. In each cell we reported the maximum distance at which the object was correctly recognized by the model, and the relative accuracy. For each compression level of the H5 file, we performed the inference once per video. "Low" and "High" refer to the light condition.

Approaching object predictions (V1 = 400 rpm)

Compression level	OBJECTS																			
	#1		#2		#3		#4		#5		#6		#7		#8		#9		#10	
	Low	High	Low	High	Low	High	Low	High	Low	High	Low	High	Low	High	Low	High	Low	High	Low	High
Not compressed	8.0% <10cm	5.3% <10cm	10.0% 40cm	5.0% 40cm	6.0% 10cm	3.9% 10cm	5.4% 50cm	—	—	—	10.0% 10cm	3.7% 20cm	5.0% 40cm	—	7.0% <10cm	5.0% 10cm	—	—	3.4% 20cm	2.2% 30cm
0 MTE	—	—	3.0% 20cm	—	—	—	3.4% 20cm	—	—	—	—	—	—	—	—	—	—	—	—	3.0% 10cm
10 MTE	—	—	3.9% 10cm	12.1% 20cm	—	—	8.5% <10cm	5.0% 30cm	—	—	2.9% 20cm	5.2% 20cm	—	—	4.0% <10cm	5.8% 10cm	—	—	1.5% 20cm	2.8% 20cm
20 MTE	4.5% <10cm	4.4% <10cm	3.8% 20cm	7.9% 30cm	—	—	3.4% 20cm	—	—	—	16.2% 10cm	5.1% 20cm	5.4% 40cm	—	23.0% <10cm	4.3% 10cm	—	—	2.3% 20cm	3.7% 30cm

Approaching object predictions (V2 = 1500 rpm)

Compression level	OBJECTS																			
	#1		#2		#3		#4		#5		#6		#7		#8		#9		#10	
	Low	High	Low	High	Low	High	Low	High	Low	High	Low	High	Low	High	Low	High	Low	High	Low	High
Not compressed	7.2% <10cm	—	3.0% 30cm	5.0% 30cm	5.3% 10cm	4.7% 10cm	4.5% 40cm	—	—	—	2.9% 10cm	13.0% 20cm	—	—	—	12.0% 10cm	—	—	5.7% 20cm	3.0% 30cm
0 MTE	—	—	—	—	—	—	3.7% 30cm	—	—	—	—	—	—	—	—	—	—	—	—	—
10 MTE	—	—	3.0% 30cm	8.7% 10cm	1.3% <10cm	13.0% 40cm	—	—	—	—	4.7% 20cm	—	—	—	2.5% <10cm	—	—	—	13.0% 20cm	
20 MTE	5.1% <10cm	—	4.5% <10cm	4.0% 20cm	8.2% <10cm	3.7% 30cm	—	—	—	—	6.8% 20cm	4.9% —	—	—	4.5% <10cm	—	—	—	7.3% 30cm	

Table 4. Maximum class probabilities at which the object was correctly recognized by the model when the drill rpm were set to V1 *(top)* and V2 *(bottom)*. For each compression level of the H5 file, we performed the inference once per video. "Low" and "High" refer to the light condition. This table shows data regarding the H5 files compressed with LineCompress.

Object predictions (V1 = 400 rpm)

Compression level	OBJECTS																			
	#1		#2		#3		#4		#5		#6		#7		#8		#9		#10	
	Low	High	Low	High	Low	High	Low	High	Low	High	Low	High	Low	High	Low	High	Low	High	Low	High
Not compressed	18.0%	86.0%	16.0%	95.0%	36.0%	40.0%	12.0%	70.0%	52.0%	37.0%	—	66.0%	13.0%	30.0%	6.0%	73.0%	—	12.0%	79.0%	79.0%
x1	8.9%	95.6%	—	84.9%	—	—	12.4%	70.2%	—	—	—	57.8%	—	—	—	10.8%	3.3%	19.8%	38.1%	50.1%
x2	10.9%	96.6%	—	77.0%	—	—	14.1%	79.3%	—	—	—	56.5%	—	5.7%	—	5.9%	3.5%	16.8%	34.9%	48.6%
x3	6.6%	46.4%	—	65.9%	—	4.0%	2.9%	54.8%	—	—	—	11.9%	—	3.9%	59.0%	9.5%	25.2%	—	—	—
x4	5.9%	38.1%	—	—	—	—	—	—	—	—	5.9%	7.5%	—	—	6.6%	46.7%	17.7%	33.3%	—	—
x5	8.7%	58.5%	—	4.9%	—	—	—	52.6%	—	—	—	11.3%	—	—	9.2%	69.4%	15.6%	—	—	—
x6	—	24.5%	—	—	—	—	—	69.5%	—	—	—	5.8%	—	—	—	16.7%	9.0%	—	—	—

Object predictions (V2 = 1500 rpm)

Compression level	OBJECTS																			
	#1		#2		#3		#4		#5		#6		#7		#8		#9		#10	
	Low	High	Low	High	Low	High	Low	High	Low	High	Low	High	Low	High	Low	High	Low	High	Low	High
Not compressed	—	72.0%	—	89.0%	17.0%	95.0%	—	43.0%	—	34.0%	—	—	—	3.0%	—	—	—	3.0%	—	38.0%
x1	—	88.8%	—	69.1%	6.2%	32.8%	—	4.5%	—	—	—	—	—	—	—	—	—	4.4%	—	7.3%
x2	—	90.6%	—	55.8%	5.7%	34.3%	—	8.8%	—	—	—	—	—	—	—	—	—	5.2%	—	5.3%
x3	—	29.9%	—	—	—	10.9%	—	13.9%	—	—	—	—	—	—	—	—	3.9%	7.1%	—	—
x4	—	23.1%	—	—	2.6%	5.0%	—	—	—	—	—	—	—	—	—	—	5.8%	12.1%	—	—
x5	—	37.7%	—	—	2.5%	10.5%	—	—	—	—	—	—	—	—	—	—	—	5.2%	—	—
x6	—	9.7%	—	—	—	4.6%	—	9.2%	—	—	—	—	—	—	—	—	—	—	—	—

In particular, we chose 10 frames that belong to the part of the video where the object is in the central area of the working space, *i.e.*, the moment in which the object is recognized the most. These data are available in Table 6. The latency values related to the recognition of object #1, in low light condition and with velocity V1, are shown in Fig. 5b.

Table 5. Maximum recognition distances when the objects move towards the camera and respective class probabilities. The drill rpm were set to V1 *(top)* and V2 *(bottom)*. In each cell we reported the maximum distance at which the object was correctly recognized by the model and the relative class probability. For each compression level of the H5 file, we performed the inference once per video. "Low" and "High" refer to the light condition. This table shows data regarding the H5 files compressed with LineCompress.

Approaching object predictions (V1 = 400 rpm)

Compression level	OBJECTS																			
	#1		#2		#3		#4		#5		#6		#7		#8		#9		#10	
	Low	High	Low	High	Low	High	Low	High	Low	High	Low	High	Low	High	Low	High	Low	High	Low	High
Not compressed	8.0% <10cm	5.3% <10cm	10.0% 40cm	5.0% 10cm	6.0% 10cm	3.9% 10cm	5.4% 50cm	—	—	—	10.0% 10cm	3.7% 20cm	5.0% 40cm	—	7.0% 10cm	5.0% 10cm	—	—	3.4% 20cm	2.2% 30cm
x1	8.6% <10cm	4.2% <10cm	8.4% 10cm	12.8% 20cm	—	5.6% 10cm	2.7% 50cm	—	—	—	—	—	—	—	5.0% <10cm	8.7% 10cm	—	—	2.0% 20cm	1.8% 20cm
x2	5.1% <10cm	9.6% <10cm	8.3% 10cm	9.7% 20cm	—	4.1% <10cm	9.6% 20cm	—	—	—	6.2% 10cm	13.0% 10cm	—	—	—	3.7% 10cm	—	—	1.0% 20cm	3.7% 20cm
x3	—	—	—	6.5% <10cm	—	—	1.8% 40cm	2.8% 20cm	—	—	—	—	—	—	7.0% <10cm	3.7% 10cm	—	—	—	—
x4	—	—	—	6.5% <10cm	—	—	1.9% 40cm	3.6% 30cm	—	—	—	—	—	—	13.1% <10cm	23.1% <10cm	—	—	—	—
x5	—	—	—	3.9% 10cm	—	—	2.5% 40cm	17.8% 20cm	—	—	5.9% 10cm	3.7% 10cm	—	—	—	9.4% <10cm	—	—	—	—
x6	—	—	—	—	—	—	1.0% 30cm	2.8% 10cm	—	—	—	—	—	—	—	4.7% <10cm	—	—	—	—

Approaching object predictions (V2 = 1500 rpm)

Compression level	OBJECTS																			
	#1		#2		#3		#4		#5		#6		#7		#8		#9		#10	
	Low	High	Low	High	Low	High	Low	High	Low	High	Low	High	Low	High	Low	High	Low	High	Low	High
Not compressed	7.2% <10cm	—	5.0% 30cm	5.3% 30cm	4.7% 10cm	4.5% 10cm	4.5% 40cm	—	—	—	2.9% 10cm	13.0% 20cm	—	—	12.0% 10cm	—	—	—	5.7% 20cm	3.0% 30cm
x1	8.6% <10cm	4.2% <10cm	8.4% 10cm	12.8% 20cm	—	5.6% <10cm	2.7% 30cm	—	—	—	—	—	—	—	13.6% <10cm	—	—	—	—	2.9% 30cm
x2	—	3.32% <10cm	—	13.4% 10cm	—	4.9% <10cm	2.0% 40cm	—	—	—	—	—	—	—	8.9% <10cm	—	—	—	—	2.5% 20cm
x3	—	—	—	—	—	—	8.7% 40cm	7.0% 10cm	—	—	—	—	—	—	42.0% <10cm	—	—	—	—	—
x4	—	—	—	—	—	—	2.4% 50cm	6.5% 10cm	—	—	—	—	—	—	38.3% <10cm	—	—	—	—	—
x5	—	—	—	—	—	—	8.9% 50cm	—	—	—	7.0% <10cm	5.7% <10cm	—	—	32.8% <10cm	—	—	—	—	—
x6	—	—	—	—	—	—	7.3% 50cm	—	—	—	—	—	—	—	8.0% <10cm	—	—	—	—	—

In Fig. 5b we reported the average inference time with respect to the nominal one. Furthermore, in order to evaluate the potential impact of using compressed weight models, we monitored the python process during the inference performed on one video, in order to achieve the CPU and memory usage (respectively in percentage and in MB), for each H5 file. For this analysis the tool `psrecord`[3] has been used to obtain the log files resulting from the sampling of the resources' usage, with a chosen sampling frequency 100 Hz (*i.e.*, 10 ms between each sample), enough to follow properly the dynamic of the inference itself (whose natural behavior is fixed at about one half second). Once the log files have been obtained, we manipulated the data and plotted them by using MATLAB. In particular, for each H5 file, we computed the average usage of the resources and compared it to the one of the non compressed H5 file (Figs. 5c and 5d). As can be observed the similar pattern seems to arise from the resources utilization of the H5 files compressed by DNNZip and by LineCompress. For example, looking at Fig. 5c it can be seen that the cost relating to the use of the first compression level (*m0* for DNNZip and *x1* for LineCompress) is not sufficient to bring advantages in terms of CPU usage while a second compression level (*m10* for DNNZip and

---

[3] `psrecord` is available online at: https://github.com/astrofrog/psrecord.

Table 6. Average inference time for each H5 file. Inference was performed on the video regarding the coffee mug in movement with velocity V1. For each H5 file we report the average inference time along all the frames of the video, and the RMSE between the average inference time and the ones measured for each frame of the video.

H5 file	Light conditions (Low/High)	Average inference time (ms)	RMSE (ms)
Not compressed	Low	622.0	10.1
	High	619.4	7.6
0 MTE	Low	622.1	11.0
	High	623.4	12.0
10 MTE	Low	614.2	12.0
	High	621.8	12.5
20 MTE	Low	615.4	10.5
	High	619.0	12.6
x1	Low	619.0	9.4
	High	618.7	13.0
x2	Low	613.4	7.8
	High	619.4	8.6
x3	Low	617.0	8.6
	High	617.6	9.3
x4	Low	623.5	14.7
	High	623.7	10.3
x5	Low	620.2	11.0
	High	621.0	14.0
x6	Low	616.1	12.5
	High	623.6	11.0

$x2$ for LineCompress) already overcomes this barrier. As you progress with the compression levels, other problems come into play related to the deterioration of inputs at the intermediate layers caused by compression at the initial layers. A dual situation arises in the case of memory usage as shown in Fig. 5d. Given that, for some level of compression, the overall performance is quite better and the loss of accuracy is not so marked.

4   Conclusions

In this work, we investigated the impact of two different weight compression techniques, originally designed for DNN hardware accelerators, in a different scenario involving general-purpose low-end hardware. After applying several weight compression levels on a MobileNet DNN model, we show how accelerator-oriented weight compression techniques can have an impact on both memory traffic pressure and inference/latency figures, still resulting in a good trade-off in terms of accuracy loss. Future work will focus on the development of tools and methodologies for automatically gathering useful information from a compression setup executed in a general-purpose architecture in order to optimize its deployment on a given hardware accelerator.

Acknowledgements. This work was supported by the Research Grants from: the Italian Ministry of University and Research (MIUR) PNR 2015 2020 within the project "MAIA Monitoraggio Attivo dell Infrastruttura", ref. ARS01_0035; MIUR PO FESR SICILIA 2014–2020 within the project "PRE-CUBE: PREdizione, PREvenzione, PRE-disposizione", ref. 086201000304; the University of Catania - Piaceri 2020–2022 - Linea 2, within the project MANGO.

References

1. Agustsson, E., et al.: Soft-to-hard vector quantization for end-to-end learning compressible representations. In: International Conference on Neural Information Processing Systems, pp. 1141–1151 (2017)
2. Ascia, G., Catania, V., Mineo, A., Monteleone, S., Palesi, M., Patti, D.: Improving inference latency and energy of dnns through wireless enabled multi-chip-module-based architectures and model parameters compression. In: 2020 14th IEEE/ACM International Symposium on Networks-on-Chip (NOCS), pp. 1–6. IEEE (2020)
3. Cavigelli, L., Rutishauser, G., Benini, L.: Ebpc: Extended bit-plane compression for deep neural network inference and training accelerators. IEEE J. Emerg. Sel. Top. Circ. Syst. **9**(4), 723–734 (2019)
4. Cheng, Y., Wang, D., Zhou, P., Zhang, T.: A survey of model compression and acceleration for deep neural networks (2017)
5. Choi, Y., El-Khamy, M., Lee, J.: Towards the limit of network quantization. CoRR abs/1612.01543 (2016)
6. Gudovskiy, D.A., Hodgkinson, A., Rigazio, L.: DNN feature map compression using learned representation over GF(2). In: European Conference on Computer Vision, September 2018
7. Han, S., Mao, H., Dally, W.: Deep compression: Compressing deep neural networks with pruning, trained quantization and huffman coding. In: International Conference on Learning Representations, October 2016
8. Krizhevsky, A., Sutskever, I., Hinton, G.E.: ImageNet classification with deep convolutional neural networks. Adv. Neural Inf. Process. Syst. **2**, 1097–1105 (2012)
9. Lahdhiri, H., et al.: Dnnzip: selective layers compression technique in deep neural network accelerators. In: 2020 23rd Euromicro Conference on Digital System Design (DSD), pp. 526–533. IEEE (2020)
10. Li, E., Zeng, L., Zhou, Z., Chen, X.: Edge AI: on-demand accelerating deep neural network inference via edge computing. IEEE Trans. Wireless Commun. **19**(1), 447–457 (2019)
11. Mazumder, A.N., et al.: A survey on the optimization of neural network accelerators for micro-AI on-device inference. IEEE J. Emerg. Sel. Top. Circ. Syst. **11**(4), 532–547 (2021)

12. Russo, E., Palesi, M., Monteleone, S., Patti, D., Mineo, A., Ascia, G., Catania, V.: DNN model compression for IoT domain specific hardware accelerators. IEEE Internet Things J. **9**(9), 6650–6662 (2022)
13. Wu, C.J., et al.: Machine learning at Facebook: understanding inference at the edge. In: 2019 IEEE International Symposium on High Performance Computer Architecture (HPCA), pp. 331–344. IEEE (2019)

Spatial Dependency in Software-Defined Networking In-Band Monitoring: Challenges and Future Perspective

Chin Jun Nan[1,2] and Tan Saw Chin[1,2(✉)]

[1] Faculty of Informatics and Computing, Multimedia University, 63100 Cyberjaya, Selangor, Malaysia
sctan1@mmu.edu.my
[2] Telekom Malaysia R&D, Jalan Persiaran Multimedia, 63100 Cyberjaya, Selangor, Malaysia

Abstract. Software-Defined Networking (SDN) enhances the current networking infrastructure to be more flexible and manageable. The traditional networking infrastructure is heavily reliant on the hardware devices resulted a difficult time controlling the network traffic flow and device configuration. In-band networking telemetry or network monitoring in SDN is focusing on the collection of the information required by the application process, managing the network by interacting with the network infrastructure with a set of application programming interfaces. These application programming interfaces will gather and retrieve the data that the monitoring applications require in order to fulfill their responsibilities by integrating all of the nodes inside the network. The order in which telemetry items are collected must be determined depending on the requests of monitoring applications, and any spatial dependency in the network must be detected. Therefore, the objectives of this paper are two folds: First, to identify the research challenges towards SDN In-band telemetry monitoring. Second, to propose the future research perspectives of the envisioned SDN telemetry monitoring.

Keywords: Software-Defined Networking (SDN) · Network monitoring · Network performance · In-band networking telemetry

1 Introduction

In-band network telemetry (INT) is a form of improved networking that can provide higher network-wide visibility [1]. The data-plane monitoring technique is able to handle short-term issues such as microbursts, load balancing, and congestion. In-band network telemetry network with programmable devices that makes low-level telemetry item easier to collect and integrate into production network flow. The header fields of the packet will refer to the telemetry instructions that need to be conducted by the devices and these commands allow the devices to collect and store packet network status data. INT has become the standard monitoring technology that can give in-depth network-wide visibility [2]. The INT notion is that network traffic packets will be created by collecting and encapsulating the low-level telemetry information. As a result, network operators

I. Awan et al. (Eds.): MobiWIS 2022, LNCS 13475, pp. 156–162, 2022.
https://doi.org/10.1007/978-3-031-14391-5_12

would troubleshoot short-term network events like micro-bursts and unbalanced load in the network. According to Nguyen et al. [3, 4] a software-defined approach, also known as software-defined networking (SDN) is becoming increasingly popular due to its flexibility in network control. The traffic information from network monitoring may be sent to the SDN controller which can calculate the network traffic. In-band network telemetry will execute monitoring over the network data planes and link each packet to a real-time network and allowing it to do fine-grained monitoring. Because it is a particularly developed framework to capture and report network characteristics from data plane, INT would allow several applications like congestion control, advanced routing, and data plane verification to be executed. INT is a new approach to SDN monitoring which it the monitoring process is performed directly on the data plane and attach the real-time network status to every packet. The primary task of INT is to gather and report the network status straight from data plane. At the same time, the network process will be made up of control parameters such as rules that specify which data in the network should be collected, and it will be set up as telemetry instructions from a central controller to other network devices.

In the network infrastructure, several nodes will be present and each node will be containing various telemetry items required by the monitoring applications. As a result, one of the issues will be determining the order of telemetry item collecting. Since the monitoring applications are having different requests for telemetry items, there may be spatial dependency while collecting telemetry items in the network. When two or more telemetry items must be gathered from the same forwarding devices or nodes, spatial dependency might be fulfilled. According to T.W. Crawford, the degree of spatial autocorrelation between independently measured values seen in geographical space is referred to as spatial dependency [14]. The research motivation of SDN in-band monitoring is to investigate how the spatial dependency affects the performance of network monitoring and the approach the in-band network monitoring discovering the best network flow for each monitoring application.

In this article, the objectives are two folds: First, to identify the research challenges towards SDN In-band telemetry monitoring. Second, to propose the future research perspectives of the envisioned SDN telemetry monitoring. The rest of this paper is therefore organized as follow: Sect. 2 presents the literature review of the related research works, Sect. 3 presents the research analysis and challenges, Sect. 4 presents the future research direction and finally, Sect. 5 presents the conclusion of this work.

2 Research Background

According to Abdulminum et al. [6], when the size of the system increase and the network requirements are changing, the movement control between hardware keys and human control of software keys becomes more difficult. The control plane of a traditional network is spread, but the communication is being done without centralized control [7]. In an SDN network, a controller will be located at the control plane and the data plane consist of the keys for data transport that has benefits such as against cyberattacks, controllable networks, and standard control activities such as transfer, creation, and distributions are all possible with SDN. Due to its central nature, it generates more efficient and effective network productivity and delivery.

A large-scale network is very complex and is hard to be managed. They could be facing a lot of short-term issues as a result of misconfigurations, hardware failure, software bugs, and load imbalance could impact the performance and revenue. SwitchPointer [8] is a network monitoring and debugging system that exploits the end-host resources, collects and monitors the telemetry data programmability. It is also used to catch up on any spurious network event occurring inside the network. SwitchPointer's main contribution is providing better network visibility for such an end-host-based system by using a switch memory as a directory. This approach is different from the in-network approach that is storing the telemetry data that is needed to diagnose network problems. SwitchPointer will switch storing the telemetry data pointers to the end host. Furthermore, Switch-Pointer debugged the spurious network event by using a distributed directory service to filter all the data that is necessary. When the network is overburdened, a problem might arise when a low-priority network flow competes with a large number of high-priority network flows on a single output port which might lead to the collection of telemetry items becoming time-consuming or even cannot find their target. The sequence in which the telemetry items are collected will be determined, which solve the priority flow problem.

One of the problems for SDN in-band monitoring will be reliability. When there is a problem during the network monitoring process, there should be a remedy available. According to Ashton et al. [9], the network management configuration of the SDN controller must be intelligent and validated in order to maximise the network availability so the network problems can be avoided and under control. Based on Vizaretta et al. [10] ONOS which is a production-grade SDN controller having unsatisfied reliability, has been discovered that the number of defects, fault detection, and resolution time were reasonably constant between versions. In legacy networks, when devices break or stop operating, the network traffic is routed through other alternative nodes in order to preserve the network flow control. Because SDN controls the whole network through a single central controller, if the central network fails, the entire network will be impacted and malfunction. ONOS is being employed because of its online availability of complete and uncensored defect reports, however there are currently insufficient samples available for ONOS to increase its accuracy of reliability estimation in SDN.

The scalability of network could be one of the challenges for SDN in-band monitoring. Layer 3 routing capabilities is utilised to link several Layer 2 networks in the traditional LAN's multi-tiered design. It does not fit well when supporting east–west traffic due to the Layer 3 devices is inside end-to-end path. Scalability of traditional local area network (LAN) is referring to the capacity of a process, network, programme, or organization to grow and manage rising demand. SDN controller must be able to compensate for network broadcast overhead and the expansion of flow table entries. It should be able to manage and support minimum 100 switches inside the network. The SDN controller is the central component of the SDN architecture, and it is responsible for creating flows, monitoring status of switches, calculating flow pathways between switches, and sending flow tables to switches to direct them in packet forwarding [12]. Early measurements of an SDN controller which is known as NOX have shown that it can manage 30 k flow initiations per second, according to Soheil et al. [13].

SDN in-band network monitoring may bring out some new network attacks due to its open interface and the attacks may affect the network performance. Various D-DOS attacks may cause the networks architecture break down and unable to function. The SYN flood attack is being described in [11], exhausting the TCP protocol's queue, is possible to knock down any organization's server. In SDN some prevention should be prepare to protect the network which include the software integrity, user authentication, network mitigation, remote access management, user authorization and network threat detection.

Due to SDN network central character, it benefits control tasks such as transfer and distribution, and it creates more efficient and effective energy, which improves network productivity and delivery. Because of its open interface, SDN in-band monitoring may result in the evolution of network attacks, which may have an impact on network topology. Aside from that, spatial dependence may be a worry in network monitoring services; if network monitoring did not incorporate spatial dependency, it would be difficult to acquire the necessary data quickly and properly. In data transportation, spatial dependence is vital for retrieving and computing the shortest pathways. To assure the shortest pathways across a network node, we will integrate spatial dependency in our model.

3 Research Analysis and Challenges

In this section, we will go through the synopsis of each publication that has been discovered and reviewed, including the aims, suggested technique and limitations. The detail shown in Table 1.

From the literature, the majority of the works discuss the use of In-Band Network Telemetry to tackle contemporary networking challenges by examine the scalability and performance of software-defined networking.

4 Future Research Direction

Aside from that, to guarantee that the telemetry items match the spatial dependence, network monitoring with Software-defined networking is suggested as future research direction as below:

1. Architecture improvement by using scalable heuristic algorithms that could determine the top boundaries for monitoring applications to tackle the detection limitation when the number of monitoring applications is being increase.
2. Modification of the algorithms or adding another algorithm could be helping to meet the monitoring needs and ensure all the telemetry items inside the network being gathered at the same time for dealing with spatial dependencies when the number of network monitoring applications is increasing.
3. The order in which the telemetry items are gathered must be specified in the design, which may address the priority flow problem.

Table 1. Summary of in-band network telemetry monitoring

Reference	Objectives	Proposed method	Limitation
[1]	To formalize the In-Band network Telemetry using the orchestration model	Evaluation of the network monitoring application's performance by checking the number of telemetry items being collected and ensure the number of spatial dependencies satisfied	The capability to detect the network anomalies reduces significantly when the number of monitoring applications is being increase
[2]	To consider monitoring needs for addressing the scalability of In-band Network Telemetry orchestration challenge	Perform the research by using a custom algorithm that is based on Greedy Randomized Adaptive Search and a local-search procedure that can avoid exceeding the local maximums	The offered solutions struggle to deal with spatial dependencies when the number of network monitoring applications is increasing
[3]	To overcome the constraints of conventional monitoring approaches, such as performance limitation	To allow real-time network monitoring, an In-Band Network Telemetry (INT) architecture has been present with implemented in an Open Network Operating System (ONOS) controller	The CPU utilization grows linearly in proportion to the amount of INT packets delivered to the ONOS
[8]	To determine if SwitchPointer could efficiently monitor and troubleshoot network problems, many of which were difficult or perhaps impossible to solve with present architectures	SwitchPointer enables existing systems to be solved by dividing time into epochs and maintaining a pointer to all end-hosts, switches incorporate the switchID and current epochID into packet header before forwarding a packet	When the network is overwhelmed, a problem may occur when a low-priority network flow competes with a large number of high-priority network flows on a single output port, causing the collection of telemetry items to become time-consuming or perhaps impossible

(continued)

Table 1. (*continued*)

Reference	Objectives	Proposed method	Limitation
[12]	To ensure adequate control plane performance and high controller availability in SDN, the workflow of active controllers, as well as the availability of control channels and their delay performance should be maintained dynamically	Managing the amount of controllers, switches, and control flows allocated to each other, as well as traffic though control channels in order to ensure load-balancing for both controllers and control traffic	The dynamic control plane includes not only dynamic control channels, but also dynamic end points, such as controllers and switches. The use of dynamic end points on a large scale necessitates the use of a cloud support system

5 Conclusion

Software-Defined Networking (SDN) enhances the current networking infrastructure to be more flexible and manageable. In-band networking telemetry in SDN is focusing on the collection of the information required by the application process, managing the network by interacting with the network infrastructure with a set of application programming interfaces. The order in which telemetry items are collected must be determined depending on the requests of monitoring applications, and any spatial dependency in the network must be detected. Based on the research challenges identified, future research perspectives of the envisioned SDN telemetry monitoring were suggested.

References

1. Hohemberger, R., et al.: Orchestrating in-band data plane telemetry with machine learning. IEEE Commun. Lett. **23**(12), 2247–2251 (2019). https://doi.org/10.1109/lcomm.2019.294 6562
2. Hohemberger, R., Lorenzon, A.F., Rossi, F.D., Luizelli, M.C.: A heuristic approach for large-scale orchestration of the in-band data plane telemetry problem. In: Barolli, L., Amato, F., Moscato, F., Enokido, T., Takizawa, M. (eds) Advanced Information Networking and Applications. AINA 2020. AISC, vol. 1151. Springer, Cham (2020). https://doi.org/10.1007/978-3-030-44041-1_35
3. Van Tu, N., Hyun, J., Hong, J.W.-K.: Towards ONOS-based SDN monitoring using in-band network telemetry. In: 2017 19th Asia-Pacific Network Operations and Management Symposium (APNOMS) (2017). https://doi.org/10.1109/apnoms.2017.8094182
4. Medina, A., Lakhina, A., Matta, I., Byers, J.: BRITE: an approach to universal topology generation. In: Proc. MASCOTS (2001)
5. Albert, R., Barabási, A.L.: Topology of evolving networks: local events and universality. Phys. Rev. Lett. **85**, 5234–5237 (2000)
6. Abdulsammad, A.A., Abdullah, M.Z.: Recent techniques in software-defined network (SDN) - IJNTR. https://www.ijntr.org/download_data/IJNTR05080019.pdf. Accessed 25 Oct 2021
7. Haji, S.H., et al.: Comparison of software-defined networking with traditional networking. Asian J. Res. Comput. Sci. https://www.journalajrcos.com/index.php/AJRCOS/article/view/30216. Accessed 26 Oct 2021

8. Tammana, P., Agarwal, R., Lee, M.: Distributed network monitoring and debugging with Switchpointer. USENIX (1970). https://www.usenix.org/conference/nsdi18/presentation/tam mana. Accessed 10 Oct 2021
9. Ashton, M., et al.: Ten things to look for in an SDN controller. Technical Report (2013). http://www.ashtonmetzler.com/How%20to%20Evaluate%20SDN%20Cont rollers.pdf. Accessed 18 Jan 2022
10. Vizarreta, P., Trivedi, K., Helvik, B., Heegaard, P., Kellerer, W., Machuca, C.M.: An empirical study of software reliability in SDN controllers. In: 2017 13th International Conference on Network and Service Management (CNSM), pp. 1–9 (2017). https://doi.org/10.23919/CNSM. 2017.8256002
11. Rana, D.S., Garg, N., Chamoli, S.K.: A study and detection of TCP SYN flood attacks with IP spoofing and its mitigations. Int. J. Comput. Technol. Appl. 3(4), 1476–1480 (2012). https://www.researchgate.net/publication/267726062_A_Studyand_Dettion_of_TCP_SYN_Flood_Attacks_with_IP_spoofing_and_its_Mitigations/citation/download
12. Dynamic control plane for SDN at scale. https://www.researchgate.net/publication/327783 339_Dynamic_Control_Plane_for_SDN_at_Scale. Accessed 27 Feb 2022
13. On scalability of software-defined networking. https://www.cs.toronto.edu/~soheil/papers/sdnscalability-ieeemag.pdf. Accessed 27 Feb 2022
14. Spatial dependence - an overview. ScienceDirect Topics. https://www.sciencedirect.com/topics/earth-and-planetary-sciences/spatial-dependence#:~:text=Spatial%20dependence%20refers%20to%20the,singular%20measure%20of%20spatial%20dependence. Accessed 16 Mar 2022

Smart Systems and Applications

What is a Smart Service?

Johannes Brill[✉] and Volker Nissen

Technische Universität Ilmenau, Helmholtzplatz 3, 98693 Ilmenau, Germany
{johannes.brill,volker.nissen}@tu-ilmenau.de

Abstract. In this paper, we argue that the traditional view of a smart service as something that is tied to a physical product is too limited. After reviewing key aspects of smart services in the literature, we propose a broader definition that retains key characteristics while opening up the concept for a broader, intangible context, such as the professional service industry. In order to make the term even more specific, a checklist is developed that classifies services as (not) smart, based on a range of different criteria. These criteria are generated from a structured literature review and supplemental interviews with subject experts. Finally, the usefulness of the new definition and the associated checklist is demonstrated with an example from automated auditing.

Keywords: Smart service · Internet of things · Digital transformation · Professional service industry · Consulting virtualization

1 Motivation, Research Problem and Methodology

The term smart service is generally understood as a service that offers added value based on data from a smart product with strong interaction between the service pro-vider and the customer [1, 3, 7, 11]. A prominent example from an industrial perspective is predictive maintenance. Aircraft turbine manufacturers such as General Electric or Rolls-Royce offer their customers a data-driven maintenance service that calculates a maintenance interval for the respective aircraft based on the engine's sensor data, flight routes, weather data, and internal company maintenance data, so that the aircraft's downtime and repair times are optimized [4].

We consider this hardware-related understanding of the term 'smart service' as too limited. This is motivated by our research focus on professional services, where highly intangible solutions are provided to customers, and themes such as service virtualization, algorithmic consulting, and automated customer self-services are currently discussed that have an association to smart services [38–40]. Consequently, in this paper we argue for a broadened definition of a 'smart service' together with a checklist of characteristics that helps to differentiate a smart service from other concepts.

The research is initially based on a structured literature review, following Webster and Watson [46]. For this work, the literature databases Google Scholar, IEEE Xplore, the Web of Science, EBSCOHost (Business Source Primer) and SpringerLink are used, where we focus on highly rated journal articles. With regards to our research focus on professional services, three search strings are used (listed below):

© The Author(s), under exclusive license to Springer Nature Switzerland AG 2022
I. Awan et al. (Eds.): MobiWIS 2022, LNCS 13475, pp. 165–178, 2022.
https://doi.org/10.1007/978-3-031-14391-5_13

1. *"Smart service" NOT "city" NOT "grid" NOT "meter" NOT "cities" NOT "home"*
2. *"Smart service consulting" OR "smart consulting service" OR "consulting automation" OR "digital consulting" OR "consulting 4.0" OR "digital consulting service" OR "virtual consulting service"*
3. *"Smart service advisory" OR "smart advisory service" OR "digital advisory" OR "digital advisory" OR "advisory 4.0" OR "advisory automation" OR "smart virtual advisory service"*

To ensure that the articles are up to date, the search is restricted to articles from 2016 onwards. Only articles in German and English were used. The results of the initial hit list (see Table 1) are then narrowed down based on relevance (title and abstract check). This search is supplemented by a forward and backward search for further literature and duplicates are removed. The search (86 articles) is finally evaluated in the form of a concept matrix (not presented here due to space limitations) in terms of the addressed industry, the service level (general services, professional services, consulting services), applied concepts and technologies (e.g., platforms, AI, blockchains, Big Data Analytics) and the adopted digitalization approach (e.g., virtualization, servitization, smart services, smart service systems).

Table 1. Initial hit list

Database	Search string	Number of initial hits	Number of hits after filtering
IEEE Xplore	1	747	405
	2	1282	383
	3	374	97
SpringerLink	1	2678	395
	2	70	70
	3	23	23
EBSCOHost (Business Source Primer)	1	412	117
	2	687	16
	3	237	8
Google Scholar	1	2280	400
	2	28	27
	3	13	11
Web of Science (Core)	1	402	277
	2	3710	43
	3	1960	19

To ensure relevance and plausibility in practice regarding the identified concepts and to evaluate and verify the completeness and suitability of the extended smart service definition and checklist, expert interviews are held following the procedure of Döring and Bortz [9] and Meuser and Nagel [34]. Nine such interviews are conducted with experienced staff from professional service firms, mainly consulting and IT service providers (see Table 2). The average work experience of the interviewees is more than eight years, while eight out of nine interview partners come from companies with more than 3,000 employees. Semi-structured interviews are used here. On the one hand, this procedure offers the advantage that the interview has a uniform structure and a common thread, and on the other hand, individual comments from the experts can be addressed in detail. Interviews are transcribed and condensed according to the methodology. The interviewees are asked about their experiences with smart services and their possible characteristics, their assessment of the extended smart service definition and the smart service checklist, as well as potential fields of application and implications for their profession and industry.

Table 2. Details about the interviewees (n = 9)

Category	Details	Number of interviewees
Profession	Consultants	6
	Other professions	3
Work experience	<5 years	4
	5–10 years	2
	>10 years	3
Company size	<3000 employees	1
	>3000 employees	8
Company Location	Germany	8
	Netherlands	1
Industry	Consulting	5
	IT service provider	2
	Insurance	1
	Logistics and process automation	1

In the following section, the current understanding of what makes up a smart service is highlighted, followed by a critical analysis of the limitations. Then a new, expanded definition is suggested that keeps key characteristics while removing unnecessary limitations. Thereafter, the old and new definition are compared. In order to ease the classification of a given service as (not) smart, a checklist is then developed. Finally, the practicability and usefulness of this checklist is shown in an example from the auditing sector, before the article is brought to a conclusion.

2   The Current Understanding of a Smart Service

Despite its widespread use, the term smart service is not clearly defined in the literature [14, 37, 44]. As a combination of the terms smart and service, the first part of the overall term presents a definitional challenge. The term smart is associated with intelligence. There are various views on smartness in the literature when smart services are discussed, which are briefly highlighted below.

The product-centric view describes smartness/intelligence as the integration of components into the product itself, as well as the networking of these products [28]. Porter and Heppelmann [42], like many other authors (e.g. Wunderlich et al. [49], Beverungen et al. [6]) highlight the relevance of a smart product as a fundamental premise for the development of a smart service. It describes an object equipped with "sensor technology and capable of being networked" [1, 36, 42] that is capable of collecting data on product state, usage, and environment [36]. Smart products include: (1) physical components (e.g., hardware), (2) smart components (e.g., sensors, data storage, software, or embedded systems), and (3) connectivity components (e.g., protocols or networks) [28].

Another perspective refers to the learning capabilities of a smart service in the context of human and machine interaction. Here, the intelligence of a technology refers to learning from machine-to-machine or human-to-machine communication [28]. The focus is on creating customized services and on how both the digital technology and the humans involved in co-production can learn [28, 32]. To this end, Huang and Rust [20] present four stages of artificial intelligence (AI). The first level (mechanical intelligence) describes the case where a system has minimal learning or adaptation capabilities, while a level two system (analytical intelligence) has data-based learning and adaptation capabilities. The third level (intuitive intelligence) encompasses the capabilities of a system to make boundedly rational decisions. The last level describes empathic intelligence, which is characterized by an ability to learn and adapt based on experience and emotion. Gavrilova and Kokoulina [14] assume in the context of smart services that intelligence has two core components. Anthropomorphic characteristics refer to smart technologies taking on human tasks that initially do not appear to be solvable by machines. In turn, the use of AI is necessary because humans are not able to collect and quickly analyze large amounts of real-time data.

The third perspective focuses on the implementation and beneficial results of a smart service and less on the availability of technical performance features. Here, customer benefit of the service and the question of how the customer uses the service are addressed. Furthermore, this view deals with the analysis of involved actors, their goals and values [28].

By contrast, the term service is described more clearly in the literature. A service is "a process that consists of a set of activities which take place in interactions between a customer and people, goods and other physical resources, systems and/or infrastructures representing the service provider and possibly involving other customers, which aims at assisting the customer's everyday practices" [18]. From a historical perspective, the compound term smart service can be seen as the result of the evolution of previous concepts, including teleservices and remote (diagnostic) services [27].

Allmendinger und Lombreglia [1] argue that a service to be 'smart' the service providers must integrate intelligence into the product to provide the service (product-centric view). Moreover, according to these authors, smart services have a fundamentally preventive character and open up new added value for the customer, primarily in the form of improved processes, product performance or the avoidance of unwanted events [1]. This is necessary because microprocessors and sensors in the products generate an enormous amount of data records that cannot be analyzed without machine intelligence [1]. The functions of a smart service range from simple monitoring tasks, remote control and optimization functions in operation, to fully autonomous action in decision-making [43].

In addition, other definitional approaches exist in the literature. Moser et al. [35] e.g., speak of "IT-supported services [...] that represent new value creation structures in the design of relationships between manufacturers and end users". Frank et al. [12] and Koldewey et al. [27] describe a smart service as a digital, data-based service built on top of a physical product. Wellsandt et al. [47] speak of a "hybrid service bundle", composed of physical and intangible parts.

Particularly against the background of Service Dominant Logic (SDL) raised by Vargo and Lush, the idea of value co-creation is promoted by some authors with regard to a smart service. In this context, customer and service provider achieve added value through strong interaction and collaboration in the service creation process [31, 45].

In addition, a smart service must be distinguished from a digital service. According to Werth et al. [48], a digital service is a service "[...] which results from the transformation of its potentially marketable production process by means of (...) technology, into a more efficient and/or effective process". Beverungen et al. [5] assume that a digital service, in contrast to a smart service, does not require the use of a smart product at all. A digital service can thus be built exclusively on information systems (e.g., a database). Götz et al. [16] name four aspects in which smart services differ from traditional services:

1. A smart service uses embedded information and communication technologies (ICT) that enable data transmission and information generation.
2. It integrates Big Data analyses and is realized through these.
3. A smart service is either fully or at least partially automated and aligned with human interaction. Such automated service actions are only possible through the integration of intelligent components such as cognitive systems.
4. From the customer's point of view, a smart service offers greater individualization of the service by reacting to environmental conditions or customer preferences (e.g., smart services adapt based on the user's location data).

3 An Extended Definition of Smart Services

3.1 Current Limitations and Conclusion

A limitation of the current smart services concept is the dependency on or necessity of a (physical) smart product as the basis for a smart service. Thus, a smart service is often understood as a hybrid service bundle consisting of digital and physical services [13, 22, 35, 47]. However, this product-centric view does not reflect the current evolution of companies towards an increasing service orientation [20]. Following Knote et al. [26], customers use a smart service because of social, monetary, or hedonistic motivations rather than the characteristics of the physical product itself [10, 26]. In addition, it is not predominantly the smart product that should be seen as the basis for the smart service. Rather, the data which is integrated via an interface to the environment as well as its analysis and aggregation are the basis of service creation [22, 23]. Consequently, a detachment of the smart service concept from an inevitable coupling to a smart product appears to be purposeful and expands the application possibilities to further subject areas, such as the professional service industry. This also supports the trend toward an increasing service orientation of companies across industry boundaries.

Another limitation of the term smart service relates to the use of communication channels and interfaces to the environment. Here, some definitions implicitly or explicitly feature Internet communication as an essential component [2, 3, 22, 44]. Other authors, however, speak more generally of information and communication technologies [16]. Basically, a smart service is characterized by providing a data-based solution of given tasks (e.g., decision making and support). Communication with other information systems is essential to provide the service to the customer. Furthermore, it is assumed that a smart service has an interface to the environment so that, for instance, requests and customer data can be integrated. Some authors explicitly assume digital platforms as interface technologies in this context [8]. This restriction appears too strict, as the data does not necessarily have to be collected and made available via a platform. The exact design of the information and communication technologies and interfaces used (e.g., platforms, chat-bots, or virtual avatars) is not restricted, but the technology selection is considered specific to the smart service use case.

Another discussion point is when a smart service is considered to be smart. From a product-centric point of view, the physical product is networked and provided with digital functions, which no longer seems appropriate in the context of increasing requirements [28]. Furthermore, this view restricts the scope of application too much. In the opinion of two of our nine interviewees, a smart service does not require any limitation of the technology but consists in particular of a beneficial solution to a specific customer problem. The technology used must be appropriate to that problem. Four of our interview partners see automation/reduction of human interaction in service provision as a key feature of a smart service. Against the background of increasing data volumes and fully automated processes, only a technology-based approach is capable of processing large volumes of data in a reasonable amount of time.

If, on the other hand, the ability to learn and adapt is considered, the goal of a smart service is to map or mimic human intelligence through artificial intelligence [24]. This approach raises the question of what technology can map these capabilities. Also, three of our interviewees mention AI as a possible, narrower demarcation criterion in the definition of a smart service. In addition, experience knowledge as part of the database can also suggest intelligence, so that sufficiently large data sets can also exhibit intelligence by means of case-based reasoning. Similarly, systems consisting of explicit expert knowledge (knowledge base) and a logic for drawing conclusions from this knowledge base could be applied in a smart service as so-called expert systems or knowledge systems [24]. Eventually, the use of such forms of AI distinguishes smart services from other services (esp. digital services, such as online banking). It is assumed that a smart service, which has the level of mechanical intelligence and, according to Huang and Rust [20], includes intelligent algorithms, has a minimum of learning or adaptation capability. The transitions here are fluid. A pure knowledge compilation based on search results, which in principle only outputs a rudimentary hit list, is not capable of learning or adaptation. However, if the hit list were to prioritize or recommend based on past searches or based on thresholds, this minimal learning or adaptive capability would be present.

Finally, referring to the interviews conducted, the term individualized as a characteristic of a smart service is in practice often associated with the development of special software solutions for individual customers and not with customer needs per se, so we prefer the term user-centric for a smart service instead.

In summary, it can be stated that the term smart service is by no means unambiguous nor uniformly defined in the literature. It is clear that the characteristics and definitions so far are unnecessarily limiting and necessitate the need for an expanded definition. Therefore, the following extended smart service definition is suggested that encompasses all three discussed perspectives of smartness (product-centric, learning and adaptability, beneficial results for the customer):

A smart service is a user-centric, context-specific service that draws data from an interface to its environment and uses artificial intelligence for task processing to provide at least one beneficial solution to a customer's problem.

3.2 Old and New Definition in Comparison

In their editorial on smart services, Allmendinger and Lombreglia [1] highlight the fundamental preventive and evidence-based nature of this type of service. For them, a key goal is the prevention of unexpected events, such as machine component failures. Our extended definition abstracts this view and speaks more generally of task processing, which renders a beneficial solution for a customer problem. This includes preventing failures of machines, but also addresses other customer problems, possibly outside manufacturing. The evidence-based character is considered by the integration of data through an interface. Allmendinger and Lombreglia [1] mention machine intelligence as an essential feature of a smart service that is used for data processing. In the extended definition, we speak of artificial intelligence, which is a more common term today, but can be equated with machine intelligence following Knote et al. [26]. In the extended definition, AI is taken up as a distinguishing criterion compared to other services.

Beverungen et al. [5], Frank et al. [12], Wunderlich et al. [49], and Porter and Heppelmann [42], among others, emphasize the inherent coupling of a smart service with a smart product. This exclusive condition is not followed by the extended smart service definition here. In fact, this relationship is not seen as a basic premise, but merely as a possible source of data for service creation. Rather, it is the data that is obtained via an interface that is decisive for tailored service creation. However, a smart service is not necessarily a purely digital service, since a smart service can contain physical components (e.g., along the lines of a smart coffee machine that prepares a desired coffee variation at a preferred temperature based on the user's voice).

While Bullinger et al. [8] address the provision of a smart service via an integrated service platform and emphasize individuality and the customer context to be included in the service creation, Anke et al. [3] cite communication via the Internet as a key feature of a smart service. The extended definition of this work does not make any delimitation at this point as to which technologies are used for the provision of a smart service. This choice depends on the individual use case of the smart service. The extended definition also uses the terms user-centric and context-specific, since the term individualization is often associated in our interviews with individual software adaptation to a specific customer context.

4   A Smart Service Checklist for Service Classification

4.1   Foundations

In the literature, there seems to be no procedure for checking a service under consideration for classification as a smart service. In order to identify the current application status of smart services in the professional service and consulting industry, a website analysis (not detailed here) of top 15 management consultancies (by revenue) and leading 15 IT consulting and system integration companies in Germany (based on [28, 29]) is carried out. In particular, the term 'smart service' and asset-based consulting solutions in the field of data and analytics as well as AI are searched for. These results as well as findings from our interviews suggest that solutions outside manufacturing exist which meet our new definition of a smart service, without currently being labeled this way. Furthermore, the reverse case also occurs, where the term smart service is used for service offerings where the smartness is at least doubtful and the term is largely used for marketing purposes or as a buzzword. Therefore, we decided to develop a checklist for classifying services as being (not) smart.

This smart service checklist (Fig. 1) represents an artifact in a Design Science sense [19, 41]. It serves to provide the user with a tool to perform an assessment, e.g., review his/her existing service portfolio to determine the level of smartness in it. The smart service checklist is focused on the assessment of a single/stand-alone service for classification as (not) smart service and does not consider combination of different services (e.g., several smart and/or not smart services). However, this aspect should be addressed in further research, but requires a common understanding of term 'smart service', for which the extended smart service definition and checklist constitutes a basis. The employed criteria and associated assessment questions are mainly derived from our extended smart service definition, which in turn incorporates results from the literature analysis as well as contributions of the nine expert interviews. Finally, the criteria/questions are checked for completeness and consistency using the requirements of method engineering compiled by Greiffenberg [17].

4.2   Explaining the Checklist

The Smart Service Checklist has four subareas of equal importance and must be answered completely for a comprehensive assessment: 1. Basic Requirements: This subarea deals

Category/Criterion	Criteria fulfilled?
Basic Requirements	
Is the object a service?	
Is the service data-based?	
Is the service basically automated?	
User Perspective	
Is the service individualized to the customer's needs (user-centric) and adapted for their use case (context-specific)?	
Does the service provide at least one solution to a (partial) problem of the customer?	
Interface	
Does the service utilize an interface to its environment in order to aquire data?	
Technology Use	
Are technologies used for service creation that essentially attempt to imitate human intelligence or does the service at least have minimal learning or adaptation capabilities?	
Evaluation	
The object of consideration is a Smart Service (all criteria above are met)	yes / no

Fig. 1. Smart service checklist

with basic assumptions and requirements that the object of consideration must meet. 2. User Perspective: It deals with issues relating to the interaction between the service provider and the customer, focusing in particular on the user orientation of the service and the resulting added value. 3. Interface: This subarea covers the interaction of the service with its environment. 4. Technology Use: This subarea focuses on the technology used for data processing or problem solving. The smart service checklist is illustrated in Fig. 1, while the four subareas are explained in more detail below.

Basic Requirements

This subsection contains three questions. First, is the object under consideration even a service. Since a smart service is by definition built on data and not based on arbitrary assumptions, a data-based service must be present to confirm the basic assumptions [8, 16, 47]. What kind of data is required for service provision depends on the individual use case and is addressed indirectly in the other categories.

Furthermore, smart services are basically automated [16]. As far as possible, the service should not include any human components, but is provided automatically using various information and communication technologies [23]. It should be emphasized here that some human interaction with the system may be present, for example, in the case of task confirmation by an employee for further service processing. But this is triggered automatically by the smart service and the service as such still runs autonomously.

User Perspective

The user perspective assesses the added value of the service and its user orientation, as demanded by Moser et al. [35]. The benefits of the smart service must outweigh the risks of using it. The scope of application ranges from simple monitoring tasks to in-depth analysis or the derivation of recommendations for action, to the independent control of systems and autonomous decision-making [15, 25, 33, 49]. Of course, the industry background is important here. Further context specificities of the service may result from varying user inputs or the necessity to analyze datasets adapted to the customer context.

Interface

A service that is classified as a smart service must have an interface to its environment in order to acquire relevant data. The exact design of this interface does not have to be further specified here, and the technologies used to implement it are variable. Keyboard may be used for human interaction with the smart service, or alternatively a chatbot or voice assistant which recognizes natural language. Even the use of virtual avatars as an interface is conceivable. Interaction via a smart product (e.g., in the form of a robot) or a digital platform would also be possible. Furthermore, there is no restriction on the origin of the data, as our interviewees point out. Data may stem from the customer, other external sources, or simply from the service provider's database.

Use of Technology

For task processing and the derivation of a solution to the (partial) problem of the customer, some form of AI must be used to classify a service as a smart service. This requires that technologies are used for service creation and task processing that essentially attempt to imitate human intelligence or render at least minimal learning or adaptation capabilities of the service. We deliberately avoid naming particular AI technologies here, as this field is highly dynamic, and similar results can be achieved using different approaches.

4.3 Demonstration of the Checklist: Automated Financial Statement Audit

As part of an annual audit, companies must submit many documents to the respective auditor. In this process, the company's compliance is checked and the accuracy of the annual financial statements is assessed by an auditing firm. As a rule, all relevant documents of the client are handed over to the auditor. These are then checked for gaps and errors regarding applicable laws and regulatory requirements as part of manual analyses by the auditors and subject matter experts. Finally, an audit opinion is issued and discussed in cooperation with the client. This service can also be provided by a software solution, or the auditor can be supported by corresponding software during the audit. For example, Optical Character Recognition (OCR)-software enables scanning of corporate documents. Using techniques based on machine learning, these can then be automatically evaluated in terms of accuracy and checked for compliance – a service already in use, as explained by some of our interviewed experts from an auditing firm. The suggested smart service checklist is now used to classify an automated financial statement audit.

We initially check if such a solution can be considered a service that is automated and based on data. Depending on the client, the data in auditing is available in different formats. It can be assumed that these are typically digital documents (e.g. invoices), reports from ERP systems and spreadsheets in standardized formats. Paper documents would first have to be digitized with OCR-software. It can thus be assumed that the audit software works on a database. With regard to automation, it should be noted that discussions or interviews with client staff are typically carried out as part of an audit. These interviews are excluded from the example because they can only be digitally mapped to an insufficient extent. AI systems are currently not yet capable of conducting complete conversations [21]. The use case is therefore limited to the evaluation and analysis of documents that are available to the auditing company in digital form. However, standardized documentation of interviews (e.g. templates filled by a consultant or auditor) could be included in the audit database. Consequently, an automated audit meets the basic requirements for a smart service.

In order to fulfill the user perspective, the service must react in a user-centric and context-specific manner adapted to the client. Audit software is able to apply relevant regulatory requirements (e.g., due to the industry, company size, or location) to the client, including for example selecting an accounting standard. The service can also check the accuracy of the client's financial statements and identify deviations in reporting periods as verified by our interview partners. Furthermore, the goal of a smart service is to provide a beneficial solution for a (partial) problem of the customer. This criterion is to be judged for the use case as follows. The customer in this case is the client of the audit firm, while the user of the audit software is the auditor. As the client must perform an audit of the annual financial statements and cannot do this independently, the auditing software solves this problem in a beneficial way in that the audit takes less time than a manual audit. Moreover, fewer resources are tied up and thus cost advantages are created as compared to classical auditing. Thus, the criteria in this dimension are fulfilled.

The audit software must have an interface to its environment for classification as a smart service. For this purpose, a digital platform is utilized in the present use case on which the client can store audit documents, which are then automatically analyzed. Other interfaces to the environment would be conceivable, such as extracting data from an ERP-system.

In the final dimension of our smart service checklist, the task processing software must apply some form of AI. In the application scenario described, OCR is initially used for text recognition. Then, due to the amount of data, Big Data and AI-techniques are employed to analyze these data sets appropriately in time, interpret the data, and identify anomalies in the client's records efficiently. Thus, this application scenario meets the technology criteria for a smart service. All mandatory criteria for a smart service are given. As a result, the automated audit of the annual financial statements is a smart service in the sense of the checklist and our underlying extended definition.

5   Conclusion

In this paper we have argued that the traditional view of a smart service as something that is tied to a physical product is too limited, as smart services can, in our view, also be found in the service sector that is inherently intangible. Therefore, after reviewing key aspects of a smart service from the literature, we proposed a broader definition that contains important key characteristics and opens up the concept for a broader context. In order to provide a more rigorous definition of the term 'smart service', a checklist was developed that classifies services either as 'smart' or 'not smart', based on a range of different criteria. These criteria were generated from a structured literature review and supplemented by interviews with subject matter experts. The practicability and usefulness of the new definition and the associated checklist was then demonstrated in a practical example from the auditing domain.

With our proposal we hope to foster a fruitful discussion to overcome the unnecessarily limited scope of smart service definitions so far. Our own research is currently centered around the question where smart services can be applied in highly intangible settings, such as management consulting. Moreover, we investigate the relationship of self-services and smart services in the context of the digital transformation of the consulting industry.

References

1. Allmendinger, G., Lombreglia, R.: Four strategies for the age of smart services. Harv. Bus. Rev. **83**(10), 1–11 (2005)
2. Anke, J.: Design-integrated financial assessment of smart services. Electron. Mark. **29**(1), 19–35 (2019). https://doi.org/10.1007/s12525-018-0300-y
3. Anke, J., Poeppelbuss, J., Alt, R.: It takes more than two to tango: identifying roles and patterns in multi-actor smart service innovation. Schmalenbach Bus. Rev. **72**(4), 599–634 (2020). https://doi.org/10.1007/s41464-020-00101-2
4. Beverungen, D., Breidbach, C.F., Poeppelbuss, J., Tuunainen, V.K.: Smart service systems: an interdisciplinary perspective. Inf. Syst. J. **29**(6), 1201–1206 (2019). https://doi.org/10.1111/isj.12275
5. Beverungen, D., Kundisch, D., Wünderlich, N.: Transforming into a platform provider: strategic options for industrial smart service providers. J. Serv. Manage. **32**(4), 507–532 (2021). https://doi.org/10.1108/JOSM-03-2020-0066
6. Beverungen, D., Matzner, M., Janiesch, C.: Information systems for smart services. Inf. Syst. e-Bus. Manage. **15**(4), 781–787 (2017)
7. Beverungen, D., Müller, O., Matzner, M., Mendling, J., vom Brocke, J.: Conceptualizing smart service systems. Electron. Mark. **29**(1), 7–18 (2019). https://doi.org/10.1007/s12525-017-0270-5
8. Bullinger, H.J., Neuhüttler, J., Nagele, R., Woyke, I.: Collaborative development of business models in smart service ecosystems. In: Portland International Conference on Management of Engineering and Technology (PICMET), pp. 1–9, IEEE, Portland (2017)
9. Döring, N., Bortz, J.: Forschungsmethoden und Evaluation. 5th edn. Springer, Wiesbaden (2016). https://doi.org/10.1007/978-3-642-41089-5
10. Edvardsson, B., Tronvoll, B., Gruber, T.: Expanding understanding of service exchange and value co-creation: a social construction approach. J. Acad. Mark. Sci. **39**(2), 327–339 (2011)
11. Fischer, M., Heim, D., Hofmann, A., Janiesch, C., Klima, C., Winkelmann, A.: A taxonomy and archetypes of smart services for smart living. Electron. Mark. **30**(1), 131–149 (2020)
12. Frank, M., Gausemeier, J., von Widdern, N., Koldewey, C., Menzefricke, J.S., Reinhold, J.: A reference process for the smart service business: development and practical implications. In: Proceedings of the 2020 ISPIM Connects: Partnering for an Innovative Community, Bangkok (2020)
13. Freitag, M., Wiesner, S.: Smart service lifecycle management: a framework and use case. In: IFIP International Conference on Advances in Production Management Systems, pp. 97–104. Springer, Cham (2018). https://doi.org/10.1007/978-3-319-99707-0_13
14. Gavrilova, T., Kokoulina, L.: Smart services classification framework. In: Proceedings of the Federated Conference on Computer Science and Information Systems, pp. 203–207. Lodz, Poland (2015)
15. Gonçalves, L., Patrício, L., Grenha Teixeira, J., Wünderlich, N.V.: Understanding the customer experience with smart services. J. Serv. Manage. **31**(4), 723–744 (2020). https://doi.org/10.1108/JOSM-11-2019-0349
16. Götz, C., Hohler, S., Benz, C.: Towards managing smart service innovation: a literature review. In: Satzger, G., Patrício, L., Zaki, M., Kühl, N., Hottum, P. (eds) Exploring Service Science. IESS 2018. LNBIP, vol. 331. Springer, Cham (2018). https://doi.org/10.1007/978-3-030-00713-3_8

17. Greiffenberg, S.: Methodenentwicklung in Wirtschaft und Verwaltung. Kovač, Hamburg (2004)
18. Grönroos, C.: Service logic revisited: who creates value? And who co-creates? Eur. Bus. Rev. **20**(4), 298–314 (2008)
19. Hevner, A.R., March, S.T., Park, J., Ram, S.: Design science in information systems research. MIS Q. **28**(1), 75–105 (2004). https://doi.org/10.2307/25148625
20. Huang, M.H., Rust, R.T.: Artificial intelligence in service. J. Serv. Res. **21**(2), 155–172 (2018). https://doi.org/10.1177/1094670517752459
21. Johannsen, F., Schaller, D., Klus, M.F.: Value propositions of chatbots to support innovation management processes. Inf. Syst. e-Bus. Manage. **19**(1), 205–246 (2021). https://doi.org/10.1007/s10257-020-00487-z
22. Jussen, P., Kuntz, J., Senderek, R., Moser, B.: Smart service engineering. In: Procedia CIRP (83), pp. 384–388 (2019). https://doi.org/10.1016/j.procir.2019.04.089
23. Kaltenbach, F., Marber, P., Gosemann, C., Bölts, T., Kühn, A.: Smart services maturity level in Germany. In: 2018 IEEE International Conference on Engineering. Technology and Innovation (ICE/ITMC), pp. 1–7. IEEE, Stuttgart (2018)
24. Kaplan, J.: Künstliche Intelligenz: Eine Einführung. 1st edn. MITP (2017)
25. Klein, M.M., Biehl, S.S., Friedli, T.: Barriers to smart services for manufacturing companies. J. Bus. Ind. Mark. **33**(6), 846–856 (2018). https://doi.org/10.1108/JBIM-10-2015-0204
26. Knote, R., Janson, A., Söllner, M., Leimeister, J.M.: Value co-creation in smart services: a functional affordances perspective on smart personal assistants. J. Assoc. Inf. Syst. **22**(2), 418–458 (2021). https://doi.org/10.17705/1jais.00667
27. Koldewey, C., Meyer, M., Stockbrügger, P., Dumitrescu, R., Gausemeier, J.: Framework and functionality patterns for smart service innovation. In: Procedia CIRP (91), pp. 851–857 (2020). https://doi.org/10.1016/j.procir.2020.02.244
28. Lee, J.Y.H., Hsu, C., Silva, L.: What lies beneath: unraveling the generative mechanisms of smart technology and service design. J. Assoc. Inf. Syst. **21**(6), 1621–1643 (2020). https://doi.org/10.17705/1jais.00648
29. Lünendonk: Lünendonk®-Liste 2021: Führende IT-Beratungs- und Systemintegrations-Unternehmen in Deutschland (2021). www.luenendonk.de/produkte/listen/. Accessed 31 Dec 2021
30. Lünendonk: Lünendonk®-Liste 2021: Führende Managementberatungs-Unternehmen in Deutschland (2021). www.luenendonk.de/produkte/listen/. Accessed 27 Nov 2021
31. Maglio, P., Kwan, S.K., Spohrer, J.: Commentary-toward a research agenda for human-centered service system innovation. Serv. Sci. **7**(1), 1–10 (2015)
32. Marinova, D., de Ruyter, K., Huang, M.H., Meuter, M.L., Challagalla, G.: Getting smart: learning from technology-empowered frontline interactions. J. Serv. Res. **20**(1), 29–42 (2017). https://doi.org/10.1177/1094670516679273
33. Martin, D., Hirt, R., Kühl, N.: Service systems, smart service systems and cyber-physical systems—what's the difference? In: 14th International Conference on Wirtschaftsinformatik. Siegen (2019).
34. Meuser, M., Nagel, U.: Das Experteninterview — konzeptionelle Grundlagen und methodische Anlage. In: Pickel, S., Pickel, G., Lauth, H.J., Jahn, D. (eds.) Methoden der vergleichenden Politik- und Sozialwissenschaft, pp. 465–479. VS Verlag, Wiesbaden (2009)
35. Moser, B., Jussen, P., Rösner, C.: Smart-service-plattformen. In: Stich, V., Schumann, J.H., Beverungen, D., Gudergan, G., Jussen, P. (eds.) Digitale Dienstleistungsinnovationen, pp. 601–624. Springer, Berlin (2019). https://doi.org/10.1007/978-3-662-59517-6_29
36. Neuhüttler, J., Fischer, R., Ganz, W., Spath, D.: Künstliche Intelligenz in Smart-Service-Systemen–Eine Qualitätsbetrachtung. In: Automatisierung und Personalisierung von Dienstleistungen, pp. 207–233. Springer, Berlin (2020). https://doi.org/10.1007/978-3-658-301 68-2_8

37. Neuhüttler, J., Fischer, R., Ganz, W., Urmetzer, F.: Perceived quality of artificial intelligence in smart service systems: a structured approach. In: QUATIC 2020: Quality of Information and Communications Technology, pp. 3–16. Faro (2020)

38. Nissen, V.: Digital transformation of the consulting industry—introduction and overview. In: Nissen, V. (ed.) Digital Transformation of the Consulting Industry: Extending the Traditional Delivery Model, pp. 1–58. Springer, Cham (2018). https://doi.org/10.1007/978-3-319-704 91-3_1

39. Nissen, V.: Das Geschäftsmodell Data Facilitator im Consulting. HMD Praxis der Wirtschaftsinformatik **58**(3), 552–564 (2021). https://doi.org/10.1365/s40702-021-00723-1

40. Nissen, V.: Einflüsse der Digitalisierung auf die Unternehmensberatung – Grundlagen und Transformationen des Geschäftsmodells. In: Corsten, H., Roth, S. (eds.) Handbuch Digitalisierung, pp. 957–986. Vahlen, München (2021)

41. Peffers, K., Tuunanen, T., Rothenberger, M.A., Chatterjee, S.: A design science research methodology for information systems research. J. Manage. Inf. Syst. **24**(3), 45–77 (2007). https://doi.org/10.2753/mis0742-1222240302

42. Porter, M.E., Heppelmann, J.E.: How smart, connected products are transforming companies. Harv. Bus. Rev. **93**(10), 96–114 (2015)

43. Strobel, G., Paukstadt, U., Becker, J., Eicker, S.: Von smarten Produkten zu smarten Dienstleistungen und deren Auswirkung auf die Wertschöpfung. HMD Praxis der Wirtschaftsinformatik **56**(3), 494–513 (2019). https://doi.org/10.1365/s40702-019-00520-x

44. van Husen, C., Razek, A.R.A.: Entwicklung von Smart Service-Leistungen mit Einsatz neuer Technologien. In: Bruhn, M., Hadwich, K. (eds) Künstliche Intelligenz im Dienstleistungsmanagement. Forum Dienstleistungsmanagement. Springer Gabler, Wiesbaden (2021). https://doi.org/10.1007/978-3-658-34324-8_9

45. Vargo, S., Maglio, P., Akaka, M.: On value and value co-creation: a service systems and service logic perspective. Eur. Manage. J. **26**, 145–152 (2008)

46. Webster, J., Watson, R.T.: Analyzing the past to prepare for the future: writing a literature review. MIS Q. **26**(2), xiii-xxiii (2002)

47. Wellsandt, S., Anke, J., Thoben, K.-D.: Modellierung der Lebenszyklen von Smart Services. In: Thomas, O., Nüttgens, M., Fellmann, M. (eds.) Smart Service Engineering, pp. 233–256. Springer, Heidelberg (2017). https://doi.org/10.1007/978-3-658-16262-7_11

48. Werth, D., Greff, T., Scheer, A.W.: Consulting 4.0. HMD Praxis der Wirtschaftsinformatik **53**(1), 55–70 (2016). https://doi.org/10.1365/s40702-015-0198-1

49. Wunderlich, N.V., et al.: "Futurizing" smart service: implications for service researchers and managers. J. Serv. Mark. **29**(6–7), 442–447 (2015). https://doi.org/10.1108/jsm-01-2015-0040

SSSB: An Approach to Insurance for Cross-Border Exchange by Using Smart Contracts

Khoi Le Quoc[1](✉), Hong Khanh Vo[1], Luong Hoang Huong[1],
Khiem Huynh Gia[1], Khoa Tran Dang[1], Hieu Le Van[1], Nghia Huynh Huu[1],
Tran Nguyen Huyen[1], The Anh Nguyen[1], Loc Van Cao Phu[1],
Duy Nguyen Truong Quoc[1], Bang Le Khanh[1], and Ha Xuan Son[2]

[1] FPT University, Can Tho, Vietnam
lekhoi456@gmail.com
[2] University of Insubria, Varese, Italy

Abstract. Traditional commercial systems face many problems in terms of transportation, information latency, and reliability, thus affecting the whole process. Blockchain technology and smart contracts have been seen as a panacea for these problems. Specifically, all information about packages, orders, and ties between relevant parties (i.e., seller and buyer) is stored in a distributed ledger. Thereby, the seller and the buyer can access the necessary information about their package. However, the most significant difference between the international trading system and the rest is the need for an arbitrator/third party (i.e., a middleman) to judge when there is a conflict between the seller and the buyer (e.g., the bank provides the letter of credit). Setting up the rules/policies is essential during the order/package creation. It helps the middleman issue penalty fees if the stakeholders violate the constraints in the contract. Due to the above reasons, this paper introduces a system based on blockchain and smart contracts named Safe Seller Safe Buyer (SSSB) system as an approach to insurance for cross-border exchange. This article also implements SSSB on the three common platforms currently supporting Ethereum's ERC20, including Ethereum, BNB Smart Chain, and Fantom. By evaluating the actual implementation of the Gas, SSSB has the cheapest fee when installed on the Fantom platform. We provide the implementation/deployment of smart contracts on the three platforms to encourage further research on this topic.

Keywords: International trade · Blockchain · Smart contract · Ethereum · Fantom · BNB Smart Chain

1 Introduction

With the development of technology, many industries are forced to reform their business processes/organizations, as well as management strategies to satisfy

© The Author(s), under exclusive license to Springer Nature Switzerland AG 2022
I. Awan et al. (Eds.): MobiWIS 2022, LNCS 13475, pp. 179–192, 2022.
https://doi.org/10.1007/978-3-031-14391-5_14

customer requirements [1]. An excellent example of the above statement is the traditional model of international trade built on the trust of stakeholders (i.e., buyers and sellers). This model has enormous risks coming from both sides. Buyers may end up buying shoddy products due to a lack of verification mechanism; besides, the seller may lose the entire goods if the buyer refuses to pay. Later, the intermediary role was assigned to the Bank (Letter of Credit). Specifically, the buyer is provided with an economic guarantee from a bank that grants credit to an exporter of the goods [2]. The seller is responsible for keeping all relevant bank statements and is only entitled to receive the money once the buyer has received the goods. This model still encounters many problems that are drawing much attention. For example, the 4 of 100 containers of cashew nuts from Vietnam exported to Italy are at risk of losing [3].

These traditional models are greatly hampered by opaque information and are subject to tedious validation of the traceability of goods, cash and information flow. The advancement of the internet led to the emergence of internet-based e-commerce, which greatly reduces the efficiency of international trade processes. A series of new models have been introduced to replace the models of exchange of goods between sellers and buyers. For example, in e-commerce, Cash-on-delivery was introduced as a temporary solution to the boom period of e-commerce [4]. Specifically, the carrier will play an extremely important role in delivering and receiving the buyer's money. The return of such funds to the seller is subject to the seller's contractual obligations and the shipping company. It is because of this vulnerability that many sellers lose all their money to the shipping company if that company goes bankrupt or refuses to pay [5].

A series of Blockchain-based models have been introduced to solve this problem, providing a secure platform for both sellers and buyers, a.k.a decentralized marketplace/exchange (we will detail the pros and cons of these approaches in the Related Work section). However, the proposed models still do not satisfy the requirements of international trade [6]. To solve this problem, we introduce a system based on Blockchain and smart contracts called SSSB (Safe Seller Safe Buyer) an approach to insurance for cross-border exchange. In the proposed model, we build three main user groups: Seller, Buyer and Middleman. The SSSB consists of eight main steps, from the seller initiating the package/order to the package/order being delivered to the buyer. Besides, to define the logical constraints in the smart contract to maintain the stable operation of the system, we also design the authorization service for the stakeholders. To design logical constraints on smart contracts, we additionally exploit Solidity language[1]. To evaluate SSSB, we implemented a test model on all three of the most popular platforms that currently support EVM, including Ethereum[2], BNB Smart

---

[1] Solidity is an object-oriented, high-level language for executing smart contracts. Smart contracts are programs that govern the behavior of accounts in the Ethereum state https://docs.soliditylang.org/en/v0.8.13/.
[2] Ethereum https://ethereum.org/en/whitepaper/.

Chain[3], and Fantom[4]. To support international trade insights (i.e., Cross-Border Exchange), we share our proof-of-concept implemented on all three platforms.

Following this introduction, a state-of-the-art is presented to help understand the limitations and challenges of the current approaches. Then, we define the architecture of Safe Seller Safe Buyer (SSSB) Architecture based on the blockchain and smart contract. In the next section, we describe the implementation process including data structure, SSSB execution algorithm, and the authorization. Section 5 focuses on the evaluation process based on deploying SSSB in the three platforms. Finally, suggestions for future research and conclusion are made in the last section.

2   Related Work

Based on the benefits of blockchain-based system, more and more protocols are introduced to protect the rights and obligations of stakeholders, for example, sellers and buyers in the Cash-on-Delivery (COD) model [7,8], doctors and patients in the medical care system [9,10], emergency [11,12], or blood donors and recipients in the humanitarian blood transfusion model [13,14].

Undoubtedly, the limitations of the traditional shipping (i.e., COD model) such as dependence on trusted third parties, order management, complicates payment processes between parties in the system, and the high-level risk of losing the deposit as well as the package [6]. Thus, blockchain technology is used (e.g., smart contract, decentralized management) to solve the problems of COD introduced in [15]. For instance, a method called localEthereum is built on the interaction between the sellers and buyers [4,16]. With blockchain technology approach, i.e., smart contract, the Ether transaction took place on a decentralized online peer-to-peer market. LocalEthereum relied on trusted third parties as the funded escrow agreed by both the seller and the buyer rather than depending on a escrow-acting contract. Therotically, OpenBazaar was similar to localEthereum. It was based on a buyer and seller-sponsored margin transaction called Multisignature escrow, introduced in [17]. The main difference between OpenBazaar and localEthereum was the way the parties participate in the COD process. This approach involves three parties: the seller, the buyer, and the moderator. The Sponsored Escrow Institution will act as a moderator in the event of a dispute. This solution is expensive and does not give buyers and sellers the right to choose their trusted arbitrator (i.e., middleman) in any dispute. In addition, the biggest shortcoming of these methods is that this is a fully trusted shipper without any incentive to take the item from the seller and deliver it to the off-chain buyer. As a result, the shipper is not tracked on the chain.

To address this problem, an approach in [18] proposed a primary mechanism based on the Ethereum platform, which helps to transport products from sellers to buyers. Besides, the shipper plays an essential role in this plan. The process

---

[3] Binance Smart Chain https://github.com/bnb-chain/whitepaper/blob/master/WHITEPAPER.md.

[4] Fantom https://fantom.foundation/research/wp_fantom_v1.6.pdf.

involves two steps as follows: (i) the key is carried with the product and delivered to the buyer, and (ii) the buyer must then enter the key using the available key's hash in smart. contract for verification. The hash of the key entered by the buyer matching the existing hash of the smart contract is a prerequisite for placing Ether in the seller's account. However, the disadvantage of this method is that it depends on the complete trust of the shipper. The shipper must ensure the key is safe until it reaches the buyer. Furthermore, there is no guarantee that all parties involved are honest, and this approach will fail if any party engages in malicious behavior, especially the shipper. The limitation of these methods is that there may still be a dispute between the seller and the buyer.

To enhance the role of the shipper in the COD model Duong et al. [19] and Le et al. [20] introduced a decentralized user model based on Blockchain technology, including buyers, sellers and carriers. These works develop transportation processes and provide mechanisms to promote and ensure the interests of the parties involved. Buyer's interests are enhanced, and penalize shippers (sellers) who intentionally commit fraud. However, the group of authors above only solves the problem on a small scale between parties in the same city or country. This model is also untested as the scope of application is extended across countries. In addition, they have not yet built a middleman to resolve disputes that may arise between the parties.

Compared with previous approaches, SSSB builds a safe environment for both sellers and buyers regardless of distance/international trade (i.e., between different countries). We also aim to resolve conflicts by establishing a system around the middleman and a clear and transparent decentralized mechanism between the parties. Participants can monitor each other and detect violations before affecting the whole system.

3   SSSB-(Safe Seller Safe Buyer) Architecture

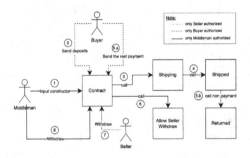

Fig. 1. SSSB architecture

The SSSB architecture is presented in Fig. 1, which includes three main actors, namely Seller, Buyer, and Middleman.

- *Seller*: who sells orders to the Buyer to get money. In SSSB, seller only withdraw the fund in the smart contract after the order is shipped to the buyer.
- *Buyer*: The Buyer is also called an Importer (in the transport industry) who spends the money to buy the Buyer's orders. In SSSB, the buyer has to transfer money to the smart contract, one for the deposit and one for the rest to complete the payment.
- *Middleman or Trustee*: who is trusted party to control i) the order being shipped to the Buyer and ii) all payments being transferred to the seller. The middleman is also known as the contract owner controlling the entire function and method, i.e., this is defined and cannot be changed in the smart contract. In this paper, we do not refer to off-chain tasks.

According to Fig. 1, SSSB has eight steps. In particular, the Middleman firstly enters the parameters defined in the paper contract (off-chain) into the smart contract and deploys it on the Fantom blockchain network. Once the smart contract is deployed, it is identified in the blockchain network by the contract address. The Buyer then transfers the deposit to this address for the smart contract in Step 2. The Buyer can transfer many times so that the amount transferred to the smart contract is equal to or greater than the previously declared deposit. The deposit held in smart contract proves that the Buyer has paid the deposit, and the seller can safely ship the other. The smart contract automatically changes state when the deposit is received and allows the Middleman to call the shipping method. In the third step, when the order has just been shipped (in off-chain), the Middleman calls the shipping function to change the order status to Shipping. After that, the order arrived (in off-chain). The Middleman calls the shipped function to change the order status to Shipped in Step 4. Next, the Buyer must transfer all the remaining amount of the order to the smart contract [Step 5.a]. However, if the Buyer does not send the remaining money by the deadline (according to off-chain), it is considered a breach of contract and loses the deposit. At this point, the middleman call the non-payment function to change the order status to `Returned` [Step 5.b]. Regardless of whether the Buyer deposits the remainder, the Seller still can withdraw funds by the middleman calling to `allowSellerWithdraw` function in the sixth step. The buyer is allowed to withdraw money by calling the contract through the `sellerWithdraw` function. In step 7, The actual amount received by the Seller depends on the condition in step 5 - already defined in the smart contract. Finally, the remaining money in the smart contract is withdrawn by the Middleman (intermediary fee) by calling the `middlemanWithdraw` function [Step 8].

4   Implementation

4.1   Data Structure

Figure 2 presents the data structure of the SSSB framework. The main collection of data is **Order** as an instance which is an order signed in the paper contract. The **Order** included data types:

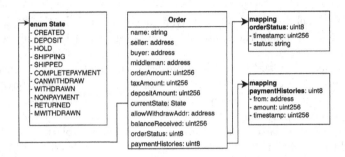

Fig. 2. Data structure

- The name of the order (`name`).
- The address (on blockchain) of seller/exporter (`seller`).
- The address (on blockchain) of buyer/importer (`buyer`).
- The address (on blockchain) of middleman/transporter/truster (`middleman`).
- The order amount signed in the smart contract (including the middleman's fee and the gas fee for blockchain network) (`orderAmount`).
- The deposit amount for the order to be shipped (`depositAmount`).
- The current status of the order (all states are predefined using enum **State**) (`currentState`).
- The address (on blockchain) is allowed to withdraw money from smart contract (`allowWithdrawAddr`).
- The list of records that store the status of order by timestamp (`orderStatus`).
- The list of records that store the transactions received from buyers by timestamp (`paymentHistories`).

All of these fields describe the details of an Order. It is also stored in a smart contract that makes it transparent for the seller, the buyer, the middleman, and others to see it. If any data field is changed, it is immediately recorded in the blockchain network.

To determine the status of the Order, it was preconceived all (11) occurrence states of Order. It is stored in enum **State** and has that has been created (`CREATED`); The full deposit has been received. And deposit is being hold in smart contract (`HOLD`); The order is shipping (`SHIPPING`); The order has arrived (`SHIPPED`); The full payment received. Buyer is allowed to receive (`COMPLETEPAYMENT`); The seller is allowed to withdraw from the smart contract (`CANWITHDRAW`); The seller has withdrawn successfully (`WITHDRAWN`); The buyer is not paying (`NONPAYMENT`); The order is being returned (`RETURNED`); The middleman has withdrawn successfully (`MWITHDRAWN`).

After storing the status of an order, it is saved to a mapping `OrderStatus`. That means a list of records that stores the status of an order for future reference. When a query with `orderStatusNumber`, the smart contract will return timestamp which is the point time that order status changed. And status referenced with enum **State** to return specific `staterecord` with a string format.

Incoming/outgoing transactions are also recorded in the mapping **payment Histories**. It's a list of records that store the payment history transactions included the address (on blockchain) sent/received from smart contract (from); the amount sending/receiving of the transaction (amount). And the point time of transaction (timestamp).

4.2 Algorithm

1: Input: name, middleman, buyer, seller, orderAmount, taxAmount, depositAmount

2: Output: currentState equal to State.MWITHDRAW

3: Begin: set currentState = State.CREATED; set balanceReceived = 0

4: **while** buyer transfers deposit >= depositAmount **do**

5:   update balanceReceived

6:   storing payment transaction to paymentHistories

7:   **if** balanceReceived < depositAmount **then**

8:     update currentState = State.DEPOSIT

9:   **else if** balanceReceived >= depositAmount && balanceReceived < orderAmount **then**

10:     update currentState = State.HOLD

11:   **else**

12:     update currentState = State.COMPLETEPAYMENT

13:   **end if**

14:   storing order's status to orderStatus

15: **end while**

16: **if** currentState == State.HOLD or currentState == State.COMPLETE PAYMENT **then**

17:   manual update currentState = State.SHIPPING

18: **end if**

19: **if** currentState == State.SHIPPING **then**

20:   manual update currentState = State.SHIPPED

21: **end if**

22: **while** receiving the rest payment until the deadline **do**

23:   **if** balanceReceived == orderAmount **then**

24:     update currentState = State.COMPLETEPAYMENT

25:     manual update currentState = State.CANWITHDRAW

26:   **else**

27:     manual update currentState = State.NONPAYMENT

28:   **end if**

29: **end while**

30: **if** currentState == State.CANWITHDRAW **then**

31:   set amountWithdraw = balanceReceived - taxAmount

32: **else if** currentState == State.NONPAYMENT **then**

33:   set amountWithdraw = balanceReceived - 2*taxAmount

34: **end if**

35: **while** seller withdrew money **do**

36:    currentState = State.WITHDRAWN
37: **end while**
38: **while** middleman withdrew money **do**
39:    currentState equal to State.MWITHDRAWN
40: **end while**

The algorithm executes sequentially from top to bottom of the SSSB framework's execution. First, the middleman inputs variables to the constructor. Set `currentState` variable to State.CREATED and set `balanceReceived` equal to 0 is the required step to initialize the first value; From lines 4 to 15, when the buyer sends money to the smart contract, the `balanceReceived` will be updated, and smart contract will record the transaction history into `paymentHistories`. If `balanceReceived` is less than `depositAmount` then set `currentState` equal to State.DEPOSIT. Until `balanceReceived` is greater than or equal to `depositAmount` but less than `orderAmount`, update `currentState` equal to State.HOLD. Besides, if `balance Received` is equal to `orderAmount`, update `currentState` equal to State.COM- PLETEPAYMENT. After that, smart contract automatic saves the order status into `orderStatus`; Next to line 16, if the order just shipped (`currentState` is equal to State.HOLD or State.COMPLETEPAYMENT), the middleman must manually update `currentState` equal to State.SHIPPING; Next to line 19, if the order has arrived (`currentState` is equal to State.SHIPPING), the middleman must manually update `currentState` equal to State.SHIPPED; From lines 22 to 29, it is necessary to wait until the deadline to receive the rest payment from the buyer transferring to the smart contract. If `balanceReceived` is equal to `orderAmount`, the smart contract automatic update `currentState` equal to State.COMPLETEPAYMENT and the middleman must manually update `currentState` equal to State.CANWITHDRAW. Conversely, if the deadline is over and the buyer does not transfer the rest of the money, the middleman needs to manually update `currentState` equal to State.NONPAYMENT. At this point, the seller is allowed to withdraw; Next to line 30, if `currentState` is equal to State.CANWITHDRAW, the amount received by the seller is `amountWithdraw` equal to `balanceReceived` minus `taxAmount`. Until `currentState` is equal to State. NONPAYMENT, the seller's actual amount received is `amountWithdraw` equal to `balanceReceived` minus (`taxAmount` multiply 2); From lines 35 to 37, after the seller completes withdrawal, the status will be automatically set `currentState` equal to State. WITHDRAW; From lines 38 to 40, the middleman is allowed to withdraw the funds. After the middleman has finished withdrawn, the status will be automatically set `currentState` equal to State.MWITHDRAWN.

4.3   Authorization

SSSB also provides the authorization service for the stakeholders in the system. The list of functions is described in Table 1. Addition to the three main users, the people is to represent the normal user who not play the seller or buyer in specific transaction.

Table 1. The permission of the stakeholders in SSSB

Function/method	Middleman	Seller	Buyer	People
constructor	Authorized	-	-	-
receive	-	Authorized	-	-
shipping	Authorized	-	-	-
shipped	Authorized	-	-	-
manualChangeStatus	Authorized	-	-	-
allowSellerWithdraw	Authorized	-	-	-
nonPayment	Authorized	-	-	-
sellerWithdraw	-	Calling the allowSellerWithdraw first	-	-
middlemanWithdraw	Calling the sellerWithdraw first	-	-	-
getBalance, orderStatus, currentStatus, getOrderAmount, paymentHistories	Authorized	Authorized	Authorized	Authorized

We verify the actor's authority on smart contract by account address (public key) in the Fantom blockchain network. The functions and methods in smart contract are described below.

- *constructor*:
  This one-time deployed method sets the variables (`name, buyer, seller, middleman, orderAmount, depositAmount, taxAmount`) containing information value in the smart contract. Therefore, only the middleman has the authorization to implement this method.
- *receive*: This method confirms a transfer of the buyer's funds to the smart contract. Only the buyer can transfer money to the smart contract, so the authorization to execute this method only belongs to the buyer.
- *shipping*: It is to make sure that the order has just been shipped and on the way to the seller. Buyer and seller have trusted the middleman. Therefore, only the middleman is authorized to call this function.
- *shipped*: Like the shipping function, this function ensures the order has arrived at the port (on buyer).
- *manualChangeStatus*: In case of off-chain issues, the on-chain needs to be updated with the state. This task belongs to the middleman authorized to call the manualChangeStatus function.
- *allowSellerWithdraw*: Only the middleman is authorized to allow the seller to withdraw funds. Of course, it already conforms to the pre-set conditions in the smart contract.
- *nonPayment*: If the order status is shipped and the buyer is overdue for payment. The order must be transferred to the return state and perform some conditional logic in the smart contract. Authorized middleman.
- *sellerWithdraw*: It is a function for the seller to withdraw money from the smart contract. Only the seller has authorized to perform this action. However, it already meets the conditions in the smart contract and needs to get the middleman's permission by calling *allowSellerWithdraw* first.

– *sellerWithdraw*: It is a function for the seller to withdraw money from the smart contract. Only the seller has authorized can perform this action. However, it already met the conditions in the smart contract and needs to get the middleman's permission by calling *allowSellerWithdraw* first.

– *middlemanWithdraw*: It is a function for the middleman to withdraw money from the smart contract. Of course, it already satisfied the conditions of the smart contract. And the middleman has been authorized this function only after the *sellerWithdraw* function is executed. In other words, when the seller completes the withdrawal can the middleman withdraw the money.

– *getBalance, getOrderAmount, currentStatus, orderStatus, paymentHistories*: These methods represent the consistency of smart contracts. Therefore, everyone has the authorization to call it.

5 Evaluation

5.1 Environment Setting

We use Solidity language and Remix IDE to program smart contracts because it is pretty popular. When implementing this solution, compiler 0.8.7+commit.e28d00a7 is stable. We also use the default EVM version and don't need optimization. The gas limit is 3000000, just enough to deploy smart contract. We also use the MIT License because we want more people to reuse our solution. Choosing a blockchain network to run smart contracts on is also an issue to be evaluated. We have measured (will be covered in the Experimental section) and decided to use the several platforms, namely Fantom, Ethereum, and BNB Smart Chain platforms.

5.2 Results

5.2.1 Define the Order's State
To prove the effectiveness of SSSB, we set up two scenarios (i.e., buyer pays and not pays the rest of payment) in the tree most common of EVM Blockchain platforms, namely Fantom, Ethereum, and Binance Smart Chain. We also provide the proof-of-concept for the further extension in this topic[5]. The main eight steps is presented below:

1. **State.CREATED:** The order has been created. The order has just been created. Only the receive method to receive the native coin is enabled. When the buyer transfers all the deposits to the smart contract, the status is automatically changed to State.HOLD. No one can withdraw or take any action in this state.

[5] The implementation/deployment of SSSB on: **Fantom platform**: https://testnet. ftmscan.com/address/0xF11Fde29e0EB94d977d44c2660F5e0227DC81462#code; **Ethereum platform**: https://kovan.etherscan.io/address/0xc3f2e07d850d913 1123513e3a106c2ce02b8fa21\#writeContract; **Binance Smart Chain platform**: https://testnet.bscscan.com/tx/0x236fd512f44fa21148e0f902e72277619e2438d 704fe9bfa7d6a8db55f1861b7.

2. **State.HOLD:** The full deposit has been received. Deposit is being hold in smart contract. After the smart contract receives the buyer's deposit. This state is enabled. In the State.HOLD state, the money will be kept in the smart contract and waiting for the seller to send the packages to the port. The middleman controls the smart contract and executes the next steps of the order. Others can not withdraw or take any action in this state.

3. **State.SHIPPING:** The order is shipping. After the packages are on board, the middleman actively changes the order status to State.SHIPPING. The middleman controls the smart contract and executes the next steps of the order. Others can not withdraw or take any action in this state.

4. **State.SHIPPED:** The order has arrived. When the order arrives at the port (by buyer), the middleman actively changes the status of the order to State.SHIPPED. At this time, the buyer needs to transfer the remaining payment of the order to the smart contract, so that the smart contract automatically changes the order status to State.COMPLETEPAYMENT. No one can withdraw or take any action in this state.

5.a. **State.COMPLETEPAYMENT:** The full payment received. Buyer is allowed to receive. After the buyer transfers the remaining payment of the order to the smart contract, it automatically changes the order status to State.COMPLETE- PAYMENT. At this time, the buyer is allowed to receive the packages. The middleman controls the smart contract and executes the next steps of the order. Others can not withdraw or take any action in this state.

5.b.1. **State.NONPAYMENT:** The buyer is not paying. If the buyer does not pay the rest of the order, the middleman will activate the State.NONPAYMENT state. At this time, the buyer is also allowed to withdraw the funds but will have to pay the returned cost. The middleman controls the smart contract and executes the next steps of the order.

5.b.2. **State.RETURNED:** The order is being returned. In the condition that the order is not paid by the buyer, when the seller withdraws all the funds they receive, the smart contract will automatically change the state to State.RETURNED. It means that the middleman should be responsible for returning the order to the port (by seller).

6. **State.CANWITHDRAW:** The seller is allowed to withdraw from the smart contract. The middleman needs to make sure the order is successfully received. Then, they can enable the seller to withdraw funds in smart contract by transferring the state to State.CANWITHDRAW. The middleman controls the smart contract and executes the next steps of the order.

7. **State.WITHDRAWN:** The seller has withdrawn successfully. When the seller withdraws all the funds they receive, the smart contract will automatically change the state to State.WITHDRAW.

8. **State.MWITHDRAWN:** The middleman has withdrawn successfully. After the buyer withdraws, the intermediary is allowed to withdraw and the smart contract will automatically change the state to State.MWITHDRAW. The contract is completed.

5.2.2 Scenario 1: Buyer Pays Full Payment

This scenario will trigger sequentially the states as 1., 2., 3., 4., 5.a., 6., 7., and 8.. In this scenario, the middleman sets the state to `State.SHIPPED`, the buyer transferred the rest of the payment to the smart contract within the deadline. Step 5.a. activated automatically by smart contract. And the middleman has to enable step 6. to allow the seller to withdraw funds from the smart contract.

5.2.3 Scenario 2: Buyer Not Pays the Rest of Payment

This scenario will trigger sequentially the states as 1., 2., 3., 4., 5.b.1., 5.b.2., 6., 7., and 8.. In this scenario, the middleman sets the state to `State.SHIPPED`, the buyer does not transfer the rest of the payment to the smart contract within the deadline. Step 5.b.1. and 5.b.2. activated by middleman will change the order's status to return. Smart contract will recalculate the cost and the middleman has to enable step 6. to allow the seller to withdraw funds from the smart contract.

Table 2. The gas for the smart contract execution of the three platforms, i.e., Fantom, Ethereum, and BNB Chain.

Gas for execution	Fantom	Ethereum	BNB Chain
Deploy contract	0.491 FTM ($0.58)	0.00600 ETH ($18,22)	0.02384 BNB ($9.90)
Sends deposits	0.059 FTM ($0.07)	0.00042 ETH ($1.28)	0.00267 BNB ($1.11)
Call shipping	0.017 FTM ($0.02)	0.00008 ETH ($0.24)	0.00079 BNB ($0.33)
Call shipped	0.017 FTM ($0.02)	0.00008 ETH ($0.24)	0.00079 BNB ($0.33)
Call allowSellerWithdraw	0.028 FTM ($0.03)	0.00013 ETH ($0.4)	0.00126 BNB ($0.52)
Call nonPayment	0.028 FTM ($0.03)	0.00013 ETH ($0.4)	0.00126 BNB ($0.52)
Call sellerWithdraw	0.043 FTM ($0.05)	0.00020 ETH ($0.63)	0.00197 BNB ($0.82)
Call middlemanWithdraw	0.028 FTM ($0.03)	0.00013 ETH ($0.4)	0.00127 BNB ($0.53)

5.2.4 Comparison

The Table 2 describes the gas fees for the SSSB functions/methods deployment and execution on the three platforms, i.e., Fantom, Ehtereum, and BNB Smart Chain[6]. Overall, Fantom's smart contract execution fee is the cheapest with only 0.08 FTM on average. In which the most expensive is deploying contract with 0.491 FTM ($0.58) and the cheapest cost is from $0.02 to $0.07. In contrast, Ethereum is the most expensive followed by BNB Smart Chain to deploy/call the same system. Specifically, we spend about $18.22 and $9.9 to deploy the contract on ETH and BNB, which is approximately 31 and 17 times higher than the cost of deploying on Fantom. The average gas for all eight functions/methods deployed on Ethereum and BNB Smart Chain are $2.73 and $1.76, respectively. This is much higher when compared to the Fantom platform with only $0.1 on average.

---

[6] The redemption value as of date April 16, 2022.

It is clear that currently the fee to maintain and execute the system on Fantom will be cheaper than the other two ecosystems. To account for this, we also refer to the time when these platforms were introduced. Specifically, FTM has the smallest age of all three (i.e., introduced in 2020) platforms, so there are not many applications established on this ecosystem. This also contributes to the cost of Fantom which is more attractive to other developers.

6 Conclusion

This paper introduced a transaction process based on Blockchain and a smart contract called SSSB (Safe Seller Safe Buyer). The primary purposes of this proposal are to solve the difficulties and dilemmas of traditional international trade. In particular, the transactions' information and metadata among the parties involved are stored on the distributed ledger, increasing the system's transparency. Sellers and buyers can access the order/package related information. In a seller and buyer dispute, the SSSB also proposes a smart contract-based conflict resolution mechanism. Besides, the role of the middleman is also emphasized in the model of SSSB. To evaluate the effectiveness of SSSB, we deployed and analyzed it on three of the common platforms, including Fantom, BNB Smart Chain, and Ethereum. Based on the evaluation results, we are able to claim that Fantom's Gas is the lowest one of all three platforms.

Regarding possible future directions, we aim to have only two key user types (i.e., buyer and seller) in the international trade but still ensure the resolution of conflicts between the parties involved. Moreover, we will consider the role of the shipper/transportation company in international trade. Furthermore, we aim for a comprehensive review, where the more complex scenarios will be considered.

References

1. Wong, S.Y., Chin, K.S.: Organizational innovation management: an organization-wide perspective. In: Industrial Management and Data Systems (2007)
2. Dolan, J.: The law of letters of credit. 4th edn, pp. 07–36 (2007)
3. TTXVN: Case of 100 containers of cashews exported to Italy: police kept 4 containers (2022). https://fomexco.com/business-news/case-of-100-containers-of-cashews-exported-to-italy-policekept-4-containers-230
4. Ethereum: How our escrow smart contract works (2022). https://www.thenational.ae/business/technology/cash-on-delivery-the-biggest-obstacle-to-e-commerce-in-uae-and-region-1
5. Waters, D.: Supply Chain Risk Management: Vulnerability and Resilience in Logistics. Kogan Page Publishers (2011)
6. Ha, X.S., et al.: DeM-CoD: novel access-control-based cash on delivery mechanism for decentralized marketplace. In: 2020 IEEE 19th International Conference on Trust, Security and Privacy in Computing and Communications (TrustCom), pp. 71–78. IEEE (2020)
7. Son, H.X., et al.: Towards a mechanism for protecting seller's interest of cash on delivery by using smart contract in hyperledger. Int. J. Adv. Comput. Sci. Appl. 10(4), 45–50 (2019)

8. Ha, X.S., Le, T.H., Phan, T.T., Nguyen, H.H.D., Vo, H.K., Duong-Trung, N.: Scrutinizing trust and transparency in cash on delivery systems. In: Wang, G., Chen, B., Li, W., Di Pietro, R., Yan, X., Han, H. (eds.) SpaCCS 2020. LNCS, vol. 12382, pp. 214–227. Springer, Cham (2021). https://doi.org/10.1007/978-3-030-68851-6_15

9. Duong-Trung, N., et al.: Smart care: integrating blockchain technology into the design of patient-centered healthcare systems. In: Proceedings of the 2020 4th International Conference on Cryptography, Security and Privacy. ICCSP, pp. 105–109 (2020)

10. Duong-Trung, N., et al.: On components of a patient-centered healthcare system using smart contract. In: Proceedings of the 2020 4th International Conference on Cryptography, Security and Privacy, pp. 31–35 (2020)

11. Son, H.X., Le, T.H., Quynh, N.T.T., Huy, H.N.D., Duong-Trung, N., Luong, H.H.: Toward a blockchain-based technology in dealing with emergencies in patient-centered healthcare systems. In: Bouzefrane, S., Laurent, M., Boumerdassi, S., Renault, E. (eds.) MSPN 2020. LNCS, vol. 12605, pp. 44–56. Springer, Cham (2021). https://doi.org/10.1007/978-3-030-67550-9_4

12. Le, H.T., et al.: Patient-chain: patient-centered healthcare system a blockchain-based technology in dealing with emergencies. In: Parallel and Distributed Computing, Applications and Technologies. PDCAT 2021. LNCS, vol. 13148. Springer, Cham (2022). https://doi.org/10.1007/978-3-030-96772-7_54

13. Quynh, N.T.T., et al.: Toward a design of blood donation management by blockchain technologies. In: Gervasi, O., et al. (eds.) ICCSA 2021. LNCS, vol. 12956, pp. 78–90. Springer, Cham (2021). https://doi.org/10.1007/978-3-030-87010-2_6

14. Le, H.T., et al.: BloodChain: a blood donation network managed by blockchain technologies. Network **2**(1), 21–35 (2022)

15. Le, H.T., et al.: Introducing multi shippers mechanism for decentralized cash on delivery system. Int. J. Adv. Comput. Sci. Appl. **10**(6), 590–597 (2019)

16. Antonopoulos, A.M., Wood, G.: Mastering Ethereum: Building Smart Contracts and DApps. O'Reilly Media (2018)

17. OpenBazaar: Truly decentralized, peer-to-peer ecommerce features (2022). https://openbazaar.org/features/

18. Two party contracts (2022). https://dappsforbeginners.wordpress.com/tutorials/two-party-contracts/

19. Duong-Trung, N., et al.: Multi-sessions mechanism for decentralized cash on delivery system. Int. J. Adv. Comput. Sci. Appl. **10**(9) (2019)

20. Le, N.T.T., et al.: Assuring non-fraudulent transactions in cash on delivery by introducing double smart contracts. Int. J. Adv. Comput. Sci. Appl. **10**(5), 677–684 (2019)

A Review: Sensors Used in Tool Wear Monitoring and Prediction

Perin Ünal[1]([✉]) [iD], Bilgin Umut Deveci[1] [iD], and Ahmet Murat Özbayoğlu[2] [iD]

[1] TEKNOPAR Industrial Automation, İvedikosb Yenimahalle, 06378 Ankara, Turkey
{punal,deveci}@teknopar.com.tr
[2] TOBB University of Economics and Technology, Söğütözü Çankaya, 06510 Ankara, Turkey
mozbayoglu@etu.edu.tr

Abstract. Tool wear prediction/monitoring of CNCs is crucial for improving manufacturing efficiency, guaranteeing product quality, and minimizing tool costs. As a computer-aided application, it has a significant role in the future and development of Industry 4.0. Sensors are the key piece of hardware used by data-driven enterprises to predict/monitor tool wear. The purpose of this study is to inform about the predominant types of sensors used for tool wear monitoring/prediction. This study serves as a resource for researchers and manufacturers by providing the recent trends in sensors for tool wear monitoring. Thus, it may help reduce the time spent on sensor selection.

Keywords: Sensors · Industry 4.0 · Accelerometer · Acoustic emission · Microphone · Current sensor · Dynamometer

1 Introduction

Sensors, in general, are devices that detect changes in the physical environment and transmit the measured data in various formats [1]. While the input of sensors may differ such as temperature, vibration, sound, flow, or movement; in the end they all output a signal. During the machining processes, the cutting tool is exposed to harsh heat and mechanical stresses due to the contact with the cutting tool, the workpiece material, and the chips. As a result, changes in shape, volume loss, and cutting tool sharpness might occur gradually or suddenly. These changes, known as tool wear, often occur at rates determined by operating conditions, workpiece material, and cutting tool material or shape [2].

Tool wear has long been a subject of concern in the machining industry. Keeping tools in good condition is a key practice for reaching maximum efficiency. Implementing tool wear prediction and monitoring systems is therefore critical. Since the machining process is too complex to model, sensor-based systems have been implemented in the machining industry [3]. The most accurate, but inefficient methods rely on direct inspection of the tool's condition using microscopes, laser devices or machine vision systems. These tools are less costly than of sensors used in indirect measurement [4]. The effectiveness of direct approaches is restricted by the fact that machining must be halted to check the tools. This prolongs the production time, hence increasing product costs. Majority of industrial direct methods have this significant drawback [5]. Indirect measurement is the measurement method where the sensors are continuously obtaining data. Using machine-learning technology, the indirect techniques examine relevant information acquired from one or more sensors to determine tool wear conditions. The machining process does not need to stop. This method is especially crucial in scenarios where direct measurement is not a possibility [6]. Modern sensors present a plethora of tool indirect monitoring ways. Indirect approaches are desirable since they do not alter the machining process and, under ideal conditions, provide excellent prediction accuracy [7]. Sensors are commonly used together to improve their prediction/classification accuracies. This method is called "sensor fusion".

Depending on the system, the machining tool (turning, milling, grinding, drilling), the material of the cutting tool, the shape, the type of sensors should be changed. In this paper, 65 studies that focus on indirect tool wear monitoring/prediction are examined. The predominant types of sensors used in these studies are acoustic emission sensors [19–30], accelerometers [31–52], microphones [49, 52–65], ampere meters [66–72] and dynamometers [15, 16, 73–80]. These sensors are briefly defined, and the models of the sensors in these studies (if given) are listed in a table. Hence, the most used sensor models in the literature for tool wear monitoring/prediction are presented. Also, the sensors' important features are examined according to their datasheets.

2 Types of Sensors Used in Tool Wear Applications

2.1 Accelerometer

Vibration is detrimental in the machining process since it reduces component life, decreases surface quality, degrades tool geometry, and induces failures. One of the most frequently used vibration monitoring equipment is the accelerometer [8]. Accelerometers measure acceleration using the piezoelectric crystals and can be attached physically, magnetically, or adhesively to a mechanical device. When the accelerometer vibrates or spins, the internal structure shifts, causing the capacitance value to change. The change of capacitance is then converted to the appropriate voltage output. The main advantage of an accelerometer is its linearity over a broad frequency range, which allows it to determine the quality of a cutting process. Gravity (g), acceleration (m/s^2), and frequency (Hz) may all be used to calculate vibration acceleration [9]. In general, single axis (uniaxial) accelerometers and triaxial accelerometers are commonly used. Triaxial accelerometers can identify the x, y, and z axes.

2.2 Acoustic Emission

Acoustic emission defines the propagation of stress waves in a material when it is exposed to lateral load and deformations occur in the material structure [43]. Thus, acoustic emission signals can predict tool wear with ease. The frequency content of AE signal produced in mechanical processes spans a wide frequency range, ranging from 50 kHz to 1 MHz [47]. Because the sampling rate needed to sample acoustic emission signals is too high, it is complex to obtain the data. With its sensitivity, it is prone to noise. Since the distance and presence of joints between the AE source and sensor are crucial due to signal degradation, the optimum mounting location of the AE sensor is the cutting tool or workpiece. Given to the changing nature of the cutting tool and workpiece, the sensor must be installed in the tool holder in practical uses. Since the acoustic emission signal is complex, it is generally visualized in frequency domain, using FFT (Fast Fourier Transform) [29].

2.3 Microphone

The generation of audible sound during machining is a frequent result of friction between the tool, the workpiece, and the flowing chips. With the increasing tool wear, it is harder to cut the workpiece, thus higher cutting forces occur. Higher cutting forces cause "chattering", which microphones can detect [10–12]. This sound, unlike acoustic emission sensors, is transmitted directly via air medium and is caught by microphones. The frequency range of an acoustic emission sensor is around 10 kHz to 10 MHz, while the frequency range of a microphone is approximately 1 Hz to 100 kHz. This makes for more convenient data acquisition compared to acoustic emission sensors. The acoustic emission sensor must be installed around the cutting site, whilst the microphone can be placed away from the cutting site. Hence, microphones can be placed in a safe place away from the machining, resulting in longer useful life. However, there are several additional sources of noise on factory floors, such as neighbouring machines and machining operations. To address this problem, directional microphones are used [13].

2.4 Current Sensor

Many monitoring systems consider motor current to be one of the most acceptable signals for machining applications [deep learning driven], since its premise is simple, and the monitoring procedure does not require the machine to be shut down. Current sensors are widely in use and cheap. The only compatibility challenge for this sensor is knowing the maximum ampere input of the machine. Generally, current sensors use the "Hall Effect" principle. Since the amount of machining power needed during cutting process is proportionate to the cutting force, there is a strong correlation between tool wear and tool wear growth. The integration of current sensors on a CNC machine is convenient since the sensor can be placed outside the machine. In conclusion, a power or current signal may be easily acquired without interfering with specific operations inside the machine, requires little hardware with no unique and costly arrangements, is dependable, and is valuable for monitoring tool wear status and predicting early tool failure [13]. Albeit all its advantages, current sensor predicts tool failure and severity later than accelerometers and acoustic emission sensors [14].

2.5 Dynamometer

Cutting force is acknowledged as the factor that best explains the cutting process in the machining industry [15]. The force pattern information is utilized to evaluate the quality and geometric profile of the cutting surface. Furthermore, oscillatory responses and peaks in the cutting-force pattern may be caused by overloading, indicating a process irregularity and an increased risk of tool failure or workpiece damage [16]. Cutting forces can be computed or evaluated in a variety of techniques, including theoretical models, capacitive, optoelectronic, strain gage, and motor currency techniques [17]. Most used dynamometers are Kistler's piezoelectric dynamometers. In theory, piezoelectric measurements use specific crystals to transform mechanical pressure into electrical energy. Compared to other systems, the piezoelectric force sensor provides exceptional accuracy, sensitivity, and stiffness, which differentiates this technique [18]. The disadvantages of using a piezoelectric force sensor are that the tool holding components must be redesigned for durable and sensitive measurement. Fragmental design results in gaps, which reduce rigidity and may create chatter vibrations through time. Using dynamometers restricts the maximum workpiece size, making this method unfeasible for manufacturers and this encourages research into alternative sensors.

3 Predominant Sensors in Literature and Their Models

Table 1. Types of predominant sensors used in tool wear monitoring/prediction.

Sensor type	Measuring method	References
Accelerometer	Direct and indirect	[25, 26, 31–52, 60, 61, 67, 68, 80]
Acoustic emission	Indirect	[19–30, 42–48, 66]
Microphone	Indirect	[28, 43, 44, 49, 52–65, 68]
Current sensor	Direct and indirect	[25, 45, 46, 66–72]
Dynamometer	Indirect	[15, 16, 25, 47–51, 54, 59, 64, 67, 73–80]

Table 1 shows the types of predominant sensors used in tool wear monitoring/prediction and their measuring methods. Depending on the installation and the sensors' communication protocol, accelerometers and current sensors may require the production to be halted to be able to obtain data. The other sensors can continuously gather data with production. References to the articles they are used are given on a column. Accelerometer is used in 30 studies, acoustic emission sensor is used in 20 studies, microphone is used in 20 studies, current sensor is used in 10 studies, and dynamometer is used in 21 studies.

Table 2. Models of accelerometers used in tool wear monitoring/prediction.

Accelerometer model	Important features	References
ENDEVCO 7201-50	Uniaxial, Charge, 50 pC/g sensitivity, ±2000 g measurement range, 0–6 kHz frequency range	[25]
PCB 35A21	Uniaxial, IEPE, 10 mV/g sensitivity, ±500 g measurement range, 0–10 kHz frequency range	[26]
IMI 608A11	Uniaxial, IEPE, 100 mV/g sensitivity, ±50 g measurement range, 0–10 kHz frequency range	[33]
CSI 350	Uniaxial, Voltage, 100 mV/g sensitivity, ±50 g measurement range, 0–10 kHz frequency range, Handheld	[34]
Mukun Tech M69	Triaxial, Voltage, 100 mV/g sensitivity, ±100 g measurement range, 0–5 kHz frequency range, Wireless	[38]
PCB 356A17	Triaxial, IEPE, 500 mV/g sensitivity, ±10 g measurement range, 0–3 kHz frequency range	[39, 40]
PCB 356A71	Uniaxial, Charge, 10 pC/g sensitivity, ±500 g measurement range, 0–5 kHz frequency range	[41]
PCB 307A	Uniaxial, IEPE, 100 mV/g sensitivity, ±50 g measurement range, 0–5 kHz frequency range	[42]
PCB 353B16	Uniaxial, IEPE, 10 mV/g sensitivity, ±500 g measurement range, 0–10 kHz frequency range	[43, 44]
Kistler 8763B	Triaxial, IEPE, 100 mV/g sensitivity, ±50 g measurement range, 0–10 kHz frequency range	[43, 44]
PCB 352C34	Uniaxial, IEPE, 100 mV/g sensitivity, ±50 g measurement range, 0–10 kHz frequency range	[45]
Kistler 8692C50	Triaxial, IEPE, 100 mV/g sensitivity, ±50 g measurement range, 0–6 kHz frequency range	[46]
PCB J356A45	Triaxial, IEPE, 100 mV/g sensitivity, ±50 g measurement range, 0–10 kHz frequency range	[47]
PCB 356A16	Triaxial, IEPE, 100 mV/g sensitivity, ±50 g measurement range, 0–5 kHz frequency range	[48]
PCB 356A15	Triaxial, IEPE, 100 mV/g sensitivity, ±50 g measurement range, 0–5 kHz frequency range	[49, 68]
PCB 352C22	Uniaxial, IEPE, 10 mV/g sensitivity, ±500 g measurement range, 0–10 kHz frequency range	[50]
PCB U353B65	Uniaxial, IEPE, 100 mV/g sensitivity, ± 50 g measurement range, 0–10 kHz frequency range	[51]
PCB 352C33	Uniaxial, IEPE, 100 mV/g sensitivity, ±50 g measurement range, 0–10 kHz frequency range	[52]

(*continued*)

Table 2. (*continued*)

Accelerometer model	Important features	References
Kistler 8752A	Uniaxial, Voltage, 100 mV/g sensitivity, ±50 g measurement range, 0–5 kHz frequency range	[60]
CTC AC230	Triaxial, IEPE, 100 mV/g sensitivity, ±50 g measurement range, 0–10 kHz frequency range	[61]

The accelerometer models used in the literature can be seen in Table 2. The important parameters of accelerometers include number of measurement axis, voltage/current input, sensitivity, measurement range and frequency range. Number of measurement axis determines the characteristics of the accelerometer, whether it detects vibration from one axis or multi-axes. Voltage/current input feature is important since it determines the signal conditioning/data acquisition equipment. The sensitivity value determines the step size of analog signal output, lower sensitivity value makes the analog output more precise. Choosing the measurement range correctly for the application is a critical for further analysis. Implementing a ±10 g accelerometer on a motor that produces ±50 g of acceleration results in significant data loss. The frequency range is important since proper data acquisition equipment is needed. With Nyquist's theorem, the sampling rate of the data acquisition hardware must be at least two times the frequency range, to prevent data loss. It is clear from the table that PCB is the most used accelerometer manufacturer. In particular, the PCB 356AXX triaxial accelerometer found the most use in tool wear monitoring/prediction.

Table 3. Models of acoustic emission sensors used in tool wear monitoring/prediction.

Acoustic emission sensor model	Important features	References
PAC WD 925	56 dB peak sensitivity, 100–900 kHz frequency range	[25]
PAC Micro80	57 dB peak sensitivity, 200–900 kHz frequency range	[26]
Kistler 8152B11/8152B111	57 dB peak sensitivity, 50–400 kHz frequency range	[27, 45, 46]
Kistler 8152B21	48 dB peak sensitivity, 100–900 kHz frequency range	[48]
Beijing Shenghua SR800	50–800 kHz frequency range	[28]
PAC U80D-87	2–400 kHz frequency range	[29, 30]
PAC R15a	80 dB peak sensitivity, 50–400 kHz frequency range	[42]
PAC WSa	55 dB peak sensitivity, 100–1000 kHz frequency range	[42]

(*continued*)

Table 3. (*continued*)

Acoustic emission sensor model	Important features	References
Kistler 8152C0	57 dB peak sensitivity, 50–400 kHz frequency range	[43, 44, 47]
Murakami-giken AE-1	8 dB peak sensitivity, 100–230 kHz frequency range	[66]

Table 3 shows the acoustic emission sensors used in the literature. The important features in selecting the acoustic emission sensors include peak sensitivity and frequency range. Higher peak sensitivity means higher Signal-to-Noise Ratio (SNR), which results in less noisy signals. Since the frequency range of acoustic emission sensors are high, high-speed data acquisition systems shall be implemented according to frequency range feature. Clearly, Kistler 8152B and 8152C are the most used acoustic emission sensors. PAC is also a commonly preferred acoustic emission sensor manufacturer.

Table 4. Models of microphones used in tool wear monitoring/prediction.

Microphone model	Important features	References
Hangzhou Aihua AWA14423	IEPE, 1/2" nominal diameter, 50 mV/Pa sensitivity, 20 Hz–20 kHz frequency range (±2 dB), free-field	[28]
PCB 130F20	IEPE, 1/4" nominal diameter, 45 mV/Pa sensitivity, 20 Hz–10 kHz frequency range (±2 dB), free-field	[43, 44]
G.R.A.S. 46AE	CCP, 1/2" nominal diameter, 50 mV/Pa sensitivity, 3.15 Hz–20 kHz frequency range (±2 dB), free-field	[49, 54, 64]
Brüel & Kjær 4957	IEPE, 1/4" nominal diameter, 11.2 mV/Pa sensitivity, 100 Hz–5 kHz frequency range (±2 dB), array	[52]
PCB 130E21	IEPE, 1/4" nominal diameter, 45 mV/Pa sensitivity, 20 Hz–10 kHz frequency range (±2 dB), free-field	[55]
ECOOPRO EO-200	Condenser	[57, 63]
ECM-1028	50 Hz–16 kHz frequency range (±3 dB), electret condenser, tie clip	[60]
SPM0408LE5H-TB	Voltage, MEMS, -18 dBV/Pa sensitivity, 100 Hz–10 kHz frequency range (±2 dB), free-field	[61]

(*continued*)

Table 4. (*continued*)

Microphone model	Important features	References
G.R.A.S. 40AE	CCP, 1/2" nominal diameter, 50 mV/Pa sensitivity, 3.15 Hz–20 kHz frequency range (±2 dB), free-field	[62]
Kretz K-818	50 Hz–16 kHz frequency range (±2 dB), condenser, free-field	[65]
Brüel & Kjær 4966	IEPE, 1/2" nominal diameter, 50 mV/Pa sensitivity, 5 Hz–20 kHz frequency range (±2 dB), free-field	[68]

In Table 4, microphone models used in the literature are listed. Important features for the microphones include voltage/current input, diameter, sensitivity, frequency range and directionality. Lower sensitivity values generate more precision. Directionality is an important feature on microphone selection. Free-field microphones achieve higher directionality that makes ambient noise less interfering with the sound source. Random-incidence microphones are able to catch sound signals from any direction. It is observed that G.R.A.S. is the most preferred microphone manufacturer with its 46AE model. PCB is also commonly selected in the literature.

Table 5. Models of current sensors used in tool wear monitoring/prediction.

Current sensor model	Important features	References
OMRON K3TB-A1015	Rated Current: 200 A	[25]
GAA-KY1	N/A	[45]
Weidmüller WAS2	Rated Current: 10 A	[46]
Hioki CT6863	Rated Current: 200 A	[66]
YHDC SCT013	Rated Current: 10 A	[67, 69]
CSA201-P030T01	Rated Current: 200 A	[68]
LT-108-S7	Rated Current: 100 A	[70]
YDF-I-A4-P1-04	Rated Current: 50 A	[71]
SECOHR 50 BCI S2	Rated Current: 50 A	[72]

Table 5 shows the current sensors used in the literature. Current sensor should be selected according to the machinery's current input. Since current sensors are widely available and has no compatibility or environmental challenges other than maximum ampere input, there is no clear favourite current sensor manufacturer.

The dynamometer models used in tool wear monitoring/prediction applications can be seen in Table 6. The important features in selecting a dynamometer include measuring

Table 6. Models of dynamometers used in tool wear monitoring/prediction.

Dynamometer model	Important features	References
Kistler 9256C1	±250 N measuring range, −26 pC/N sensitivity on x and z axes, −13 pC/N on y axis	[26]
Kistler 9255B	±20 kN measuring range on x and y axes, −10 kN to +40 kN measuring range on z axis, −8 pC/N sensitivity on x and y axes, −3, 7 pC/N on z axis	[15, 47, 50, 73]
Kistler 9017B	±20 kN measuring range on x and y axes, −10 kN to +40 kN measuring range on z axis, −8 pC/N sensitivity on x and y axes, −3,7 pC/N on z axis	[48]
Kistler 9257B	±5 kN measuring range on x, y and z axes, −7,5 pC/N sensitivity on x and y axes, −3,7 pC/N on z axis	[49, 75, 77–80]
PCB 740B02	IEPE, Uniaxial, 100 pk µε measurement range, 50 mV/µε sensitivity	[51]
Kistler 9272	±5 kN measuring range on x and y axes, −5 kN to + 20 kN measuring range on z axis, −7,8 pC/N sensitivity on x and y axes, −3,5 pC/N on z axis	[64]
Kistler 9257A	±5 kN measuring range on x, y and z axes, −7,5 pC/N sensitivity on x and y axes, −3,7 pC/N on z axis	[16, 74]

range and sensitivity. Kistler is the favourite manufacturer amongst the literature for dynamometers. Kistler 9257B is the most used sensor model.

4   Conclusion

In the existing literature for tool wear monitoring/prediction, there are five predominant sensors used. These are accelerometers, acoustic emission sensors, microphones, current sensors and dynamometers.

The least invasive (interfering with production) sensor is current sensor, the most invasive sensor is dynamometer. Hence, dynamometers are commonly used for laboratory research. The most accurate information about the production process is also given by dynamometers.

Since the frequency bandwidth reached by acoustic emission sensors are high, in ideal conditions, they predict tool wear with ease. But since it is too dependent on the cutting tool and workpiece, it is too prone to noise, hard to implement and hard to obtain data, it is mostly used in laboratory conditions. Albeit microphones do not reach the same level of bandwidth as acoustic emission sensors, microphones are more likely to be used in production environments. It is more convenient to implement and obtain data from, and it can be placed away from the machining process.

Accelerometers are commonly used in tool wear applications and have well predictive abilities. Although current sensors are easily implemented in production environments, they do not perform as well as accelerometers and acoustic emission sensors in terms of severity. Current sensors lag a while compared to other sensors. Most costly approach for tool wear monitoring is the use of dynamometer systems. Except current sensors, every sensor type has a "favourite" manufacturer according to the literature.

References

1. Javaid, M., et al.: Sensors for daily life: a review. Sens. Int. **2**, 100121 (2021)
2. IAzmi, A.I.: Monitoring of tool wear using measured machining forces and neuro-fuzzy modelling approaches during machining of GFRP composites. Adv. Eng. Softw. **82**, 53–64 (2015)
3. Sharif Ullah, A.M.M.: Modeling and simulation of complex manufacturing phenomena using sensor signals from the perspective of Industry 4.0. Adv. Eng. Inform. **39**, 1–13 (2019)
4. Mehta, S., et al.: Measurement and analysis of tool wear using vision system. In: 2019 IEEE 6th International Conference on Industrial Engineering and Applications (ICIEA). IEEE (2019)
5. Pagani, L., Parenti, P., Cataldo, S., Scott, P.J., Annoni, M.: Indirect cutting tool wear classification using deep learning and chip colour analysis. Int. J. Adv. Manuf. Technol. **111**(3–4), 1099–1114 (2020). https://doi.org/10.1007/s00170-020-06055-6
6. Alhadeff, L.L., et al.: Protocol for tool wear measurement in micro-milling. Wear **420**, 54–67 (2019)
7. Yu, H., et al.: An improved tool wear monitoring method using local image and fractal dimension of workpiece. Math. Prob. Eng. **2021**, 11 p. (2021). https://doi.org/10.1155/2021/9913581. Article ID 9913581
8. Shen, Z.-A., et al.: Real-time estimation of machine cutting tool wear. J. Chin. Inst. Eng. **45**, 1–14 (2022)
9. Kuntoğlu, M., Salur, E., Gupta, M.K., Sarıkaya, M., Pimenov, D.Y.: A state-of-the-art review on sensors and signal processing systems in mechanical machining processes. Int. J. Adv. Manuf. Technol. **116**(9–10), 2711–2735 (2021). https://doi.org/10.1007/s00170-021-07425-4
10. Sener, B., et al.: A novel chatter detection method for milling using deep convolution neural networks. Measurement **182**, 109689 (2021)
11. Serin, G., Sener, B., Ozbayoglu, A.M., Unver, H.O.: Review of tool condition monitoring in machining and opportunities for deep learning. Int. J.Adv. Manuf. Technol. **109**(3–4), 953–974 (2020). https://doi.org/10.1007/s00170-020-05449-w
12. Seyrek, P., et al.: An evaluation study of EMD, EEMD, and VMD for chatter detection in milling. Procedia Comput. Sci. **200**, 160–174 (2022)
13. Nath, C.: Integrated tool condition monitoring systems and their applications: a comprehensive review. Procedia Manuf. **48**, 852–863 (2020)
14. Tamang, S.K., Chandrasekaran, M., Sahoo, A.K.: Sustainable machining: an experimental investigation and optimization of machining Inconel 825 with dry and MQL approach. J. Braz. Soc. Mech. Sci. Eng. **40**(8), 1–18 (2018). https://doi.org/10.1007/s40430-018-1294-2
15. Kious, M., et al.: Influence of machining cycle of horizontal milling on the quality of cutting force measurement for the cutting tool wear monitoring. Prod. Eng. **2**(4), 443–449 (2008)
16. Haber, R.E., et al.: An investigation of tool-wear monitoring in a high-speed machining process. Sens. Actuators A **116**(3), 539–545 (2004)
17. Liang, Q., et al.: Methods and research for multi-component cutting force sensing devices and approaches in machining. Sensors **16**(11), 1926 (2016)
18. Totis, G., Sortino, M.: Development of a modular dynamometer for triaxial cutting force measurement in turning. Int. J. Mach. Tools Manuf. **51**(1), 34–42 (2011)
19. Patra, K.: Acoustic emission based tool condition monitoring system in drilling. In: Proceedings of the World Congress on Engineering, vol. 3 (2011)

20. Snr, D.E.D.: Sensor signals for tool-wear monitoring in metal cutting operations—a review of methods. Int. J. Mach. Tools Manuf. **40**(8), 1073–1098 (2000)
21. Li, X.: A brief review: acoustic emission method for tool wear monitoring during turning. Int. J. Mach. Tools Manuf. **42**(2), 157–165 (2002)
22. Arul, S., Vijayaraghavan, L., Malhotra, S.K.: Online monitoring of acoustic emission for quality control in drilling of polymeric composites. J. Mater. Process. Technol. **185**(1–3), 184–190 (2007)
23. Hutton, D.V., Hu, F.: Acoustic emission monitoring of tool wear in end-milling using time-domain averaging. J. Manuf. Sci. Eng. **121**, 8–12 (1999)
24. Gómez, M.P., et al.: Assessment of cutting tool condition by acoustic emission. Procedia Mater. Sci. **1**, 321–328 (2012)
25. Zhang, X., Wang, S., Li, W., Lu, X.: Heterogeneous sensors-based feature optimisation and deep learning for tool wear prediction. Int. J. Adv. Manuf. Technol. **114**(9–10), 2651–2675 (2021). https://doi.org/10.1007/s00170-021-07021-6
26. Feng, J., et al.: Tool wear monitoring for micro-end grinding of ceramic materials. J. Mater. Process. Technol. **209**(11), 5110–5116 (2009)
27. Zhou, J.-H., et al.: Tool wear monitoring using acoustic emissions by dominant-feature identification. IEEE Trans. Instrum. Meas. **60**(2), 547–559 (2010)
28. Zhang, K.-F., Yuan, H.-Q., Nie, P.: A method for tool condition monitoring based on sensor fusion. J. Intell. Manuf. **26**(5), 1011–1026 (2015). https://doi.org/10.1007/s10845-015-1112-y
29. Alexandre, F.A., et al.: Tool condition monitoring of aluminum oxide grinding wheel using AE and fuzzy model. Int. J. Adv. Manuf. Technol. **96**(1–4), 67–79 (2018). https://doi.org/10.1007/s00170-018-1582-0
30. Moia, D.F.G., Thomazella, I.H., Aguiar, P.R., Bianchi, E.C., Martins, C.H.R., Marchi, M.: Tool condition monitoring of aluminum oxide grinding wheel in dressing operation using acoustic emission and neural networks. J. Braz. Soc. Mech. Sci. Eng. **37**(2), 627–640 (2014). https://doi.org/10.1007/s40430-014-0191-6
31. Hanachi, H., Yu, W., Kim, I.Y., Liu, J., Mechefske, C.K.: Hybrid data-driven physics-based model fusion framework for tool wear prediction. Int. J. Adv. Manuf. Technol. **101**(9–12), 2861–2872 (2018). https://doi.org/10.1007/s00170-018-3157-5
32. Prasad, B.S., Sarcar, M.M.M., Satish Ben, B.: Development of a system for monitoring tool condition using acousto-optic emission signal in face turning—an experimental approach. Int. J. Adv. Manuf. Technol. **51**(1), 57–67 (2010)
33. Rajesh, S., et al.: Multi-response optimization of machining parameters on red mud-based aluminum metal matrix composites in turning process. Int. J. Adv. Manuf. Technol. **67**(1), 811–821 (2013)
34. Orhan, S., et al.: Tool wear evaluation by vibration analysis during end milling of AISI D3 cold work tool steel with 35 HRC hardness. NDT & E Int. **40**(2), 121–126 (2007)
35. Zhou, M., et al.: Vibration-assisted precision machining of steel with PCD tools. Mater. Manuf. Processes **18**(5), 825–834 (2003)
36. Abdullah, A., Shabgard, M.R.: Effect of ultrasonic vibration of tool on electrical discharge machining of cemented tungsten carbide (WC-Co). Int. J. Adv. Manuf. Technol. **38**(11), 1137–1147 (2008)
37. Cong, W.L., et al.: Vibration amplitude in rotary ultrasonic machining: a novel measurement method and effects of process variables. J. Manuf. Sci. Eng. **133**(3), 034501 (2011)
38. Zhang, C., et al.: Tool condition monitoring and remaining useful life prognostic based on a wireless sensor in dry milling operations. Sensors **16**(6), 795 (2016)
39. Guo, K., et al.: Development and testing of a wireless rotating triaxial vibration measuring tool holder system for milling process. Measurement **163**, 108034 (2020)

40. Guo, K., Sun, J.: An integrated wireless vibration sensing tool holder for milling tool condition monitoring with singularity analysis. Measurement **174**, 109038 (2021)
41. Hassan, M., Sadek, A., Attia, M.H.: Novel sensor-based tool wear monitoring approach for seamless implementation in high speed milling applications. CIRP Ann. **70**(1), 87–90 (2021)
42. Zhang, B., Katinas, C., Shin, Y.C.: Robust tool wear monitoring using systematic feature selection in turning processes with consideration of uncertainties. J. Manuf. Sci. Eng. **140**(8), 081010 (2018)
43. Sun, I.C., Cheng, R.C., Chen, K.S.: Evaluation of transducer signature selections on machine learning performance in cutting tool wear prognosis. Int. J. Adv. Manuf. Technol. **119**, 6451–6468 (2022). https://doi.org/10.1007/s00170-021-08526-w
44. Sun, I., Cheng, R.-C., Chen, K.-S.: Evaluation of transducer signature selections on machine learning performance in cutting tool wear prognosis. Int. J. Adv. Manuf. Technol. **119**, 1–18 (2022)
45. Chen, B., et al.: Reliability estimation for cutting tools based on logistic regression model using vibration signals. Mech. Syst. Sig. Process. **25**(7), 2526–2537 (2011)
46. Kuntoğlu, M., Sağlam, H.: Investigation of signal behaviors for sensor fusion with tool condition monitoring system in turning. Measurement **173**, 108582 (2021)
47. Duo, A., et al.: Drilling process monitoring: a framework for data gathering and feature extraction techniques. Procedia CIRP **99**, 189–195 (2021)
48. Jemielniak, K., et al.: Tool condition monitoring based on numerous signal features. Int. J. Adv. Manuf. Technol. **59**(1), 73–81 (2012)
49. Niu, B., Sun, J., Yang, B.: Multisensory based tool wear monitoring for practical applications in milling of titanium alloy. Mater. Today Proc. **22**, 1209–1217 (2020)
50. Lamraoui, M.E.B.M., Thomas, M., El Badaoui, M.: Cyclostationarity approach for monitoring chatter and tool wear in high speed milling. Mech. Syst. Sig. Process. **44**(1–2), 177–198 (2014)
51. Scheffer, C., Heyns, P.S.: Wear monitoring in turning operations using vibration and strain measurements. Mech. Syst. Signal Process. **15**(6), 1185–1202 (2001)
52. Gomes, M.C., et al.: Tool wear monitoring in micromilling using support vector machine with vibration and sound sensors. Precis. Eng. **67**, 137–151 (2021)
53. Ai, C.S., et al.: The milling tool wear monitoring using the acoustic spectrum. Int. J. Adv. Manuf. Technol. **61**(5), 457–463 (2012)
54. Shankar, S., Mohanraj, T., Rajasekar, R.: Prediction of cutting tool wear during milling process using artificial intelligence techniques. Int. J. Comput. Integr. Manuf. **32**(2), 174–182 (2019)
55. Seemuang, N., McLeay, T., Slatter, T.: Using spindle noise to monitor tool wear in a turning process. Int. J. Adv. Manuf. Technol. **86**(9–12), 2781–2790 (2016). https://doi.org/10.1007/s00170-015-8303-8
56. Ubhayaratne, I., et al.: Audio signal analysis for tool wear monitoring in sheet metal stamping. Mech. Syst. Sig. Process. **85**, 809–826 (2017)
57. Kothuru, A., Nooka, S.P., Liu, R.: Application of audible sound signals for tool wear monitoring using machine learning techniques in end milling. Int. J. Adv. Manuf. Technol. **95**(9–12), 3797–3808 (2017). https://doi.org/10.1007/s00170-017-1460-1
58. Ravikumar, S., Ramachandran, K.I.: Tool wear monitoring of multipoint cutting tool using sound signal features signals with machine learning techniques. Mater. Today Proc. **5**(11), 25720–25729 (2018)
59. Aliustaoglu, C., Metin Ertunc, H., Ocak, H.: Tool wear condition monitoring using a sensor fusion model based on fuzzy inference system. Mech. Syst. Sig. Process. **23**(2), 539–546 (2009)
60. Silva, R.G., et al.: The adaptability of a tool wear monitoring system under changing cutting conditions. Mech. Syst. Sig. Process. **14**(2), 287–298 (2000)
61. Lin, Y.-R., Lee, C.-H., Lu, M.-C.: Robust tool wear monitoring system development by sensors and feature fusion. Asian J. Control **24**, 1005–1021 (2022)

62. Alonso, F.J., Salgado, D.R.: Application of singular spectrum analysis to tool wear detection using sound signals. Proc. Inst. Mech. Eng. Part B J. Eng. Manuf. **219**(9), 703–710 (2005)
63. Li, Z., Liu, R., Dazhong, W.: Data-driven smart manufacturing: tool wear monitoring with audio signals and machine learning. J. Manuf. Process. **48**, 66–76 (2019)
64. Salgado, D.R., Alonso, F.J.: An approach based on current and sound signals for in-process tool wear monitoring. Int. J. Mach. Tools Manuf. **47**(14), 2140–2152 (2007)
65. Huda, F., Karjuni, K., Rusli, M.: Cutting tool wear analysis using sound signal and simple microphone. IOP Conf. Ser. Mater. Sci. Eng. **830**(4), 042028 (2020)
66. Uekita, M., Takaya, Y.: Tool condition monitoring for form milling of large parts by combining spindle motor current and acoustic emission signals. Int. J. Adv. Manuf. Technol. **89**(1–4), 65–75 (2016). https://doi.org/10.1007/s00170-016-9082-6
67. Zhang, X.Y., et al.: A multi-sensor based online tool condition monitoring system for milling process. Procedia CIRP **72**, 1136–1141 (2018)
68. Feng, T., et al.: A new time–space attention mechanism driven multi-feature fusion method for tool wear monitoring. Int. J. Adv. Manuf. Technol. **120**, 1–16 (2022)
69. Zhang, X.: Deep learning driven tool wear identification and remaining useful life prediction. Dissertation, Coventry University (2020)
70. Ou, J., et al.: A novel order analysis and stacked sparse auto-encoder feature learning method for milling tool wear condition monitoring. Sensors **20**(10), 2878 (2020)
71. Tang, J., Li, W.X., Zhao, B.: The application of GA-BP algorithm in prediction of tool wear state. IOP Conf. Ser. Mater. Sci. Eng. **398**(1), 012025 (2018)
72. da Silva, R.H.L., da Silva, M.B., Hassui, A.: A probabilistic neural network applied in monitoring tool wear in the end milling operation via acoustic emission and cutting power signals. Mach. Sci. Technol. **20**(3), 386–405 (2016)
73. Lin, S.C., Lin, R.J.: Tool wear monitoring in face milling using force signals. Wear **198**(1–2), 136–142 (1996)
74. Wang, G., et al.: Tool wear monitoring based on cointegration modelling of multisensory information. Int. J. Comput. Integr. Manuf. **27**(5), 479–487 (2014)
75. Chen, J.C., Chen, J.C.: An artificial-neural-networks-based in-process tool wear prediction system in milling operations. Int. J. Adv. Manuf. Technol. **25**(5), 427–434 (2005)
76. Ertunc, H.M., Oysu, C.: Drill wear monitoring using cutting force signals. Mechatronics **14**(5), 533–548 (2004)
77. Chen, J.C., Susanto, V.: Fuzzy logic based in-process tool-wear monitoring system in face milling operations. Int. J. Adv. Manuf. Technol. **21**(3), 186–192 (2003)
78. Karandikar, J., et al.: Tool wear monitoring using naive Bayes classifiers. Int. J. Adv. Manuf. Technol. **77**(9), 1613–1626 (2015)
79. Patra, K., et al.: Artificial neural network based tool condition monitoring in micro mechanical peck drilling using thrust force signals. Precis. Eng. **48**, 279–291 (2017)
80. Kene, A.P., Choudhury, S.K.: Analytical modeling of tool health monitoring system using multiple sensor data fusion approach in hard machining. Measurement **145**, 118–129 (2019)

Advanced Information Systems

Towards the Use of IT Technologies for Health Literacy and Health Information Competences – A Case Study

Marta Chmielewska-Anielak[1], Aneta Poniszewska-Marańda[1,2(✉)] (iD),
and Agnieszka Renn-Zurek[1]

[1] University of Humanities and Economics in Lodz, Lodz, Poland
{manielak,arenn}@ahe.lodz.pl
[2] Institute of Information Technology, Lodz University of Technology, Lodz, Poland
aneta.poniszewska-maranda@p.lodz.pl

Abstract. We live in a knowledge-based society, when the ability to find and apply the right information is a basic skill in every life need. Hence, today it cannot be said that someone who is not able to find and use information enabling them to take care of their own health, is a health competent person. Health literacy (HL) is the ability to understand and use the information related to health and disease. To improve the HL of people it is possible to use the IT/ICT tools and methods. The paper presents the case study of use of IT technologies for health literacy and health information competences supporting that was realized in the framework of EU project, named ELILY2.

Keywords: Health literacy · eHealth literacy · E-learning course · E-learning platform

1 Introduction

High level of health literacy (HL) is the ability to understand and use the information related to health and disease. An important issue is examining the level of human health competences. This serves to better target the interventions of public health institutions (medicine, nursing) to the HL spheres in which the greatest deficiencies are identified. One of the basic needs and challenges in the current health care system should be shaping human Health Literacy (HL). In simple terms, it is the ability to understand and use information about health and disease. Broadly understood, Health Literacy includes cognitive mechanisms and social skills that affect the motivation and skills of individuals to access, search, understand and use the information on this basis, which is to translate into improving and maintaining good health.

Health Literacy means more than just reading a leaflet or making an appointment. According to WHO, these are all cognitive mechanisms and social skills that affect the motivation and abilities of individuals to effectively obtain, process and use information to maintain or improve health. The high level of health

I. Awan et al. (Eds.): MobiWIS 2022, LNCS 13475, pp. 209–222, 2022.
https://doi.org/10.1007/978-3-031-14391-5_16

competences gives the knowledge of how and where to look for information on the impact of various factors on health. Moreover, these competences are related to the skills of critical assessment of health factors, and in a favourable environment they allow for their modification. The level of health competences and their development is important from the perspective of health promotion, as well as disease prevention or treatment. For professionals operating in these areas, it seems important to know the ways and benefits of improving HL or the effects of its low level.

We live in a knowledge-based society, when the ability to find and apply the right information is a basic skill in every life need. Hence, today it cannot be said that someone who is not able to find and use information enabling them to take care of their own health, is a health competent person. Information literacy consists of the skills to find and evaluate information as well as an appropriate amount of knowledge about the sources of information, the principles of its processing and ordering. This term, used primarily in information science, struggles to make its way in health sciences, where it hides under various guises, e.g. as an element of health literacy or computer literacy. Health information competences (HIC), however, is a narrower term than health competences. The latter, in addition to information skills, include, among others basic knowledge of health, diseases and their treatment, as well as skills such as reading, writing and calculating skills, social communication skills, etc. In turn, having a HIC is much more than the ability to use a computer and computer programs, because the necessary knowledge and skills they concern the content of the information.

As defined by the Medical Library Association, health information literacy is "a set of skills needed to: accept the need for health information, identify likely sources of information and use them to retrieve relevant information, assess the quality of information obtained, and apply it to a specific situation; and to analyse, understand and use this information to make decisions beneficial to health". This cycle of activities is determined by individual characteristics and environmental conditions (the presence and access to information sources, the "friendliness" of these sources, the degree of information processing, the presence of intermediaries assisting in finding and processing information, etc.), and the efficiency of their implementation is influenced by psychosocial factors and mechanisms on which both competences and information behaviour depend.

Because of the great development of IT/ICT technologies the health literacy and health information competences and their realisation could be supported by these technologies. of course it can be done at different levels and by different forms – by mobile application, web application, learning platforms, IT-oriented courses of health literacy [3].

The paper presents the case study of use of IT technologies for health literacy and health information competences supporting that was realized in the framework of EU project, named ELILY2. The paper is structured as follows: Sect. 2 presents the description and main ideas of ELILY 2 project. Section 3 describes the e-learning course concept of ELILY2 project while Sect. 4 deals with the e-learning course platform dedicated to ELILY2 project.

2   Case Study Presentation: ELILY2 Project

ELILY2 project aims to develop blended health literacy training for nurses working with older people. There is no evidence on how Health or eHealth Literacy knowledge and skills are included in the nursing education and if they are incorporated in the nursing studies. Reviews in USA schools of nursing revealed limited and inconsistent health literacy content in nursing curricula. However, although nurses' health literacy knowledge and communication skills are essential for improving patients' health literacy, nurses do not have adequate knowledge and experience regarding health literacy practices [7].

A significant barrier to health promotion, disease prevention, and health maintenance is inadequate HL, which is highly prevalent across the older population in Europe. Health literacy "entails people's knowledge, motivation and competencies to access, understand, appraise, and apply health information in order to make judgments and take decisions in everyday life concerning healthcare, disease prevention and health promotion to maintain or improve quality of life during the life course" [1]. In a European HL survey conducted in eight countries, higher proportions of people with limited HL were found among those who were between 66 and 75 years of age (58.2%) or 76 years or older (60.8%) [2]. Data demonstrated that patients with limited HL were at an increased risk for worse health outcomes, less understanding about their health issues, and more difficulties following treatment plans [6].

The US Department of Health and Human Services (2021) refers to the increase of HL of the population as a core objective of Healthy People 2030, encouraging the education of health care professionals and the inclusion of HL in health care program curricula. Nurses are the primary healthcare professionals who interact with patients, communicate with them, and educate them on various health issues. In related studies, nurses were not familiar with the HL definitions, did not know that older adults were considered a high-risk group of low HL, and did not recognise the consequences of low HL. Nurses reported difficulties in using screening tools, identifying patients with low HL levels, assessing their readability level and HL interventions, and effectively using written communication strategies. More years of experience at work entailed more challenges in their interaction with low HL patients [7].

Furthermore, according to the relevant research, nursing professionals may be aware of the term health literacy but only a small percentage (smaller then ¡40%) understands how the ability of patients to navigate in the health care system, to read medical material and follow the recommended treatment is linked to health literacy of the patients and their families [4]. According to a European project among 12 European countries, the first two reasons on tasks left unfinished included the communication and education of the patients and their families by nurses [5]. With this project, we aim:

- to enhance the knowledge and skills of nurses, nurses students regarding the concepts of health and ehealth literacy, how to identify low health and ehealth literate of older people and families, users of health care services,

- to enhance indirectly the health literacy and ehealth literacy skills of older people and their families,
- to provide a practice IT platform for this type of training,
- to raise awareness of the users' health literacy and ehealth literacy topic within the healthcare sector.

The blended training centred on IT platform was planned to develop in three core dimensions: ways and tools to identify the low health and ehealth literate patients, ways and tools to educate patients with low health and ehealth literacy and a tailored online course modules for nurses to enhance their own ehealth literacy skills.

3   E-learning Course Concept of ELILY2 Project

In order to support the transferability and broader exploitation of the training programme of ELILY project the e-learning course platform was developed for the training programme. From the e-course, nurses and other health care professionals can go through the training contents specially adapted to be usable and understandable remotely. The e-learning course, available in five partners' languages (English Greek Polish Lithuanian, Czech), are accessible for free from a dedicated e-learning platform. For each module of the course, the user can go through interactive resources, including [7]:

- background information, including, where appropriate, video-tutorials and step-by-step guides,
- online exercises to practice the acquired skills,
- self-assessment tools,
- online glossary and access to the FAQ library.

Upon completion of the course, the participants are be able to download an attendance certificate as well as an open-badge.

The steps of creation of the e-learning course platform were as follows [7]:

1. Adaptation of modules for e-learning course: partners, based on a standard structure provided by the lead partner, adapted the contents of developed course modules in order to make them accessible via e-learning (Fig. 1). The training material were next integrated with the development of dedicated multimedia resources, such as video tutorials.
2. Design of the e-learning course (specifications): the lead partner created the technical infrastructure of the course, designed the attendance certificate, created the open-badges, uploaded the training material and made the beta-test of the course before its release.
3. Testing of the e-learning course was the part of blended learning testing methodology. Pilot testing were organised for at least 50 nurses or other health care professionals before its final release. Feedbacks were gathered and next the training was fine-tuned where appropriate.

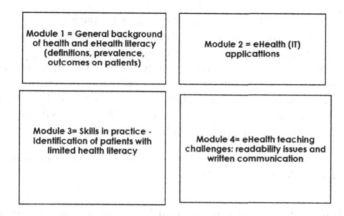

Fig. 1. First version of eHealth literacy training among nurses working with older people [7]

After the deep research of the needs of nurses and other health workers working with older people and heir families, the following four modules for the HL and eHL training among nurses was developed [7]:

1. *Module 1* includes two core items and it is focused on the training of nurses and nursing students on the concepts of HL and eHL, eHealth, mHealth. The factors associated with HL and eHL, the importance of nursing practice, the prevalence of limited HL and eHL and outcomes for nurses and older people should be discussed. The nurse-older person relationship were introduced. Trainees will be competent to describe the dimensions of concepts, prevalence, identify factors and barriers, realise the impact and understand the importance of using reliable sources.
2. *Module 2* includes five items and is focused on enhancing communication skills. It aims to teach nurses to identify low HL older adults using instruments and behaviour observations. The trainees will be introduced to the most frequently used instruments for measuring the level of HL and eHL of older adults. Most communication strategies, privacy and security issues for social media has to be learned. Interactive exercises focus on the teach-back method, Ask Me 3 and plain communication.
3. *Module 3* includes four items and aims to train nurses and nursing students to assess the readability of online health information, verify patients' understanding of written information, plan intervention as an interactive exercise and understand the cultural aspects and strategies to promote HL and eHL. The trainees will be competent to evaluate the readability of written health materials and revise them to ensure clarity and simplicity, develop individualized action plans for patients' education, identify different concepts of cultural sensitivity and diversity, use appropriate material and integrate cultural sensitive communication strategies.

4. *Module 4* includes two core items and focuses on patient safety, explaining the impact of low HL on patients' outcomes, medicine adherence, discussing safety issues at home environment and introducing the available assisted living technologies. Trainees will be competent to identify the adverse outcomes of low HL on patient safety, explain the issue of remote monitoring of patients and eHealth principles, describe available technologies and applications for older people, recognize red flags behaviours related to patient safety and explain the impact of low HL in compliance in treatment.

The next subsections present the concept and content of four designed modules of e-learning platform for ELILY project.

3.1   Module 1: Introduction to Health Literacy and eHealth Literacy

The aim of the module is to introduce the general background of Health literacy and eHealth literacy. The objectives of this module are as follows:

- to present health professionals to Health literacy and eHealth literacy and to the related concepts and factors,
- to explain the importance of health literacy and ehealth literacy for nursing practice and especially for the care of older persons,
- to address the prevalence of limited health literacy and ehealth literacy among nurses and the lack of knowledge on relevant issues,
- to indicate the importance of evaluating the reliability of online sources and ways to perform it.

The learning outcomes of the module 1 specify what the trainees will be able to do by the end of the module and they are as:

- Describe the dimensions of health literacy, ehealth literacy, mhealth literacy and related concepts.
- Be aware of the prevalence of low health literacy and ehealth literacy among nurses.
- Identify the factors and barriers associated with health literacy and ehealth literacy.
- Realize that patients' health literacy and ehealth literacy are often overestimated by nurses and that such issues are not taken adequately into consideration when providing care to older people.
- Realize the impact of health literacy and ehealth literacy on care provided to older people.
- Understand the importance of using reliable sources.
- Recognize reliable and accurate online health information and scientific resources.

3.2   Module 2: Patients with Limited Health Literacy

The aim of the module is to identify the patients with limited health literacy. The objectives of this module are as follows:

- to enable trainees to identify low health literacy older adults, through the use of instruments and behaviour observation,
- to improve participant's digital and face to face communication skills.

The learning outcomes of the module 2 specify what the trainees will be able to do by the end of the module and they are as:

- Describe instruments of health literacy and eHealth literacy assessment.
- Incorporate direct behaviour observation to identify patients with low health literacy and recognize "red flag" behaviours which may suggest a patient has low health literacy.
- Elicit patients' prior understanding of their health issues in a non-shaming manner.
- Utilize communication strategies by:
  - recognizing, avoid, and constructively correct the use of medical jargon,
  - orally communicate accurately and effectively in patients' preferred language,
  - integrating plain language principles for oral communication and feedback with patients.
- Use a patient-centred approach in every contact with the patients.
- Demonstrate advanced digital skills regarding the use of social media.
- Consider privacy and security issues while using the internet to obtain or share health information.

3.3   Module 3: Feasibility and Readability Issues and eHealth Challenges

The aim of the module is to explore the feasibility and readability issues and eHealth challenges. The objectives of this module are as follows:

- to assess the difficulty of written information materials and simplify written information materials,
- to administer tools and use methods of verification of the patients' understanding of health care information written material,
- to reflect and use culturally sensitive communication and strategies.

The learning outcomes of the module 3 specify what the trainees will be able to do by the end of the module and they are as:

- Evaluate the readability/difficulty of written health materials and revise them to ensure clarity and simplicity, e.g. using familiar lay terms, phrases, and concepts.
- Incorporate a combination of techniques on written materials to increase patient's understanding..

- Develop individualized action plans to patient using online resources (patient-centred approach).
- - Understand and discuss cultural differences:
  - identify the different concepts of cultural sensitivity and diversity in context – specific professional practice,
  - seek and use culturally and socially appropriate materials to increase written communication with patients,
  - integrate cultural sensitive communication strategies into collaboration with the patient in family.

3.4   Module 4: Health Literacy and Patient Safety

The aim of the module is to discuss how Health literacy is related with patient safety. The objectives of this module are as follows:

- to explain the impact of HL and eHL on patient safety for older people living in the community,
- to clarify health literacy and medicine adherence,
- to describe safety issues at the home environment,
- to discuss available technologies applications, assisted living technologies, other rehabilitation technologies,
- to use and assess the resources regarding patient education.

The learning outcomes of the module 4 specify what the trainees will be able to do by the end of the module and they are as:

- Identify negative outcomes of low health literary on patient safety for effective patient education..
- Explain the issue of remote monitoring of patients and various types of electronic medical records for a better patients understanding of the principles of ehealth.
- Describe and use the available technologies and applications for elderly for increase patients level of health literacy.
- Recognize reliable and accurate online health information and scientific resources for increase patients level of health literacy related to patient safety.
- Recognize the "red flag" behaviours related to patient safety for identification a patient has low health literacy.
- Explain the impact of low health literacy on outcomes on patients to increase patients compliance in treatment.
- Be aware of the importance of using modern technologies in the field of health literacy for effective patient education.

The next section presents the content of all modules created on the online course platform fulfilling the aim, objectives and learning outcomes of each module presented above.

4   E-learning Course Platform Dedicated to ELILY2 Project

Each of four modules of e-learning course dedicated for nurses and nurse students is divided into steps and each step into pages. Each step described below is presented in the separate page, creating together the sequence of steps/pages with two transitional test-quizzes as the conditions that have to be passed to proceed and one final test-quiz and questionnaire as the final evaluation of the trainees and the learning module (Fig. 2).

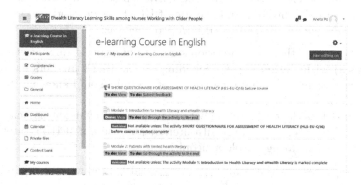

Fig. 2. E-learning course platform dedicated to ELILY2

4.1   Module 1 of E-Learning Course Platform

First step is divided into two pages containing the introduction information such as:

- Page 1 provides the short introduction information about the project, module 1 and trainings.
- Page 2 provide the short question-survey of multiple choice with the message depending on the user's answer encouraging him/her to realize the online course.

Second step presents the introduction to the topics of health literacy and eHealth literacy and is divided into two pages as:

- Page 1 provides the presentation with the definitions and concepts of health literacy, eHealth literacy, mHealth literacy.
- Page 2 provides two short videos to underline the importance of both concepts: eHealth literacy and mHealth literacy.

Third step presents the prevalence of low Health Literacy among nurses and the use of HL strategies and practices, when caring for older people. It is divided into three pages:

- Page 1 provides the presentation with published studies for the prevalence of low Health Literacy and eHealth Literacy among nurses and the use of HL strategies and practices, when caring for older people.
- Page 2 provides the short question-survey containing two questions (multiple choice) with the messages depending on the user's answers encouraging him/her to continue the online course and showing its importance.
- Page 3 provides the test-quiz containing 5 questions about the knowledge from step 2 and step 3. If the trainee pass the test he/she can go to step 4. If not, he/she has to go back to step 2.

Fourth step describes the factors and barriers associated with nurses' health literacy and eHealth literacy and the use of HL strategies and practices, when caring for older people. It is divided into two pages as:

- Page 1 provides the short question-survey containing 4 questions (multiple responses) with the messages depending on the user's answers encouraging him/her to continue the online course of Module 1 and showing its importance.
- Page 2 provides the presentation with the factors and barriers associated with nurses' health literacy and eHealth literacy and the use of HL strategies and practices, when caring for older people.

Fifth step presents the health literacy, eHealth literacy and potential outcomes on nurses and older people. It contains four pages as:

- Page 1 provides the short question-survey with the messages depending on the user's answer encouraging him/her to continue the online course of Module 1.
- Page 2 provides the presentation on the impact of health literacy and eHealth literacy on nurses and older people.
- Page 3 provides the crossword puzzle to find the hidden outcomes associated with health literacy and eHealth literacy.
- Page 4 provides the test-quiz containing 5 questions about the knowledge from step 4 and step 5. If the trainee pass the test he/she can go to step 6. If not, he/she has to go back to step 4.

The sixth step describes the searching for reliable online health information. It has two pages as:

- Page provides the short question-survey of multiple responses with the messages depending on the user's answers encouraging him/her to continue the online course and showing its importance.
- Page 2 provides the presentation with the basic steps of searching and evaluating reliable health information.

The seventh step is the last one of the module 1. It contains the page with questionnaire to collect feedback on the module and the page with the test-quiz containing 8 questions about the knowledge from steps 2–3, steps 4–5 and step 6. The exemplary views of the created platform for Module 1 are given in Figs. 3 and 4

Fig. 3. E-learning course platform dedicated to ELILY2 – exemplary view of module 1

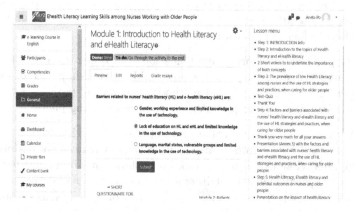

Fig. 4. E-learning course platform dedicated to ELILY2 – exemplary view of questions in module 1

4.2 Module 2 of E-Learning Course Platform

First step is provides the short introduction information about the project, module 2 and trainings. Second step learns the most used instruments for measuring health literacy and eHealth literacy available nationally. It contains 2 pages as:

- Page 1 provides the short question-survey of multiple choice with the message depending on the user's answer encouraging him/her to continue the online course – to realize Module 2 (Fig. 5).
- Page 2 provides the presentatin about the available assessment tools for measuring the health literacy and eHealth literacy to show the general view of instruments with an objective measurement approach, instruments with a subjective measurement approach and instruments with a mixed measurement approach.

Third step presents the training on how to identify common signs that indicate low health literacy. It has four pages as:

- Page 1 provides two cases of patients (diagnosed with type 2 diabetes) with different level of health literacy. The task of the trainee is to analyse the cases according to the following questions: (a) What attitudes towards health do patients present? (b) Which of the presented cases indicates low and high health competences? (c) Which patient will get health benefits and which one is at risk of developing complications? (d) Which patient will have a greater need for educational support and is willing to cooperate with the educator?
- Page 2 provides the answers to questions from the previous page presented in the form of Worksheet to identify the low and high health literacy.
- Page 3 provides the short question-survey of multiple choice with the messages depending on the user's answers encouraging him/her to continue the online Module 2 of the course and showing its importance.
- Page 4 provides the test-quiz containing 3 questions about the knowledge from step 2 and step 3. If the trainee passes the test he/she can go to step 4. If not, he/she has to go back to step 2.

Forth step presents the oral communication and cooperation with low health literacy adults – Oral/-Best practices-skill-building workshop (use of plain language, teach-back method, askMe3 method) encouraging patients and families to ask 3 specific questions to providers. It has the following pages:

- Page 1 provides the presentation of what communication is, types of communication and why is important for nurse-patient relationship. Moreover, it also explains what is the teach back and askMe3 methods and how to use plain language, during patient interaction. Next it provides the leaflet with the description what communication is, types of communication and three methods of communication during patient interaction: plain language, teach-back and askMe3 methods
- Page 2 provides the video about the use of "plain language" method explaining what the method is and how we can use it.
- Page 3 provides the video about the use of "teach-back" method explaining what the method is and how we can use it.
- Page 4 provides the video about the use of "askMe3" method explaining what the method is and how we can use it.

Fifth step presents he communication skills of social media (how to use Viber, WhatsApp, Skype, Messenger and other social media tools during the provider-patient interaction, assessing fake news, unreliable resources). It has the pages:

- Page 1 provides the presentation on three topics: (1) available professional teleconference tools used in the communication with other professionals or patient and alternative ways to exchange information, (2) guidelines for nurse-patient relationship through social media and (3) fake news problem in healthcare. Next provides the ICN (International Council of Nurses) guidelines for nurse-patient relationship on social media.

- Page 2 provides Online communication tools: WhatsApp vs Facebook Messenger vs Skype.
- Page 3 provides the test-quiz containing 5 questions about the knowledge from step 4 and step 5. If the trainee pass the test he/she can go to step 6. If not, he/she has to go back to step 4.

Sixth step describes the privacy and security issues (e.g. exchange of information, personal data, medical data). It has the following pages:

- Page 1 provides the short question-survey of multiple responses with the messages depending on the user's answers encouraging him/her to continue the online course and showing its importance.
- Page 2 provides the presentation with the most major issues regarding privacy and security issues, while using social media.

The seventh step is the last one of the module 2. It contains the page with questionnaire to collect feedback on the module and the page with test-quiz containing 8 questions about the knowledge from steps 2–3, steps 4–5 and 6.

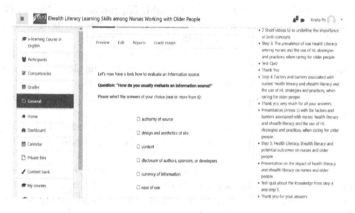

Fig. 5. E-learning course platform dedicated to ELILY2 – exemplary view of choices

Modules 3 and 4 are given in the similar forms as modules presented above according to their structure given in Sect. 3.

5 Conclusions

Nurses are the largest group of health care professionals and spend a considerable amount of time with the patients, having major impact on their caring experience. This is also the case for the older people's care. This type of care demands specialist skills to meet the older people's needs. Especially nurses working in the community settings, are the first health care professionals who come in contact with large groups of people, making assessments and recognizing early signs of poor health and other problems, acting as gatekeepers for the Health care services. The creation of e-learning courses and platform adapted to the needs of nurses and other healthcare workers can increase their knowledge and experiences in the contacts with patients that helps in increasing of health literacy and health information competences of the societies. The e-learning course platform dedicated to ELILY2 project presents the example of sue tools that are adapted to the current needs of their potentials users as well as their technical possibilities and resources.

Acknowledgements. The paper was realised and supported by Erasmus+ project eLily2-RN_ehealth LIteracy Learning skills among Nurses working with older people, no 2020-1-CY01-KA202-065962.

References

1. Sorensen, K., Van den Broucke, S., Fullam, J., Doyle, G., Pelikan, J., Slonska, Z.: Health literacy and public health: a systematic review and integration of definitions and models. BMC Public Health **12**(8), 80 (2012)
2. Sorensen, K., Pelikan, J., Rothlin, F., Ganahl, K., Slonska, Z., Doyle, G.: Health literacy in Europe: comparative results of the European health literacy survey (HLS-EU). Eur. J. Public Health. **25**(6), 1053–8 (2015)
3. Poniszewska-Marańda, A., Szukalska, A., Wilczyński, Ł: Learner-centred pedagogical approach based on smart city concept to enhance the development of STEM skills of children. In: Barolli, L., Poniszewska-Maranda, A., Enokido, T. (eds.) CISIS 2020. AISC, vol. 1194, pp. 210–221. Springer, Cham (2021). https://doi.org/10.1007/978-3-030-50454-0_20
4. Macabasco-O'Connell, A., Eileen, K., Fry-Bowers.: Knowledge and perceptions of health literacy among nursing professionals. J. Health Commun. **16**(3), 295–307 (2011)
5. Jones, T., Hamilton, P., Murry, N.: Unfinished nursing care, missed care and implicitly rationed care: state of the science review. Int. J. Nurs. Stud. **52**, 1121–37 (2015)
6. Saunders, C., Palesy, D., Lewis, J.: Systematic review and conceptual framework for health literacy training in health professions education. Health Prof. Educ. **5**, 13–29 (2019)
7. Webpage of eLily2 project. https://www.elily2.eu/. Accessed May 2022

A Systematic Literature Review on Relationship Between Internet Usage Behavior and Internet QoS in Campus

Zhang Lei[1]([⊠]) [iD] and Nor Shahniza Binti Kamal Bashah[2]

[1] Anhui Business and Technology College, Hefei Anhui 231100, China
zhangleiahbvc@gmail.com
[2] Faculty of Computer and Mathematical Sciences, Universiti Teknologi MARA,
40450 Shah Alam, Malaysia
shahniza@uitm.edu.my

Abstract. The Internet user population has drastically increased for many years. The Internet usage behavior and the Internet Quality of Service (QoS) are relatively used in most discussions about Internet users' experience and satisfaction. Even though much research has been done to improve the Internet QoS without jeopardizing the user experience, there is still a lack of studies to identify the relationship between both elements. This paper aims to conduct a systematic literature review of the relationship between Internet usage behavior and Internet QoS on campus. For this purpose, some literature search was conducted in several databases such as ACM, IEEE Explore, and Scopus. There were 47 articles selected and 36 articles met the inclusion criteria. The results show direct and indirect relationships between Internet usage, user behavior, and Internet QoS on campus. Based on these results, component variables for constructing an Internet usage behavior model on campus are proposed, and a set of direct and indirect relationships between these variables. This study complements the few previous investigations of these collaborative relationships.

Keywords: Internet usage · User profiling · User behavior model · Internet QoS

1 Introduction

With the popularization of mobile communication networks and wireless network technologies, the application with the support of the internet network is increasingly diversified, such as information retrieval, Internet TV, video call, online games, online shopping and live broadcasting, etc. The diversified internet application has increased demand for network quality (Tang et al. 2019). The network bandwidth is mainly fixed and cannot be adjusted to resolve the sharp increase in users' needs. On the other hand, the existing network is challenging to meet the QoS requirements of complex and diverse network applications. Subsequently, a series of unpredictable challenges and problems will come along with the low efficiency of the campus network, such as the security problem, network management problem, network operation stability, and network control capabilities.

I. Awan et al. (Eds.): MobiWIS 2022, LNCS 13475, pp. 223–236, 2022.
https://doi.org/10.1007/978-3-031-14391-5_17

Several studies have been conducted to understand how people utilize the Internet (Larose et al. 2001). Through previous scholars' research on students' Internet usage behavior on campus, self-efficacy and self-disparagement measures were established (Xu et al. 2019). For example, the link between Internet usage and academic achievement has been revealed, and machine learning is used to predict student academic performance based on usage statistics. Understanding users' internet usage behavior is essential for the quality of service (QoS) analysis on the internet (Polpinij and Namee 2019).

Thus, this paper aims to analyze state of the art on the relationship between Internet usage behavior and Internet Quality of Services (QoS). The literature has mainly analyzed, on the one hand, Internet usage behavior and, on the other, improving Internet QoS.

This paper starts with an explanation of the motivations for this work. Next, some related works are briefly reviewed. The central part of the paper explains how the systematic literature review for this research is conducted. The results from the systematic literature review are then analyzed and described thoroughly. Further works are given in the conclusion.

2   Motivation

Many factors motivated this work, derived from the previous analysis of related works.

2.1   Insufficient Bandwidth

Most campuses face insufficient bandwidth, partly because the Management ignores information construction. Internet bandwidth is expensive, and campuses do not have enough funds to pay for the bandwidth. Over the past five years, the average tariff per unit bandwidth of fixed broadband and per unit traffic of mobile networks has decreased by more than 95%. The dedicated line's average tariff per unit bandwidth has been reduced by more than 70%. Various fee reduction measures have benefited more than 1 billion users per year, with a cumulative profit of more than 109.9 billion US dollars. The annual cost of a 1 Gbps dedicated network also needs a bonus of $78500, and many campuses still cannot afford such high network costs.

2.2   Maximum Excess on Multimedia Files

Most students use cell phones to play games online accounted for 37%, QQ and WeChat for 98%, pay attention to the film, television, and literary developments for 23%, and browse web news for 93%, which shows that the focus of students in campuses is on games, emotional communication and making friends (Xing-Hua et al. 2018). In terms of the time period of Internet access, 39.75% of students choose to go online on double holidays, and 16.89% choose to go online before 10:00 pm. The percentage of those who choose to go online after school hours is 14.2%. Those who choose to go online overnight account for 8.9%, and those who choose to go online in the afternoon account for 20.73% (Xin-ying et al. 2019). Many students have similar Internet usage behaviors and are highly concentrated in specific time periods, which significantly impacts the change in Internet demand.

Consequently, this study aims to identify the relationship between Internet usage behavior and Internet QoS in previous research articles through a systematic literature review to find research gaps and improvement methods.

3   Related Works

There are two main areas for further improvement in the research on Internet usage behavior. One is that the data set of users' Internet usage behavior is relatively concentrated, and the investigation is only aimed at students from one University (Abbad 2021); Another is the lack of detailed and rigorous statistical analysis, especially on the time period and app (Apuke and Iyendo 2018a). In the former case, some researchers believe that offline applications can be considered in future research to reflect user access patterns (Ashibani and Mahmoud 2018), and it would be interesting to evaluate the proposed method on real data sets rather than synthetic data sets (Abdelhak et al. 2019). In the latter case, scholars believe that the customer behavior model should be optimized to reevaluate the data center (Weiwei et al. 2021).

Previous literature on the research field of Internet QoS mainly focused on the Internet of things or in a particular application, such as identifying potential website customers (Luo et al. 2017) and the impact on students' lifestyles on campus (Asimah 2020). Most literature on the quality of service selection assumes that the QoS is static (Wendong Wang et al. 2015). However, the natural environment tells us that these attributes are highly dynamic and uncertain. Limited by the "best-effort" principle and connectionless transmission protocol, the existing IP networks of many schools cannot meet the different QoS needs of users.

A few studies on Internet usage behavior and Internet QoS show that it may be interesting to continue to analyze the potential relationship between these variables. This research helps to strengthen the theoretical framework of the reciprocal relationship between user analysis, Internet behavior, user behavior model, and Internet QoS and expands the previous research on the relationship between Internet usage behavior and Internet QoS. In addition, the study helps to determine the most commonly used terms, the research methods used, and the industry and country of each paper.

3.1   Survey of Internet Usage

Several studies have applied uses and gratifications to explain Internet usage. Like Bandura's social cognitive theory, the uses and gratifications framework explains media use in terms of expected positive outcomes or gratifications.

Some researchers focused on the MOOC platform or the learning management system log data that record students' system operation to analyze and predict final grades in a specific course (Pacheco et al. 2020; Yang 2021). As an effective tool, a questionnaire survey is always used to collect Internet usage data to reveal the association between online behaviors and academic achievement (Apuke and Iyendo 2018b). In addition, to reveal the relationship between Internet usage and academic performance, some studies used special smartphone applications to track students' activities (Bogdan Ghita 2018; Wendong Wang et al. 2015). Utilize event logs to discover user behavior patterns on the internet or networking (Polpinij and Namee 2019).

Measures of self-efficacy and self-disparagement were developed for the domain of Internet behavior. The adverse outcomes of online behavior were analyzed for their impact on the Internet. Reveal the association between Internet usage behaviors and academic performance and predict undergraduates' academic performance from the usage data by machine learning (Xu et al. 2019). Understanding users' internet usage behavior is essential for the QoS analysis on the internet (Polpinij and Namee 2019).

In a survey of 171 college students, the social-cognitive model explained 60% of the available variance in Internet usage using multiple regression analysis. A set of features, including online duration, Internet traffic volume, and connection frequency, were extracted, calculated, and normalized from the actual Internet usage data of 4000 students. Three standard machine learning algorithms of the decision tree, neural network, and support vector machine were used to predict academic performance from these features (Xu et al. 2019). To have user behavior patterns from the event logs, this work aims to extract an exciting way of inappropriate user behaviors through internet usage patterns mining. The primary mechanism of the proposed method is the Generalized Sequential Pattern (GSP) algorithm, which is an algorithm of sequential pattern mining (Polpinij and Namee 2019).

Future studies should include more data on online behavior. For example, Internet resource types, the temporal distribution of access to different resources, etc., could be considered, and the involvement of more demographic data is recommended (Xu et al. 2019). We use only the Firewall event logs labeled as "not allow" for our study (Polpinij and Namee 2019).

3.2 Survey of User Profiling

User profiling is a set of structured data and information to describe a user in an interactive environment between a user and a system and explain the user's history details. Behavioral profiling-based authentication is established mainly because users present a unique behavior, such as working on a specific application (Ashibani and Mahmoud 2018). User profiling has been studied by analyzing application usage data, recommended systems, targeted advertisement services, and resource optimization programs (Abakumova et al., 2019).

Identifying user patterns is a crucial technique of user profiling, so it has been studied for various applications. The information parsed from digital devices (e.g., smartphones (Li et al. 2018) (Li et al. 2018), desktops (Benmoussa et al. 2017)) or online data (e.g., social network van) (Dumpit and Fernandez 2017) has been used for finding usage patterns.

User profiling aims to predict the characteristics of the user from digital evidence extracted from digital devices (e.g., smartphones, laptops, tablets). User profiling is vital in many areas such as software engineering, business, social network, etc.; in particular, it is essential in the digital forensics field. (Kwon et al. 2021). Many researchers have studied user profiling, whose goal is to explore how applications are correlated with the user's personal information and derive features from inferring users' characteristics (Weiwei et al. 2021). By inferring user patterns from user profiling, investigators can detect anti-forensics behavior that is the practice of circumventing forensic analysis procedures, making them unreliable or impossible such as file deletion, hiding, or data modification (Wendong Wang et al. 2015). It is consistent with anomaly detection that detects unexpected events or abnormal behavior (Abakumova et al. 2019). User profiling can enhance traditional forensic examination techniques. Investigators can identify similar cases and accomplices by analyzing the perpetrator's profile extracted from digital evidence. Also, they can anticipate possible crimes in the future and develop strategies to respond to possible crimes (Oztoprak 2015).

Entity Profiling with Binary Predicates (EPBP) model analyzes non-volatile data remaining on digital devices. The proposed model defines that a user has two properties: tendency and impact, which indicate application usage patterns (Kwon et al. 2021). Identifying user patterns is a crucial technique of user profiling, so it has been studied for various applications.

The researchers have focused only on specific applications, devices, or operating systems by analyzing the order of execution or volatile data such as network traffic and online content. The number of messages, call time, location information, or app usage time was used as a feature. Although the features are indicators that reveal users' characteristics, they have the disadvantage of being dependent on applications. Another challenge is the need for techniques that can be applied to heterogeneous devices (Kwon et al. 2021).

3.3 Survey of Behavior Model

Digital Citizenship is a module consisting of procedures and training for technology users to be intelligent when engaging with technology. There are nine elements in digital citizenship which are Digital Etiquette, Digital Law, Digital Access, Digital Commerce, Digital Communication, Digital Literacy, Digital Rights and Responsibilities, Digital Security and Safety, and Digital Health and Wellness (Maliki et al. 2021).

User profiling has been used to recognize user behavior. Web browsing data such as visited URLs and time spent on each website is essential to understanding user's online behavioral patterns (Matthijs and Radlinski 2011) used URL, title, browsing queries, first visit time, visit duration, last visit time, and count in their research (Kalimeri et al. 2019). Perform tasks like clustering, statical analysis, association rule, and classification to find interesting patterns. Pattern analysis: after performing the upper two, research is done using knowledge query tools like SQL or data cubes to perform OLAP operations (Kumar and Meenu 2017b). A questionnaire survey is always used to collect Internet usage data to reveal the association between online behaviors and academic achievement (Apuke and Iyendo 2018b). To show the relationship between Internet usage and academic performance, some studies used special smartphone applications to track students' activities (Giunchiglia et al. 2018).

One of the challenges is users' lack of cybersecurity knowledge and awareness, leading to fraud, especially when surfing unauthorized websites. Therefore, awareness among users about using the internet is crucial to avoid these issues. One coping mechanism is to understand the user's behavior (Maliki et al. 2021). Reveal the association between Internet usage behaviors and academic performance, and predict undergraduate academic performance from the usage data by machine learning (Xu et al. 2019). Internet usage data that contains several behavioral records can reflect students' learning perceptions, study state, physical activity, future job prospects, etc. Behaviors in a learning management system can be utilized as effective predictors for students' academic success (Xing et al. 2016).

Develop a user's security behavior profile using features in browsing history data and characteristics in Digital Citizenship elements as guidelines for the user behavior classification using Support Vector Machine (SVM) (Maliki et al. 2021). Implement a weblog Expert tool on a web server log file (an educational institution's web log data) to find the behavioral pattern and profiles of users interacting with a website (Kumar and Meenu 2017a). A set of features, including online duration, Internet traffic volume, and connection frequency, were extracted, calculated, and normalized from the actual Internet usage data of 4000 students. Three standard machine learning algorithms of the decision tree, neural network, and support vector machine were used to predict academic performance from these features (Xu et al. 2019).

If tested with different domain categories and the total number of users used in the dataset, the results may change. The implementation is limited to user privacy consent (Maliki et al. 2021).

4   Research Methodology

To study the relationship between Internet use behavior and Internet QoS, this Research will finally build a user internet behavior model from the following aspects.

1. To identify factors that contributed to internet usage behavior among campus users
2. To construct user profiling on internet usage behavior
3. To develop an internet usage behavior model based on its QoS
4. To validate the internet usage behaviour model from a Subject Matter Expert (SME)

Various methods for the construction of user behavior models have been proposed. Figure 1 depicts the research framework and how the research activities achieve the research objectives. It implements both mixed methods (qualitative and quantitative research methods) to represent the above needs visually.

4.1   Conceptual Study/knowledge Acquisition

The concepts analyzed in this paper are Internet usage, user behavior model, and Internet QoS. Keywords were derived from the literature search statement and formed into sets related to the type of study, the sources and the repositories. Overall, the search string was defined as (internet usage OR user profiling OR usage behavior model) AND Internet QoS. All searches were performed in IEEE Xplore, ACM, ScienceDirect, and Springer Link.

A manual search was executed, and the results were stored in EndNote, a reference management tool. EndNote was used to remove duplicates and manage a large number of references. The inclusion and exclusion criteria were defined as follows:

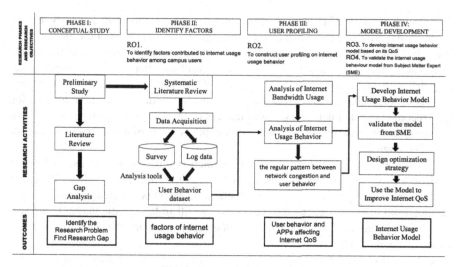

Fig. 1. Research framework

- Inclusion Criteria: The manuscript must be oriented to network technology, based on the Internet QoS study. The study is not required to mention the 'usage behavior model', but it must be a peer-reviewed journal article, a book chapter, or a conference paper (including workshops and colocated events, if and only if they were peer-reviewed). Additionally, it must be a full paper (i.e., not an extended abstract, poster, short paper, emerging results, or positions).
- Exclusion Criteria: Manuscripts were excluded if published before 2015 or were research on Internet QoS in other disciplines, such as Internet of things and software engineering. The studies based on the Internet QoS were excluded if they: used a single repository, employed an existing dataset without explaining how it was obtained, and the articles were published on some public platforms (e.g., GitHub) but not in journals.

This SLR includes search, selection and filtering processes. All studies obtained from the systematic search were collected in an EndNote library, and its integrated tools were used to remove duplicates automatically. Then, a first screening excluded articles after reading titles, abstracts and keywords only, while the second screening involved reading the full text and completing a quality assessment (in terms of sections, disclosure of steps and methodology detail). A total of 47 studies were selected and 36 articles met the inclusion criteria. Each paper was reviewed by a single author, which poses a threat to the reliability of the study. To avoid the impact of a single-author review on the study, this study sent the collected references to other researchers for secondary screening. It took the forward snowball method as the minimization strategy in data collection.

4.2 Identify Factors

This section mainly introduces how to construct the user behavior data set, including the paper data generated by the systematic literature review, questionnaires data generated by the user questionnaire and the log data generated by the user when surfing the Internet.

Through systematic literature review, extract data from the identified primary studies; To clarify the problem, this paper also briefly defines the objectives of this field and the research problems to be solved. Some related work discussed in Sect. 2 has investigated the research problems related to the overall process of the relationship between Internet usage behavior and Internet QoS. These are: (a) which databases are easier to mine, and the conclusion is that about 19% of Internet usage behavior research uses Internet log files (recorded through network gateway devices or Internet of things devices), 28% of Internet QoS research use surveys, and (b) in-depth analysis of data extraction methods and technologies.

The questionnaire is designed to find the relationship between the use of Internet bandwidth and users' behavior of using the Internet in time, app and place. To realize the randomness of questionnaire data collection, researchers selected no less than 500 students from other majors, grades and classes to fill in the questionnaire. Use Excel software to summarize and sort out the questionnaire results, and the outcome is the user questionnaire data set.

Collect all users' Internet access log data using the Internet behavior management device or network monitoring tool. Form the user log data set combined with the time-line diagram of network bandwidth utilization in the gateway device. Combine the questionnaire data and log data and output the user behavior data set through analysis tools.

4.3 User Profiling

Based on the user behavior data set, analyze the Internet bandwidth use and user internet behavior through equipment or network monitoring tools, Excel and SPSS software, find out the law between network congestion and user behavior, and determine the user behavior and app affecting Internet QoS.

Through the previous analysis results, find ways to improve the user experience of Chinese students using the campus networks.

4.4 Model Development/construction

User profiling will be used to recognize user behavior. Web browsing data such as visited URLs and time spent on each website is essential to understand user's online behavioral patterns used URL, title, browsing queries, first visit time, visit duration, last visit time, and count in their research.

This study develops a users' Internet behavior model using MATLAB and deep learning software based on users' Internet behavior analysis. The primary purpose is to establish the relationship model between campus network behavior and Internet QoS (Fig. 2).

Send the established Internet behavior model to experts in Internet information technology to verify the scope of the model's elements and the model's accuracy.

Based on the Internet usage model, the network strategy to improve the QoS of campus networks is designed. The network strategy is deployed to the network equipment to verify the role of the Internet model in improving the QoS of the Internet.

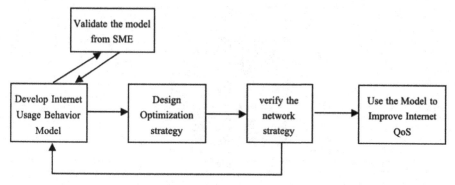

Fig. 2. Model development process

5   Result and Discussion

This section presents the results of the Systematic Literature Review (SLR).

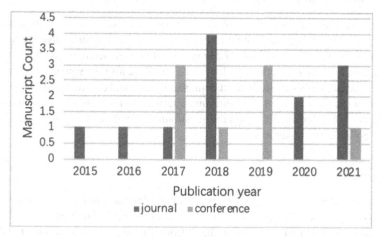

Fig. 3. Manuscript count

Figure 3 shows the number of Internet usage behavior and Internet QoS studies identified within 2017–2021 that fit the inclusion criteria. The prevalence of conference and workshop papers (both labeled 'Conferences') is due to the highly respected IT Conference, collocated with the Institute of Electrical and Electronics Engineers (IEEE). The interest in this type of research increased considerably by 2017, but the numbers dropped slightly afterward. Besides the surge of interest, another potential reason for the popularity of this type of research is the rise of the Internet of things technology. This rise in publication numbers indicates that the researcher considers Internet usage behavior and Internet QoS studies highly relevant.

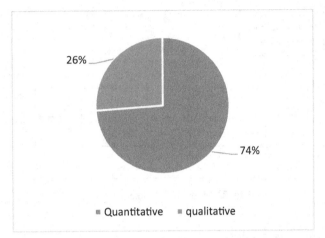

Fig. 4. Percentage of qualitative and quantitative studies on internet usage behavior

5.1 Qualitative Studies, Quantitative Studies and Tools Used

It can be observed that 74% of the research on Internet usage behavior is quantitative research and only 26% is qualitative research (Fig. 4). In all quantitative studies, 56% conducted user behavior analysis, 37.5% constructed user behavior models, and 25% obtained user to access data through logs. 50% of all qualitative studies used the questionnaire method. Only one study used both quantitative and qualitative studies. Among the research on Internet QoS, 69% are quantitative research and 31% are qualitative research. In all the studies, 56% used the questionnaire method, 47% used user analysis, and 25% constructed a user model.

5.2 Countries

The selected research on Internet usage behavior and Internet QoS related to the research questions of this paper shows that the vast majority of research countries are concentrated in Asia, with 12 from China, 3 from India, 3 from Turkey, 2 from Malaysia and 2 from Australia. In the research field, 16 studies are based on the education industry, 8 are based on the information technology industry, and 4 are based on the sociology industry. The research on Internet QoS mainly focuses on the information technology industry and the Internet of things industry, and only one research on Internet QoS is in the education industry.

5.3 Relationship Between Internet Usage Behavior and Internet QoS

Literature review shows that most studies on Internet QoS have mentioned Internet use behavior, but few studies have clearly described their relationship. Among them, the number of people who connect Internet QoS with user analysis is more, while with user behavior model is less. On the other hand, in the research of Internet usage behavior, the number of user behavior models is much higher than that in the study of Internet QoS.

Some studies have pointed out that the improvement of Internet QoS needs to be realized through network configuration, such as the load balancing method of infrastructure mode wireless network (Soo et al. 2019), Routing optimization (Zhang and Gorlatch 2021) and routing parameters of IoT sensors (Sagar et al. 2021). Most studies believe that to improve Internet QoS; there is a need to analyze users' Internet usage behavior (Kumar and Meenu 2017a; Ye et al. 2021) or users' logs of accessing the Internet (Wen et al. 2018).

Overall, the research on Internet usage behavior improves the Internet QoS, whether in a single enterprise or Internet Service Providers. In recent years, due to the increasing use of mobile devices, the research on the relationship between mobile Access Point (AP) usage behavior and Internet QoS has gradually become a new research hotspot. However, it can be seen that the research on the relationship between Internet usage behavior and Internet QoS is less carried out within the scope of the campus network. The reason may be that the Internet usage behavior on campus has apparent characteristics of time tide (Yakıncı et al. 2018), and there are many kinds of application software accessing the Internet (Li et al. 2018; Yu et al. 2018), which brings a lot of uncertainty to the research, but it still has significant research value and space.

5.4 Characteristics of the Articles

Most of the studies analyzed were quantitative. These studies use the primary data set of user behavior log data or questionnaire dataset. For data analysis, many studies use clustering analysis and support vector machines. These methods are recommended to analyze the relationship between Internet usage behavior and Internet QoS. In addition, although quantitative research is still in progress, some qualitative research (for example, unified theory of acceptance and use of technology (UTAUT) or collaborative borrowing-based packet marking (CBBPM) algorithm will also help to understand the formula and reason for the relationship between the two. Such qualitative research may also help to supplement the results of quantitative analysis.

The review shows that it is still interesting to continue to carry out further research in the education industry so that it can be compared with the Internet of things industry and find solutions for developing countries facing the same dilemma of insufficient Internet bandwidth and low Internet QoS, and provide a reference for follow-up research.

5.5 Practical Implication

This research can provide guidance for the operation and maintenance managers of campus networks, let them understand the importance of analyzing users' Internet usage behavior, and improve the Internet QoS. Network operation and maintenance managers may notice that improving Internet QoS can be implemented by adjusting network routing strategy and network equipment performance or building a user behavior model, and can improve Internet QoS to satisfactory results without considering increasing network bandwidth. No matter which method is adopted, it is always essential to create a technique and way to reflect the improvement of campus network QoS. In addition, network operation and maintenance managers may understand that their plans to improve the

Internet QoS based on analyzing users' Internet usage behavior may help save money and improve management efficiency.

5.6 Theoretical Implications

This study shows future researchers the terms used to measure Internet usage behavior and its relationship with Internet QoS, the research methods used, and the industries and countries analyzed. In addition, it is also pointed out that it is meaningful to consider user analysis and build a behavior model when examining the relationship between Internet usage behavior and Internet QoS. Future researchers may consider different directions and methods of Internet QoS improvement in the campus network environment. This future research may supplement a few studies on the relationship between Internet usage behavior and Internet QoS in other ways than network configuration optimization and user behavior analysis. In addition, this work complements the previous author's work on improving Internet QoS in education by including user analysis and user behavior model.

6 Conclusions

The analysis of Internet usage behavior may have a positive indirect impact on Internet QoS through the study of user questionnaires, the analysis of user internet behavior log and the establishment and adjustment of the user behavior model. In other words, there is a need to identify the characteristics of users' Internet usage behavior and the user factors affecting Internet QoS, to improve Internet QoS. At the same time, improving Internet QoS is also directly related to non-user factors such as network routing adjustment, equipment performance improvement and network bandwidth increase, which are not the focus of this article. This paper proposes the following relationships, which are helpful to expand and supplement the previous literature: (a) the direct relationship between Internet QoS, network routing and network equipment performance; (b) The indirect relationship between Internet QoS and Internet usage behavior; (c) Through the development of user behavior model and targeted network strategy adjustment, find out the countermeasures for the adverse impact of excessive Internet usage behavior on Internet QoS. In the future, it may be interesting to conduct a more in-depth analysis of the direct and indirect relationship between all Internet usage behavior and these variables in this study.

References

Abakumova, I.V., Denisova, E., Kruchkova, A., Klimova, N., Borokhovski, E., Vorobyova, E.V.: Students Internet usage: psychological and pedagogical aspects. SHS Web Conf. **70** (2019). https://doi.org/10.1051/shsconf/20197006002

Abbad, M.M.M.: Using the UTAUT model to understand students' usage of e-learning systems in developing countries. Educ. Inf. Technol. **26**(6), 7205–7224 (2021). https://doi.org/10.1007/s10639-021-10573-5

Abdelhak, E., Feth-Allah, H., Mohammed, M.: QoS uncertainty handling for an efficient web service selection. In: Proceedings of the 9th International Conference on Information Systems and Technologies (2019)

Apuke, O.D., Iyendo, T.O.: University students' usage of the internet resources for research and learning: forms of access and perceptions of utility. Heliyon 4(12), e01052 (2018). https://doi.org/10.1016/j.heliyon.2018.e01052

Apuke, O.D., Iyendo, T.O.: University students' usage of the internet resources for research and learning: forms of access and perceptions of utility. Heliyon 4(12), e01052 (2018b)

Ashibani, Y., Mahmoud, Q.H.: A behavior profiling model for user authentication in IoT networks based on app usage patterns. IEEE 18(2018), 2841 (2018). https://doi.org/10.1109/IECON.2018.8592761

Asimah, A.: Internet usage and its effect on the lifestyle of university students. Inf. Knowl. Manage. (2020). https://doi.org/10.7176/ikm/10-7-05

Benmoussa, M., Ouaissa, M., Lahmer, M., Chana, I., Rhattoy, A.: QoS analysis of hierarchical routing protocols for wireless sensor networks. In: Proceedings of the Second International Conference on Internet of things, Data and Cloud Computing (2017)

Bogdan Ghita, T.B.: Internet of profiling – traffic, users and applications. IEEE 18/2018 (2018)

Dumpit, D.Z., Fernandez, C.J.: Analysis of the use of social media in higher education institutions (HEIs) using the technology acceptance model. Int. J. Educ. Technol. High. Educ. 14(1), 1–16 (2017). https://doi.org/10.1186/s41239-017-0045-2

Giunchiglia, F., Zeni, M., Gobbi, E., Bignotti, E., Bison, I.: Mobile social media usage and academic performance. Comput. Hum. Behav. 82, 177–185 (2018)

Kalimeri, K., Beiró, M.G., Delfino, M., Raleigh, R., Cattuto, C.: Predicting demographics, moral foundations, and human values from digital behaviours. Comput. Hum. Behav. 92, 428–445 (2019). https://doi.org/10.1016/j.chb.2018.11.024

Kumar, M., Meenu, M.: Analysis of visitor's behavior from web log using web log expert tool. IEEE, 17/2017a (2017a)

Kumar, M., Meenu, M.: A survey on pattern discovery of web usage mining (2017b)

Kwon, H., Lee, S., Jeong, D.: User profiling via application usage pattern on digital devices for digital forensics. Exp. Syst. Appl. 168 (2021). https://doi.org/10.1016/j.eswa.2020.114488

Larose, R., Eastin, M.S., Gregg, J.: Reformulating the Internet paradox: social cognitive explanations of Internet use and depression (2001)

Li, C., Yu, K., Wu, X.: Co-clustering analysis of mobile users' usage behavior on apps. In: Proceedings of the 2nd International Conference on Telecommunications and Communication Engineering - ICTCE 2018 (2018)

Luo, X., Wang, J., Shen, Q., Wang, J., Qi, Q.: User behavior analysis based on user interest by web log mining. In: 2017 27th International Telecommunication Networks and Applications Conference (ITNAC). Article retrieved from (2017)

Maliki, N.A., Zainal, A., Abdoh Ghaleb, F.A., Kassim, M.N.: User security behavioral profiling using historical browsing website. In: 2021 International Conference on Data Science and Its Applications (ICoDSA) (2021)

Matthijs, N., Radlinski, F.: Personalizing web search using long term browsing history. In: Proceedings of the Forth International Conference on Web Search and Web Data Mining, WSDM 2011, Hong Kong, China, 9–12 February 2011 (2011)

Oztoprak, K.: Profiling subscribers according to their internet usage characteristics and behaviors. In: 2015 IEEE International Conference on Big Data (Big Data) (2015)

Pacheco, F., Exposito, E., Gineste, M.: A framework to classify heterogeneous Internet traffic with machine learning and deep learning techniques for satellite communications. Comput. Netw. 173 (2020). https://doi.org/10.1016/j.comnet.2020.107213

Tang, P., Wang, C., Wang, X., Liu, W., Zeng, W. and Wang, J.: Object detection in videos by high quality object linking. IEEE Trans. Pattern Anal. Mach. Intell. 42(5), 1272–1278 (2019)

Polpinij, J., Namee, K.: Internet usage patterns mining from firewall event logs. In: Proceedings of the 2019 International Conference on Big Data and Education – ICBDE 2019 (2019)

Sagar, A.K., Banda, L., Sahana, S., Singh, K., Kumar Singh, B.: Optimizing quality of service for sensor enabled Internet of healthcare systems. Neurosci. Inf. 1(3) (2021). https://doi.org/10.1016/j.neuri.2021.100010

Tang, P., Wang, C., Wang, X., Liu, W., Zeng, W., Wang, J.: Object detection in videos by high quality object linking. IEEE Trans. Pattern Anal. Mach. Intell. 42(5), 1272–1278 (2019)

Wang, W., Guo, J., Li, Z., Zhao, R.: Behavior model construction for client side of modern web applications. Tsinghua Sci. Technol. 26(1), 112–134 (2021). https://doi.org/10.26599/tst.2019.9010043

Wang, W., Tian, Y., Gong, X., Qi, Q., Hu, Y.: Software defined autonomic QoS model for future Internet. J. Syst. Softw. 110, 122–135 (2015). https://doi.org/10.1016/j.jss.2015.08.016

Wen, T., Bao, J., Ding, F.: QoS-aware web service recommendation model based on users and services clustering. In: Proceedings of the International Conference on Information Technology and Electrical Engineering 2018 (2018)

Xin-ying, Z., Chao, J., Yun-ju, Z.: Study for coexistence and development of mobile internet technology with traditional teaching mode (2019)

Xing-Hua, L.I., Chao, M.A., Committee, Y.L.: research on college students' behavior and habits in new social media——Taking Weibo, WeChat, QQ and Other Online Instant Social Platforms as an Example. Education Teaching Forum (2018)

Xing, W., Chen, X., Stein, J., Marcinkowski, M.: Temporal predication of dropouts in MOOCs: reaching the low hanging fruit through stacking generalization. Comput. Hum. Behav. 58, 119–129 (2016)

Xu, X., Wang, J., Peng, H., Wu, R.: Prediction of academic performance associated with internet usage behaviors using machine learning algorithms. Comput. Hum. Behav. 98, 166–173 (2019). https://doi.org/10.1016/j.chb.2019.04.015

Yakıncı, Z.D., Gürbüz, P., Yetiş, G.: Internet usage habits and internet usage in educational studies of vocational school students. J. Comput. Educ. Res. 6(11), 33–46 (2018). https://doi.org/10.18009/jcer.330925

Yang, J.: Effective learning behavior of students' internet based on data mining. In: 2021 IEEE 2nd International Conference on Big Data, Artificial Intelligence and Internet of Things Engineering (ICBAIE) (2021)

Ye, F., Lin, Z., Chen, C., Zheng, Z., Huang, H.: Outlier-resilient web service QoS prediction. In: Proceedings of the Web Conference 2021 (2021)

Yu, D., Li, Y., Xu, F., Zhang, P., Kostakos, V.: Smartphone app usage prediction using points of interest. Proc. ACM Interact. Mob. Wearable Ubiquitous Tech. 1(4), 1–21 (2018). https://doi.org/10.1145/3161413

Zhang, Y., Gorlatch, S.: Optimizing energy efficiency of QoS-based routing in software-defined networks. In: Proceedings of the 17th ACM Symposium on QoS and Security for Wireless and Mobile Networks (2021)

Model Checking Intelligent Information Systems with 3-Valued Timed Commitments

Ghalya Alwhishi$^{(\boxtimes)}$, Nagat Drawel, and Jamal Bentahar🆔

Concordia Institute for Information Systems Engineering, Concordia University,
Montreal, Canada
{g-alwhis,n-drawe}@encs.concordia.ca, bentahar@ciise.concordia.ca

Abstract. Intelligent Information Systems (IIS) and their applications have gained recently increasing interest in various domains. Their verification to enhance their reliability in uncertain settings constitutes a major challenge that is still attracting the research community to work on and investigate. This paper focuses on modeling and verifying IIS, taking the healthcare domain, namely a smart healthcare system as a typical example. We use the powerful concept of social conditional commitments to model the interactions among the stakeholders and capture the business logic properties of the system in the presence of uncertainty. We start by proposing $3v-CTL^{cc}$, a new modeling language that extrapolates the two-valued timed commitment logic CTL^{cc} to the three-value space. We define a new semantics of the commitment modality in this new logic. We also simulate and model the system and introduce a set of specifications. We verify the system model against these specifications using a model checking reduction approach. The effectiveness of the proposed approach is evaluated by implementing it on the MCMAS-SC model checker.

Keywords: 3v-Model checking · Conditional commitments · Intelligent information systems · Smart health system

1 Introduction

Nowadays, Intelligent Information Systems (IIS) and their applications in various settings such as data mining, cloud computing, big data, and Internet of Things (IoT) are the focus of many research efforts. The use of these systems to solve real world problems is on rise [15,16,20,34], particularly when the medical and health domains are considered [17,24]. However, despite the growing number of various IIS applications, they still encounter many challenges in the modelling of their components' behaviors. Communication is a fundamental aspect for these systems to coordinate the behaviors of various components towards solving problems that are difficult for an individual intelligent component to tackle. In the presence of uncertainty, this communication has been recently modeled by

I. Awan et al. (Eds.): MobiWIS 2022, LNCS 13475, pp. 237–251, 2022.
https://doi.org/10.1007/978-3-031-14391-5_18

means of social commitments [33]. Social commitments are agreements between two intelligent components, and they result from communicative actions between their interactions. Indeed, commitments offer social and observable meaning to the protocols messages exchange. That is, unlike the traditional protocols that capture legal orderings of messages exchanged among agents with a low-level presentation, commitment protocols give flexibility and a high-level meaning of these messages [13].

Many approaches that provide social modelling for commitments among intelligent components can be found in the literature. For instance, commitments are used to model the contractual obligations of various multi-agent system (MAS) applications [6,11]. In fact, commitments are a vital element that can be applied to capture the IIS dynamic messages, in which one component engages towards another component to bring about certain property. For example, "*an intelligent bill sensor commits to send alert to a mobile phone application when a level of medication reading that exceeds the limit in the body is detected*".

Nevertheless, verifying social commitments in systems that are treated under the assumption of uncertainty is an important and challenging issue, especially, when they are developed in critical applications. Model checking [7] is a well-known verification technique that has attracted several contributions with a significant industrial implication [3,9,10]. The main goal of this technique is to detect the violations of properties in the system behavior and to verify whether the system satisfies its desired specifications.

Although the number of proposals on commitments modeling and verification is significant, they differ, however, in the application domains they addressed and the formal logics they implemented. Most of these approaches treated commitments in an absolute manner, i.e., considering only two values: True (T) and False (F). Thus, the commitment is either fulfilled or definitely not. However, in many contexts, it is quite difficult to determine with absolute certainty whether a proposition about the behavior of an intelligent component is true or false. A rich domain of truth values for representing uncertain information and for capturing more realistic scenarios is of significant importance.

The three-valued logic (or 3-valued for short) is extended from classical logics, and is used to model various systems by adding additional truth values. The system model and its specifications take truth values over 3-valued lattice (T, M, F). The additional truth value M is assigned for *don't know* or *undefined* to deal with missing or uncertain information. In this paper, we are primarily concerned with the issues of reasoning about and verifying uncertainty of commitments in the context of IIS using the model checking approach, which has not been deeply investigated yet for these systems.

This work presents a new method for modeling and verifying IIS. We consider a concrete example, namely a smart healthcare system application. In fact, the verification of IIS is subject to uncertainty where one part of the system action(s) might not always lead to the fulfillment of the commitment. Our modeling approach employs the conditional commitments that are represented in the interaction among the system components. We propose a new logic called

$3v - CTL^{cc}$ (3-valued Computation Tree Logic for Conditional Commitments) to enable reasoning about uncertainty in IIS environments. We extrapolate the two-valued timed commitment logic CTL^{cc} presented in [11] to the three-value space extending $3v - CTL$ [5,19]. We report the implementation of the verification approach using a smart hospital system model as example using the model checker MACMAS-sc introduced in [11] after reducing our proposed model logic $3v - CTL^{cc}$ to the classical CTL^{cc}.

2   Related Work

Model checking IIS has been investigated by some researchers with the aim to ensure that the intelligent system works as expected and fulfil the requirements. In [21], a new model checking framework is proposed and applied to a smart system in the medical domain to help qualify medical risk and assist medical teams to make better informed decisions. In [8], the authors proposed a framework for model checking the uncertainties of an intelligent software system described by a Petri net for regular components and neural networks for intelligent components. In this work, three main steps are conducted 1) build an adaptive Petri net model, 2) transform the adaptive Petri net model to a hybrid Petri net, and 3) use a model checker to check the Petri net model. The work in [18] presented a feedback-control statistical system checking to analyze and model check Cyber-Physical intelligent Systems (CPS). The proposed approach is efficiently estimated the probability of rare events in realistic CPS applications that cannot be estimated using static-analysis techniques. On the other hand, model checking commitments has been introduced in several proposals. In [11], a new approach of model checking social conditional commitments was conducted. The authors in this work extended CTL with modalities that allow for reasoning about conditional commitments and their fulfillment. Moreover, a new technique for model checking the logic of knowledge and commitment in MAS was proposed in [1]. Several other approaches were recently proposed in this field such as in [12,14]. An extended approach of model checking called three-valued model checking was proposed to enable reasoning about uncertainty [4,31,32] and [28]. The work in [5] introduced the main approach in multi-valued model checking which includes the three-valued approach. In another work [19], the authors handled the deficiencies in [5]. However, none of the above mentioned approaches is considering social commitments for IIS applications.

3   Background

3.1   Intelligent Information Systems

Intelligent Information Systems (IIS) deal with searching, accessing, retrieving, and integrating large collections of information and knowledge from multiple heterogeneous sources to make informed decisions. IIS perform intelligent information processing (IIP) by the integration of artificial intelligence, intelligent agents, and other technologies [2]. IIP techniques involve the establishing of theories, methodologies, and algorithms to process complex systems information to make the function of IIS simulate the mental aspects of humans [23]. For example, considering online marketing, IIS are used to reach their potential customers by accessing insightful consumer data, targeting customers preferences, and tracking their shopping habits. Generally, to be considered intelligent, an information system should have the following properties: (1) operates with other agents in the same environment; (2) has cognitive abilities such as action control and using languages; (3) exhibits mental state as a human; and (4) can adapt in complex environments [21].

IIS play a fundamental role in improving the efficiency of cloud and IoT-based systems, where intelligent information processes are needed to provide high-quality services [25, 26, 29]. Cloud and IoT-based systems, such as smart homes, smart cities, smart cars, and smart healthcare [35], provide the connectivity of physical devices in order to exchange information from one device to the other through the Internet. The smart healthcare system we consider in this paper as a typical scenario aims to provide the best services to the patients and health teams. Figure 1 shows the overview of this system where the patient is connected with wearable smart devices. These devices are equipped with sensors to capture data and share them through the Internet to accomplish specific tasks. The received data go through a complex data analysis process and end with intelligently classified decisions and diagnoses. The health data are then shared smoothly with the patient and/or the health care team.

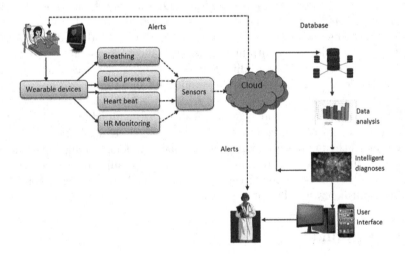

Fig. 1. Overview of a smart healthcare system

3.2 Timed Conditional Commitments Logic (CTL^{cc})

The concept of social commitments can be used in IIS applications where an intelligent system component commits to perform a particular act towards another component when the latter fulfils a particular condition. For example, consider a smart inhaler that helps patients monitor their asthma. The smart inhaler commits to send an early alert signal to the patient having asthma attacks when the smart inhaler sensor detects a high pollution area. In this work, we employ a model checking method where IIS is modeled using a formal model $\mathcal{M}$ and the requirements are specified as temporal logic formulae using timed social commitments. A model checker checks then whether $\mathcal{M} \models \phi$ or not, i.e., whether the system model $\mathcal{M}$ satisfies the requirement ϕ or not.

Let us define the IIS system model based on the timed conditional commitment logic CTL^{cc} defined from the model of communicative conditional commitments [11].

Definition 1. *IIS Model of CTL^{cc}: an IIS model with timed conditional commitments is a tuple $\mathcal{M} = (S, R_t, \{\sim_{i \to j} | (i,j) \in A^2\}, I, V)$ where:*

- *S is a set of global states of the IIS system;*
- *$R_t \subseteq S \times S$ is a total transition relation for the IIS dynamics;*
- *$I \subseteq S$ is a set of initial global states;*
- *$V : AP \to 2^S$ is a valuation function where AP is a set of atomic propositions;*
- *For each pair of agents $(i,j) \in A^2, \sim_{i \to j} \subseteq S \times S$ is a social accessibility relation defined in the usual way as in [11].*

Syntax. The syntax of CTL^{cc} is defined as follows:
$\phi ::= p \mid \neg\phi \mid \phi \vee \phi \mid EG\phi \mid EX\phi \mid E(\phi U\phi) \mid CC,$
$CC ::= CC_{i \to j}(\phi, \phi)$

where p is a constant and ϕ is a formula. The syntax $EG\phi$ for example means "there exists a path where the formula ϕ globally holds in the system". The formula $CC_{i \to j}(\phi, \psi)$ means "agent i commits towards agent j to paring about ψ if the condition ϕ holds".

Semantics. The semantics of this logic is an extension of the CTL logic semantics [22]. Here, we only include the semantics of the commitment modality. The satisfaction relation denoted by $(\mathcal{M}, s) \models \phi$ where $\mathcal{M}$ is an IIs model, s is a global state and ϕ is a conditional commitment formula is defined as follows:

- $(\mathcal{M}, s) \models CC_{i \to j}(\psi, \varphi)$ iff (1) $\exists s' \in S$ s.t. $s \sim_{i \to j} s'$ and $(\mathcal{M}, s') \models \psi$ and (2) $\forall s' \in S$ s.t. $s \sim_{i \to j} s'$ and $(\mathcal{M}, s') \models \psi$, we have $(\mathcal{M}, s') \models \varphi$.

4   Modeling Uncertainty in IIS with Conditional Commitments

IIS models are subject to uncertainty due to incomplete information about the actual system. The missing information stems from system abstraction, system space partition, unexpected system behaviours affected by the environment or an incomplete understanding of system properties. To reason about uncertainty in IIS models, we propose to use a 3-valued logic, which is more expressive and more flexible than classic 2-valued logics.

4.1   3-Valued Propositional Logic

This logic is an extension of the 2-valued logic known as the Kleene's logic, with truth values (T, M, F) where T stands for *True*, M stands for *Maybe* and F stands for *False*. The value M represents the uncertain information in the system that could be in the transitions between states or in the formulae. The truth table of this logic is represented in Fig. 2(a). The three-valued lattice logic [27,36] relies on the three-valued lattice (see Fig. 2(b)). This lattice is defined as algebraic structure $(L_3, \sqcup, \sqcap)$ where every two elements a and b in L_3 have supremum or (join) denoted by $(a \sqcup b)$ and infimum or (meet) denoted by $(a \sqcap b)$ where the symbols $\sqcup$ and $\sqcap$ operate like $\vee$ and $\wedge$ respectivily in the Kleene's logic.

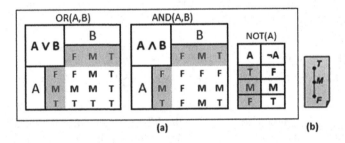

Fig. 2. (a) The truth table of Kleene's logic; (b) Three-valued lattice

4.2   3-Valued CTL^{cc}

In this section, we introduce our new logic for timed conditional commitments called 3-valued CTL^{cc} ($3v - CTL^{cc}$). This logic will be used for reasoning about uncertainty in IIS models. By doing so, we explain how uncertain or missing information affect the satisfaction of conditional commitment formulae in IIS models.

$3v - CTL^{cc}$ IIS Model: The 3-valued IIS model is obtained from the CTL^{cc} IIS model by extending it with the lattice structure $(L_3, \sqcup, \sqcap)$ and replacing the valuation V by $\mathbb{O} : S \rightarrow (AP \rightarrow L_3)$ total labeling function that maps states in S into L_3-valued sets on the set of atomic propositions AP. Thus, $(\mathbb{O}(s))(a) = l$ means the atomic variable a has value l from L_3 in state s where $a \in AP$.

Syntax. $3v - CTL^{cc}$ is syntactically equivalent to CTL^{cc}, but formulae are evaluated considering the three-valued lattice.

Semantics. The semantics of this logic is an extension to the three-valued case of the multi-valued logic introduced in [5]. As shown bellow, we added the 3v-semantic of the CTL^{cc} to the semantics of χCTL.

Given a $3v - CTL^{cc}$ IIS model K and 3v-formula, the truth degree of the satisfaction of strong conditional commitment formulas are defined as follows:

- $\| a \| (s) = (\mathbb{O}(s))(a)$ where $a \in AP$ and $\mathbb{O} : S \to (AP \to L_3)$ is a total labeling function that maps states in S into L_3 on a set of atomic propositions AP.
- $\| \varphi \vee \psi \| (s) = \| \varphi \| (s) \sqcup \| \psi \| (s)$ means in which truth degree, φ or ψ holds in state s.
- $\| \varphi \wedge \psi \| (s) = \| \varphi \| (s) \sqcap \| \psi \| (s)$ means in which truth degree, φ and ψ holds in state s.
- $\| \neg \varphi \| (s) = \overline{\| \varphi \|}(s)$ means in which truth degree, φ doesn't hold in state s.
- $\| EX\varphi \| (s) = pre_{\exists}^{R}(\| \varphi \|)(s) = \bigsqcup_{t \in S} \left(\| \varphi \| (t) \sqcap \mathbb{R}(s,t) \right)$ where $pre_{\exists}^{R}(\| \varphi \|)(s)$ stands for the backward image of state s that determines the value of φ in the next state. The semantics expresses in which truth degree there exists a path in the system where φ holds in the next state.
- $\| AX\varphi \|(s) = pre_{\forall}^{R}(\| \varphi \|)(s) = \bigsqcap_{t \in S} \left(\| \varphi \| (t) \sqcup \neg \mathbb{R}(s,t) \right)$ where $pre_{\forall}^{R}(\| \varphi \|)(s)$ stands for the backward image of state s that determines the value of φ in the next state of all paths.

- $\| EG\varphi \| = \nu \mathbb{Z}. \| \varphi \| \sqcap_L \| EX\mathbb{Z} \|$ where $\nu \mathbb{Z}$ stands for the greatest fixed point of the globally operator G. The semantics expresses in which truth degree there exists a path in the system where φ globally holds.

- $\| E[\varphi \cup \psi] \| = \mu \mathbb{Z}. \| \psi \| \cup_L (\| \varphi \| \sqcap_L \| EX\mathbb{Z} \|)$ where $\mu \mathbb{Z}$ stands for the smallest fix point of $\varphi \cup \psi$. The semantics expresses in which truth degree there is a path where φ holds until ψ holds.

The following is the new semantic where we define the truth degrees of the conditional commitment formula satisfaction in the system.

- $\| CC_{i \to j}(\psi, \varphi) \| (s) = T$ iff (1) $\exists s^{'} \in S$ s.t. $s \sim_{i \to j} s^{'}$ and $\| \psi \| (s^{'}) = T$ and (2) $for all s^{'} \in S$ s.t. $s \sim_{i \to j} s^{'}$ and $\| \psi \| (s^{'}) = T$ we have $\| \phi \| (s^{'}) = T$. This semantic means: The satisfaction degree of the formula $CC_{i \to j}(\psi, \varphi)$ in state s is "true" if the truth degree of ψ and ϕ in the accessible state $s^{'}$ is T.
- $\| CC_{i \to j}(\psi, \varphi) \| (s) = M$ iff
    - (1) $\exists s^{'} \in S$ s.t. $s \sim_{i \to j} s^{'}$ and $\| \psi \| (s^{'}) = M$ and
    - (2) $\forall s^{'} \in S$ s.t. $s \sim_{i \to j} s^{'}$ and $\| \psi \| (s^{'}) = M$ we have $\| \phi \| (s^{'}) = M \vee T$
      This semantic means: the satisfaction degree of the formula $CC_{i \to j}(\psi, \varphi)$ in state s is M if the truth degree of ψ in the accessible state $s^{'}$ is M and the truth degree of ϕ is M or T as $M \sqcap M = M$ and $M \sqcap T = M$
      OR

– (1) $\exists s' \in S s.t.\ s \sim_{i \to j} s'$ and $\| \psi \| (s') = T$ and

(2) $\forall s' \in S s.t.\ s \sim_{i \to j} s'$ and $\| \psi \| (s') = T$ we have $\| \phi \| (s') = M$. This semantics means: the satisfaction degree of the formula $CC_{i \to j}(\psi, \varphi)$ in state s is M if the truth degree of ψ in the accessible state s' is T and the truth degree of ϕ is M as $T \sqcap M = M$.

Example: Consider the three-valued model of IIS system scenario where the formulae take truth values over the three-valued lattice as shown in Fig. 3. The formulae φ and ψ represent specific positions of the physician agent (Phy) and the patient (Pat). Let the model represent a specific scenario of an "intelligent pill" that works as normal medication with monitoring technology. The scenario works as follows: (1) the "intelligent pill" sends information about the medication level in the patient's body to a sensor; (2) when the sensor reads high level of medication, it sends a risk alert to the physician (ψ); and (3) the physician commits towards the patient to recommend a new treatment (φ).

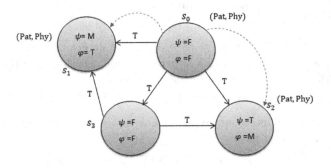

Fig. 3. A scenario of a 3-v intelligent pill model $\mathcal{M}$

In this model, it is uncertain in s_1 whether the sensor sent a risk alert to the physician or not ($\psi = M$) and, it is uncertain in s_2 whether the physician commits to recommend a treatment or not ($\varphi = M$). The truth degree of the commitment formula *"the physician commits to recommend a treatment for the patient, if the sensor sent an alert"* in state s_0 is denoted by $\| CC_{phy \to pat}(Alert, Treat) \|$ (s_0). The truth degree of this formula is determined by the truth degrees of ψ and φ in the next states. To obtain the truth degrees, we need to extract the three-valued sets (3v-sets) of (ψ) and (φ), and the three-valued relations between the system states (3v-relations).

3v-Sets: The 3v-sets are denoted by a total function $\mathbb{S} : O \to L_3$ where O is a set of elements. For a given element x, $\mathbb{S}(x)$ denotes the degree of the membership of x in $\mathbb{S}$. Fore example, Fig. 4(a) shows the mv-sets of ϕ where ϕ has the value T in s_1, the value M in s_2, and the value F in s_0 and s_3. These values are mapped to the same values in the 3-valued lattice. The same applies for ψ. To obtain the mv-sets of $\psi \wedge \phi$, we take the meet of mv-sets of ψ with mv-sets of ϕ. For example, in (a) the value of ϕ in s_1 is T and in (b) the value of ψ in the same state is M. Based on that, we obtain $\psi \wedge \phi = M$ in state s_1 that mapped to the value M in L_3 as shown in (c).

3v-Relations: The 3v-relations denoted by $\mathbb{R}$ are 3v-sets on $S \times S'$ where S and S' are set of states. For example, in Fig. 4(d), we map all the states that have relation values T, F and M to the same values of L_3 (to simplify the model, we eliminate the value F from the false transitions). For example, the relation from s_0 to s_1 denoted by (s_0, s_1) has value T and mapped to the same value in L_3, while the relation from s_1 to s_0 denoted by (s_1, s_0) has the value F and mapped to the same value in L_3. The value M in L_3 is empty because the model has no M values on the transitions between states.

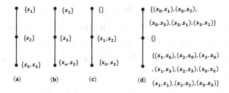

Fig. 4. (a): mv-sets of ϕ; (b): mv-sets of ψ; (c): mv-sets of $\psi \wedge \phi$; (d): the mv-relations of states

To determine the truth degree of $\psi \wedge \phi$ in the next state starting from s_0, we apply the semantics of $\parallel EX(\psi \wedge \phi) \parallel (s_0)$ as follows:

$$\parallel EX(\psi \wedge \phi) \parallel (s_0) = \bigsqcup_{t \in S} \Big(R(s_0, t) \sqcap \parallel \phi \wedge \psi \parallel (t) \Big) = \Big(R(s_0, s_0) \sqcap \parallel \phi \wedge \psi \parallel (s_0) \Big) \sqcup$$

$$\Big(R(s_0, s_1) \sqcap \parallel \phi \wedge \psi \parallel (s_1) \Big)$$

$$\sqcup$$

$$\Big(R(s_0, s_2) \sqcap \parallel \phi \wedge \psi \parallel (s_2) \Big) \quad (1)$$

$$\sqcup$$

$$\Big(R(s_0, s_3) \sqcap \parallel \phi \wedge \psi \parallel (s_3) \Big)$$

$$= (F \sqcap F) \sqcup (T \sqcap M) \sqcup (T \sqcap M) \sqcup (T \sqcap F) = \boldsymbol{M}$$

5   Model Checking $3v - CTL^{cc}$

This section is devoted to evaluate the effectiveness of our proposed work. Specifically, we apply the proposed verification approach in smart healthcare domain.

5.1   Case Study: A Smart Hospital System

A smart hospital system with "patient hospitalization" scenario is shown in Fig. 5. The process starts when a patient arrived at the hospital and checked-in using his smartphone application. The system immediately notifies the nurse and directs the patient to the appointment room. The patient then follows the direction if their health condition permits them to do so. Otherwise, a nurse will eventually responds to the patient. At the same time, a notification is sent to the bed washer report to disinfect the bed and make it ready for immediate use. Once the patient arrives to his room, all essential clinical information is automatically displayed on the digital room. Various components are involved. (1) Electronic Health Record (EHR) receives data from the sensors of the smart devices that are already connected to the patient. (2) A smart wristband is enabled with indoor tracking system as well as the smart bed. (3) Machine learning algorithms receive all this information, analyze it, and send signals when the patient's condition requires prompt intervention from the medical team. For example, the sensor immediately sends a signal to the physician if a high blood pressure is detected. Moreover, a meal recommendation according to the dietary restrictions is received by the patient at the lunchtime. The system also notifies a nurse for providing the patient with the medicine at a scheduled time.

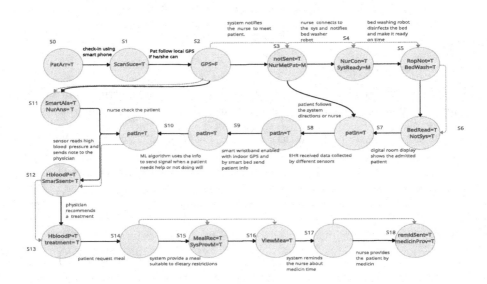

Fig. 5. A smart hospital system $\mathcal{K}$

5.2   System Properties

In this section, we emphasize the properties related to the concept of conditional social commitments. Concretely, over this system, we verified 10 properties classified into three categories, *Safety*, *Liveness* and *Reachability*. The idea of our proposed verification technique is to reduce the 3v-model to two classical models following the reduction technique presented in [4]. The advantages of this approach over some other verification techniques such as the ones introduced in

[19,30] are the reuse of the exiting model checking tools and the efficiency in dealing with the state explosion problem. Technically, this reduction process is accomplished in two steps. First, by moving the negation to the level of atomic propositions, second, by assign negative and positive version for every atomic proposition to generate an optimistic cut that considers M as True and a pessimistic cut that considers M as False. Finally, we use the MCMAS-SC model checker to run each cut and check the obtained results. That is, if the optimistic and pessimistic answers are equal, the answer $(TorF)$ is returned, otherwise, the result returned is (M). The classification of the system specifications is as follows:

- Safety properties express some thing bad will never happen
  (1) *"It is not the case that the system smart alarm sends a signal to the nurse and the nurse does not commit to respond."*
  $\varphi_1 = \neg\ EF\ CC(Nurse, System, SmartAlram, \neg NurAnswer)$
  (2) *"The bad situation is when the bed is not ready and the washer robot commits to send the ready signal to the system"*
  $\varphi_2 = \neg\ EF\ CC(Robot, System, \neg BedReady, NotSys)$
- Liveness properties express the good events that eventually happen
  (3) *"In all possible executions, the nurse commits to provide medicine to the patient, when the system sends a reminder message through the smartphone."*
  $\varphi_3 = AF\ CC(Nurse, Patient, RemindSent, MidicinProv)$
  (4) *"In all possible executions, the system commits to be ready, when the nurse needs to send or receive the required information."*
  $\varphi_4 = AF\ CC(System, Nurse, NurCon, SysReady)$
- Reachability properties express that a predetermined state will be reached in the system.
  (5) *"The nurse commits to meet the patient when the system sends a notification that the patient is arrived and checked in."*
  $\varphi_5 = EF\ CC(Nurse, System, NotSent, NurMeetPat)$
  (6) *"The smart robot commits to wash the bed when the system sends a wash signal."*
  $\varphi_6 = EF\ CC(Robot, System, RobNot, BedWash)$
  (7) *"the physician commits to see the patient for treatment if the smart slice sends a reading of high blood pressure."*
  $\varphi_7 = EF\ CC(Physician, Patient, HbloodPr, Treatment)$
  (8) *"the smart sensor connected to the patient's body commits to the patient's alert when the first reads high blood pressure."*
  $\varphi_8 = EF\ CC(Sensor, Patient, HbloodP, SmartSenAlarm)$
  (9) *"The nurse commits to respond, when an alarm is sent by the system via smartphone"*
  $\varphi_9 = EF\ CC(Nurse, System, SmartAlram, NurAnswer)$
  (10) *"The patient commits to choose the meal or refuse when the system recommends meals according to the dietary restrictions."*
  $\varphi_{10} = EF\ CC(patient, system, ViewMeal, Answer)$

Table 1. The smart hospital model verification results

Pro.	Opt.	Pes.	Result	Op.T(s.)	Pes.T(s.)
1.	T	T	T	0.025	0.024
2.	T	T	T	0.027	0.026
3.	T	T	T	0.048	0.045
4.	T	F	M	0.016	0.015
5.	T	F	M	0.014	0.012
6.	T	T	T	0.014	0.012
7.	T	T	T	0.013	0.011
8.	T	T	T	0.014	0.013
9.	T	T	T	0.013	0.011
10.	F	F	F	0.011	0.09

5.3   Verification Results

Our experiments are performed on Intel(R) Core(TM) i5-8250U with 1.60 GHz processor and 1.80 GHz RAM. After verifying the two classical systems, we obtained the following results: φ_1 and φ_2 are satisfied on the model, the reachability properties $\varphi_6, \varphi_7, \varphi_8$ and φ_9 as well as the liveness property φ_3 are also satisfied. However, the property φ_{10} is not satisfied in the model. Moreover, it is uncertain if properties φ_4 and φ_5 are satisfied because of the conflicted results. Table 1 illustrates the results with the execution time in seconds for each formula verified over the optimistic and pessimistic cuts.

To check the scalability of the performed technique, we conducted 6 experiments reported in Table 2. The experiments started with 7 and ended with 42 agents. In this table, the number of agents #Age, the number of reachable states #States, the execution time in the second T(Sec.) and the memory in use in bytes are given for each cut. We eliminated the number of reachable states and the memory in use of the pessimistic cut as it has the same values as the optimistic one. The results of the reachable states in Table 2 reflect that the state space increases exponentially with the increase in the number of agents, while the memory usage increases polynomially. The execution time for each cut increases logarithmically which reflects the high scalability of our approach.

Table 2. Scalability results of running the optimistic and pessimistic cuts 6 times each. Starting with 7 agents and ends with 42 agents

#Age.	#States.	T(Sec)	M.(B)	Pes.T(Sec)
7	174	0.017	11937984	0.014
14	2668	0.422	16328976	0.207
21	44856	0.839	17286656	0.799
28	779440	2.904	36506192	2.622
35	1.37423e+07	7.756	38296640	7.533
42	2.44159+08	10.183	38996572	9.263

6   Conclusion and Future Work

In this paper, we have applied a practical and scalable verification approach for verifying an IIS application through a smart hospital system, with social conditional commitments under uncertain behaviours. We introduced a new logic called $3v-CTL^{cc}$ by extending χCTL, the multi-valued CTL, with a new modality for conditional commitments extracted from CTL^{cc}. The new logic is used for reasoning about uncertainty in intelligent systems with conditional commitments. We implemented our framework using a reduction approach and discussed the obtained results, including the scalability. For future work, we identify the following directions: 1) we plan to extend our experiments by considering more agents and including other aspects of the IIS system scenarios to simulate more complex situations; 2) we aim to extend our logic by investigating additional conditional commitment modalities such as fulfillment, cancellation, release, delegation and assignment actions to capture more complex and realistic cases; 3) as our work handled uncertainty in the properties (i.e., in states), we plan to verify IIS with commitments under uncertainty in both the properties and the transitions between states; and 4) we plan to extend our semantics over arbitrary lattice that can take more than three values so that we can verify IIS by considering different truth levels depending on the application under investigation.

References

1. Al-Saqqar, F., Bentahar, J., Sultan, K., Wan, W., Khosrowshahi Asl, E.: Model checking temporal knowledge and commitments in multi-agent systems using reduction. Simul. Model. Pract. Theory **51**, 45–68 (2015)
2. Alzoubi, H.M., Alshurideh, M., Ghazal, T.M.: Integrating BLE beacon technology with intelligent information systems IIS for operations' performance: a managerial perspective. In: Hassanien, A.E., et al. (eds.) AICV 2021. AISC, vol. 1377, pp. 527–538. Springer, Cham (2021). https://doi.org/10.1007/978-3-030-76346-6_48
3. Bentahar, J., Meyer, J.C., Wan, W.: Model checking communicative agent-based systems. Knowl. Based Syst. **22**(3), 142–159 (2009)

250   G. Alwhishi et al.

4. Bruns, G., Godefroid, P.: Model checking partial state spaces with 3-valued temporal logics. In: Halbwachs, N., Peled, D. (eds.) CAV 1999. LNCS, vol. 1633, pp. 274–287. Springer, Heidelberg (1999). https://doi.org/10.1007/3-540-48683-6_25

5. Chechik, M., Devereux, B., Easterbrook, S., Gurfinkel, A.: Multi-valued symbolic model-checking. ACM Trans. Softw. Eng. Methodol. **12**(4), 371–408 (2003)

6. Chopra, A.K., Singh, M.P.: Multiagent commitment alignment. In: Proceedings of the 8th International Conference on Autonomous Agents and Multiagent Systems, vol. 2, pp. 937–944 (2009)

7. Clarke, E.M., Emerson, E.A., Sifakis, J.: Model checking: algorithmic verification and debugging. Commun. ACM **52**(11), 74–84 (2009)

8. Ding, Z., Jiang, W., Jiang, M., Jin, Z., Jiang, H.: Model checking the uncertainties in software systems introduced by intelligent components. In: 2018 IEEE International Symposium on Software Reliability Engineering Workshops (ISSREW), pp. 130–131. IEEE (2018)

9. Drawel, N., Bentahar, J., Laarej, A., Rjoub, G.: Formalizing group and propagated trust in multi-agent systems. In: Proceedings of the Twenty-Ninth International Joint Conference on Artificial Intelligence, IJCAI, pp. 60–66 (2020)

10. Drawel, N., Qu, H., Bentahar, J., Shakshuki, E.: Specification and automatic verification of trust-based multi-agent systems. Futur. Gener. Comput. Syst. **107**, 1047–1060 (2020)

11. El Kholy, W., Bentahar, J., El-Menshawy, M., Qu, H., Dssouli, R.: Conditional commitments: reasoning and model checking. ACM Trans. Softw. Eng. Methodol. **24**(2), 1–49 (2014)

12. El Kholy, W., Bentahar, J., El-Menshawy, M., Qu, H., Dssouli, R.: Smc4ac: a new symbolic model checker for intelligent agent communication. Fund. Inform. **152**(3), 223–271 (2017)

13. El-Menshawy, M., Bentahar, J., Dssouli, R.: Verifiable semantic model for agent interactions using social commitments. In: Dastani, M., El Fallah Segrouchni, A., Leite, J., Torroni, P. (eds.) LADS 2009. LNCS (LNAI), vol. 6039, pp. 128–152. Springer, Heidelberg (2010). https://doi.org/10.1007/978-3-642-13338-1_8

14. El-Menshawy, M., Bentahar, J., El Kholy, W., Laarej, A.: Model checking real-time conditional commitment logic using transformation. J. Syst. Softw. **138**, 189–205 (2018)

15. Hammoud, A., Otrok, H., Mourad, A., Dziong, Z.: Stable federated fog formation: an evolutionary game theoretical approach. Futur. Gener. Comput. Syst. **124**, 21–32 (2021)

16. Hammoud, A., Sami, H., Mourad, A., Otrok, H., Mizouni, R., Bentahar, J.: AI, blockchain, and vehicular edge computing for smart and secure IoV: challenges and directions. IEEE Internet Things Mag. **3**(2), 68–73 (2020)

17. Javaid, M., Khan, I.H.: Internet of Things (IoT) enabled healthcare helps to take the challenges of COVID-19 pandemic. J. Oral Biol. Craniofacial Res. **11**(2), 209–214 (2021)

18. Kalajdzic, K., Jegourel, C., Lukina, A., Bartocci, E., Legay, A., Smolka, S.A., Grosu, R.: Feedback control for statistical model checking of cyber-physical systems. In: Margaria, T., Steffen, B. (eds.) ISoLA 2016. LNCS, vol. 9952, pp. 46–61. Springer, Cham (2016). https://doi.org/10.1007/978-3-319-47166-2_4

19. Li, Y., Lei, L., Li, S.: Computation tree logic model checking based on multi-valued possibility measures. Inf. Sci. **485**, 87–113 (2019)

20. Malek, Y.N., et al.: On the use of IoT and big data technologies for real-time monitoring and data processing. Procedia Comput. Sci. **113**, 429–434 (2017)

21. Martins, J., Barbosa, R., Lourenço, N., Robin, J., Madeira, H.: Online verification through model checking of medical critical intelligent systems. In: 2020 50th Annual IEEE/IFIP International Conference on Dependable Systems and Networks Workshops (DSN-W), pp. 32–37. IEEE (2020)
22. Peled, E.M.C.O.G.D.A.: Model Checking. Cyber Physical Systems Series, MIT Press (1999)
23. Quan, W.: Intelligent information processing. Comput. Sci. Eng. **21**(6), 4–5 (2019)
24. Rahman, M.S., Peeri, N.C., Shrestha, N., Zaki, R., Haque, U., Ab Hamid, S.H.: Defending against the novel coronavirus (COVID-19) outbreak: how can the internet of things (IoT) help to save the world? Health Policy Technol. **9**(2), 136 (2020)
25. Rjoub, G., Bentahar, J., Wahab, O.A., Bataineh, A.S.: Deep and reinforcement learning for automated task scheduling in large-scale cloud computing systems. Concurr. Comput. Pract. Exp. **33**(23), e5919 (2021)
26. Rjoub, G., Abdel Wahab, O., Bentahar, J., Bataineh, A.: A trust and energy-aware double deep reinforcement learning scheduling strategy for federated learning on IoT devices. In: Kafeza, E., Benatallah, B., Martinelli, F., Hacid, H., Bouguettaya, A., Motahari, H. (eds.) ICSOC 2020. LNCS, vol. 12571, pp. 319–333. Springer, Cham (2020). https://doi.org/10.1007/978-3-030-65310-1_23
27. Roman, S.: Lattices and Ordered Sets. Springer, NY (2008). https://doi.org/10.1007/978-0-387-78901-9
28. Rosenmann, A.: A multiple-valued logic approach to the design and verification of hardware circuits. J. Appl. Log. **15**, 69–93 (2016)
29. Sami, H., Otrok, H., Bentahar, J., Mourad, A.: AI-based resource provisioning of IoE services in 6G: a deep reinforcement learning approach. IEEE Trans. Netw. Serv. Manage. **18**(3), 3527–3540 (2021)
30. Shoham, S., Grumberg, O.: Multi-valued model checking games. In: Peled, D.A., Tsay, Y.-K. (eds.) ATVA 2005. LNCS, vol. 3707, pp. 354–369. Springer, Heidelberg (2005). https://doi.org/10.1007/11562948_27
31. Shoham, S., Grumberg, O.: A game-based framework for CTL counterexamples and 3-valued abstraction-refinement. In: Hunt, W.A., Somenzi, F. (eds.) CAV 2003. LNCS, vol. 2725, pp. 275–287. Springer, Heidelberg (2003). https://doi.org/10.1007/978-3-540-45069-6_28
32. Shoham, S., Grumberg, O.: 3-valued abstraction: more precision at less cost. Inf. Comput. **206**(11), 1313–1333 (2008)
33. Sultan, K., Bentahar, J., Yahyaoui, H., Mizouni, R.: Model checking agent-based communities against uncertain group commitments and knowledge. Expert Syst. Appl. **177**, 114792 (2021)
34. Sun, D., Zhang, G., Zheng, W., Li, K.: Key technologies for big data stream computing. In: Big Data - Algorithms, Analytics, and Applications (2015)
35. Tissaoui, A., Saidi, M.: Uncertainty in IoT for smart healthcare: challenges, and opportunities. In: Jmaiel, M., Mokhtari, M., Abdulrazak, B., Aloulou, H., Kallel, S. (eds.) ICOST 2020. LNCS, vol. 12157, pp. 232–239. Springer, Cham (2020). https://doi.org/10.1007/978-3-030-51517-1_19
36. Xu, Y., Ruan, D., Qin, K., Liu, J.: Lattice-valued logic. Stud. Fuzziness Soft Comput. **132** (2003). https://doi.org/10.1007/978-3-540-44847-1

Author Index

Printed in the United States
by Baker & Taylor Publisher Services